Design and Manage to
LIFE CYCLE COST

Design and Manage to
LIFE CYCLE COST

Benjamin S. Blanchard
Virginia Polytechnic Institute and State University

M/A Press   Portland, Oregon

© Copyright by M/A Press, 1978

10   9   8   7   6   5   4   3   2   1

Library of Congress Cataloging in Publication Data

Blanchard, Benjamin S.
    Design and manage to life cycle cost.

    Bibliography: p.
    Includes index.
    1. Costs, Industrial.   2. Cost effectiveness.
3. Product life cycle—Accounting.   I. Title.
II. Title: Life cycle cost.
HD47.B49   658.1'553   77-18875
ISBH 0-930206-00-2

Printed in the United States of America

M/A Press
30 N.W. 23rd Place
P.O. Box 10766
Portland, OR 97210

CONTENTS

CHAPTER 3   THE ELEMENTS OF COST ANALYSIS

CHAPTER 4   COST ANALYSIS APPLICATIONS IN
THE SYSTEM/PRODUCT LIFE CYCLE

CHAPTER 5 THE INTEGRATED MANAGEMENT ASPECTS OF LIFE CYCLE COSTING AND ITS APPLICATIONS

APPENDICES

INDEX

PREFACE

The combination of current economic trends, rising inflation, the on-going reduction in "buying power", budget limitations, etc., has created an increasing awareness and interest in system/product cost. Through this awareness and interest, we have come to the realization that in numerous instances we do not actually know the total cost to date of many of our systems and products currently in the inventory and being utilized by the consumer. In other cases where systems and products are being evaluated, the measured costs far exceed initial expectations, particularly with respect to those elements of cost associated with sustaining system operation and logistics support. Also, it has been recognized that the greatest impact on total cost results from decisions made at the early stages of the system/product life cycle.

In essence, experience has indicated that we must orient our thinking in terms of total life cycle cost, and not just a segment of cost such as the development cost of a system, the purchase price of a product, or the production cost of an item. Further, we can accomplish much in the area of resource conservation by minimizing overall life cycle cost in the process of designing, producing, and utilizing new

systems and products of the future. Thus, life cycle cost
becomes parmount in the decision-making process from the
beginning, and total cost must be considered as a major
evaluation criterion factor along with other parameters such
as system/product performance, effectiveness, size and weight,
capacity, producibility, supportability, and so on.

   The purpose of this book is to provide emphasis in life
cycle costing--both from the standpoint of introducing cost
as a major parameter in the design and development of a new
system or product; and as a management technique employed to
aid in the decision-making process. Life cycle cost analyses
are appropriate in all phases of the system/product life
cycle (i.e., product planning and conceptual design,
preliminary system design, detailed design and development,
production, construction, operations, and logistics support),
and the concept of life cycle costing presented in this book
is applicable to all types of systems and products. Life
cycle cost analyses are accomplished to varying degrees
depending on the complexity of the system (or product) and
the nature of the problem at hand.

   This book covers the subject of life cycle costing through:
(1) an introduction to terms and definitions and some
fundamental principles of costing in Chapters 1 and 2;
(2) the applications and the process of accomplishing life
cycle cost analyses in Chapter 3; (3) some actual case study
illustrations of various types of life cycle cost analyses in
Chapter 4; and (4) a discussion of the integrated management
aspects of life cycle costing functions pertaining to program
applications in Chapter 5. The appendices include a typical
cost breakdown structure, interest tables, a description of
sample cost models, and a selected bibliography. As life
cycle cost analyses will actually vary from one application
to the next, this book obviously can not respond to all
situations; however, enough information and guidance is
provided to illustrate the process that one would follow in
completing a life cycle cost analysis.

   This book is designed for use in the classroom or by

practicing professionals. Current methods and techniques
are introduced, many practical problems are included, and
numerous references are noted. The text material is
arranged in such a manner as to guide the analyst, engineer,
or manager on a day-to-day basis in dealing with life cycle
costing activities. The intent is to provide a broad
understanding of the subject area.

   I wish to thank Mr. Elmer L. Peterson, Headquarters,
U. S. Air Force, for his assistance in providing references
and in identifying major areas of life cycle costing
activity; and a special appreciation to my secretary,
Mrs. Carolyn Stoner, for her dedication and support in the
preparation of the text materials.

                         Benjamin S. Blanchard

Chapter 1

INTRODUCTION TO LIFE CYCLE COSTING

Life cycle costing per se is not new. Industries, businesses, government agencies, institutions, and individuals alike have been dealing with various facets of cost for years. These costs have covered such functions as research, design and development, production, construction, testing, consumer operations, and support of a given system or product.[1] In general, however, these various facets of cost have been viewed in a fragmented manner, with very little attention being directed toward the overall broad spectrum of cost presented on an integrated basis; i.e., life cycle cost.

Recently, the "tight" economy, budget limitations, inflationary trends, etc., have created an increasing awareness of system/product costs. Further, experience dealing with "cause and effect" relationships has indicated

---

[1] For definition purposes, "a system may be considered as a nucleus of elements structured in such a manner as to accomplish a function designed to satisfy an identified need. A system may vary in form, fit, and function and is discussed at various levels. A system can be considered to be a product, but not all products are systems, since the above characteristics may not prevail (e.g., a radio without an operator)." B. Blanchard, Engineering Organization And Management, Prentice-Hall, Inc., 1976, Page 5.

that decisions made early in the system life cycle have a
significant impact on the subsequent costs of production and
the sustaining life cycle support of that system. Thus,
system/product costs must be viewed from the total life cycle
standpoint. This trend toward cost consciousness, presented
in the context of the system/product life cycle, has resulted
in the increased universal emphasis on life cycle costing.

1.1 THE CURRENT DILEMMA

The total cost of systems and products has been increasing
at an alarming rate. This is primarily due to a combination
of inflation and cost growth from causes such as the:
    A. Cost growth due to engineering changes occurring
throughout the design and development of a system or product
(for the purposes of increasing performance, sophistication,
etc.)
    B. Cost growth due to production and/or construction
changes.
    C. Cost growth due to program schedule changes.
    D. Cost growth due to changes in the logistics support
capability of a given system or product.
    E. Cost growth due to initial estimating inaccuracies and
changes in estimating procedures.
    F. Cost growth due to increased program documentation
requirements and paperwork.
    G. Cost growth due to unforeseen problems.
    It has been stated on occasion that cost growth due to
these various other causes has ranged from 5 to 10 times the
rate of inflation increase over the past several decades.
Figure 1-1 illustrates some basic cost growth trends for
different systems. The cost growth projections relate the
initial estimate of system cost to subsequent cost estimates
of the same system at later points in the life cycle. Cost
growth trends will of course vary from system to system.
    At the same time when considerable system/product cost

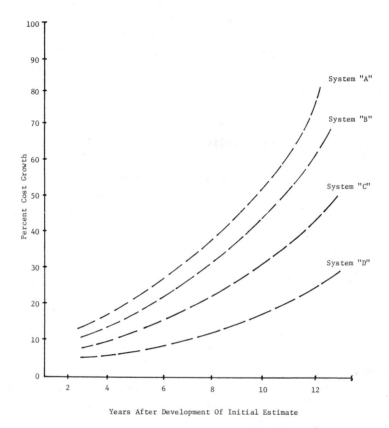

Figure 1-1 Cost Growth Trends

growth is being realized, budget allocations for many
categories of systems are decreasing from year to year.   The
net result is that <u>less funds are available</u> for:

A.   Acquiring and operating new systems or products.

B.   Maintaining and supporting both new systems as well
as those already in the inventory.

The available funds (i.e., "buying power"), when including
inflation and cost growth and converted to constant dollars,
are decreasing at a rapid rate as illustrated in Figure 1-2.

The current economic posture is further complicated by some

additional problems which are related to the actual
determination of system/product costs.

   A. In many instances, the bulk of total system costs are
not visible, particularly those costs associated with system/
product operational use by the consumer (or user), life
cycle maintenance and logistics support, and ultimate system
retirement and disposal.

   B. On-going techniques associated with cost estimation are
not adequate (i.e., the predicting of future life cycle
costs).

   C. Cost factors are often improperly applied. For instance:

      1. Costs are identified and often included in the
wrong category.

      2. Variable costs are treated as fixed costs; fixed
costs are treated as variable costs; indirect costs are
treated as direct costs; recurring costs are treated as
nonrecurring costs; and so on.

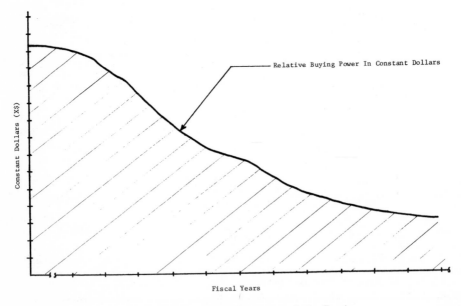

Figure 1-2 Estimated Typical Procurement Outlay Trends

 3. Incorrect cost estimating relationships are assumed
and applied.

 D. Existing accounting systems do not always permit a
realistic and timely assessment of life cycle cost.

 E. Budgeting practices are often inflexible relative to
the shifting of funds from one category to another to
facilitate economic improvements in the total system/product
acquisition and utilization process.

 Relative to total cost visibility, the problem can be
related to the "iceberg effect" illustrated in Figure 1-3.
One must not only address those initial acquisition costs
that are readily visible (i.e., research and development cost,
production cost, etc.), but consideration of support costs
is also essential. Lack of consideration in this area in the
past has caused major problems.

 In essence, our current dilemma is caused by a combination
of inflation and cost growth factors (with reduced budgets)
on one hand and our inability to properly deal with total
system/product cost on the other hand. Emphasis in life
cycle costing should alleviate some of the problems currently
being experienced.

1.2 THE CONCEPT OF LIFE CYCLE COSTING

 By way of introduction to the concept of life cycle costing,
it seems appropriate at this time to direct some attention
to a few significant terms and definitions. The objective,
of course, is to provide a common language for the purposes
of communication and in developing a better understanding of
the subject matter. Additional terms and definitions are
introduced throughout subsequent sections of this text.

1.2.1 The System/Product Life Cycle

 Fundamental to the concept of life cycle costing is a

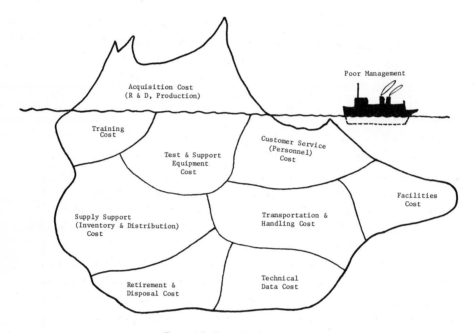

Figure 1-3 Total Life Cycle Cost

basic understanding of the system/product life cycle. The
life cycle actually commences with the initial identification
of a consumer need and extends through system planning,
research, design and development, production or construction,
evaluation, consumer use, system logistics support in the
field, and ultimate system retirement and material disposal.
The system life cycle (sometimes identified as the "consumer-
to-consumer cycle") and the major steps applicable to each
phase are illustrated in Figure 1-4.[2] These steps follow a
logical evolutionary flow of system acquisition and
utilization, and the activities associated with each step
represent a full-scale effort.

---

[2] Figures 1-4 and 1-5 are extracted from: B. Blanchard,
Engineering Organization And Management, Prentice-Hall, Inc.,
1976, Pages 16 and 17. (By Permission).

In reality, each system (or product) is somewhat unique in itself and the specific requirements of "what tasks have to be accomplished" are different. A large system, such as a transportation system or a processing plant requiring new development, may evolve through all of the steps illustrated by Path "A" in Figure 1-5. That is, there is planning (including a market analysis, a technical feasibility study, a product design and production plan, etc.); a research function to investigate different approaches by which

CONSUMER	IDENTIFICATION OF NEED	"Wants or desires" for products (because of obvious deficiencies/problems or made evident through basic research results).
PRODUCER	PRODUCT PLANNING FUNCTION	Marketing analysis; feasibility study; advanced product planning (product selection, specifications and plans, acquisition plan-research/design/production, evaluation plan, product use and logistic support plan); planning review; proposal.
	PRODUCT RESEARCH FUNCTION	Basic research; applied research ("need" oriented); research methods; results of research; evolution from basic research to product design and development.
	PRODUCT DESIGN FUNCTION	Design requirements; conceptual design; preliminary system design; detailed design; design support; engineering model/prototype development; transition from design to production.
	PRODUCTION AND/OR CONSTRUCTION FUNCTION	Production and/or construction requirements; industrial engineering and operations analysis (plant engineering, manufacturing engineering, methods engineering, production control); quality control; production operations.
	PRODUCT EVALUATION FUNCTION	Evaluation requirements; categories of test and evaluation; test preparation phase (planning, resource requirements, etc.); formal test and evaluation; data collection, analysis, reporting, and corrective action; retesting.
CONSUMER*	PRODUCT USE AND LOGISTICS SUPPORT FUNCTION	Product distribution and operational use; elements of logistics and life cycle maintenance support; product evaluation; modifications; product phase-out; material disposal, reclamation, and/or recycling.

(Left vertical label: THE SYSTEM/PRODUCT LIFE CYCLE)

*Some of the specific supporting functions indicated may be accomplished by the producer throughout and/or at various stages in the product life cycle.

Figure 1-4 The System/Product Life Cycle

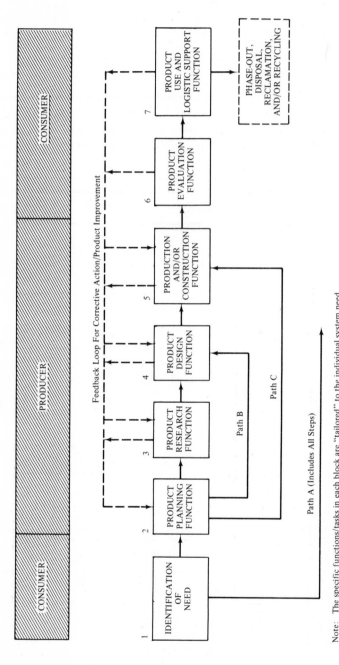

Note: The specific functions/tasks in each block are "tailored" to the individual system need. Only those activities that are actually necessary are accomplished.

Figure 1-5 System/Product Life Cycle Application
(Source: B. S. Blanchard, *Engineering Organization and Management*, Prentice-Hall, Inc., 1976. By Permission.)

technical objectives can be accomplished; a design function covering preliminary system design and the detailed design of equipment, a process, facilities, and/or software; and so on. On the other hand, a relatively small product such as a washing machine or a radio, where the design concept is basically fixed, need not be processed through all of the steps in Figure 1-4, buy may transition directly from the planning function to production as illustrated in Path "C" of Figure 1-5. Additional research and detailed design may not be necessary in this instance.

When dealing with the aspect of life cycle cost, the analyst must: (1) initially address the overall total life cycle as illustrated in Figure 1-4; (2) "tailor" the approach shown to the applicable system or product under consideration; and (3) restructure the information in Figure 1-4 to be compatible with the appropriate requirement, including all of the basic functions that must be performed. The results will ultimately establish the basis for development of the cost breakdown structure and the accomplishment of life cycle cost analyses discussed in Chapters 2 and 3, respectively.[3]

1.2.2   Life Cycle Cost (LCC)

Life cycle cost refers to all costs associated with the system or product and applied to the defined life cycle. Life cycle cost includes (but is not necessarily limited to) the following:[4]

---

[3] Describing the system/product life cycle may appear to be rather elementary; however, experience has indicated that many different interpretations of "what constitutes the life cycle" may exist. Since this establishes the major reference point for life cycle costing, it is essential that a common understanding prevail as to what is meant by the "life cycle", and what is included (or excluded).

[4] Life cycle costs may be categorized in a variety of ways. Cost categorization is discussed further in Chapter 2 and in Appendix A.

1. Research and development (R & D) cost -- initial
planning; market analysis; feasibility studies; product
research; engineering design; design documentation; software;
test and evaluation of engineering models; and associated
management functions.

2. Production and construction cost -- industrial
engineering and operations analysis; manufacturing
(fabrication, assembly, and test); facility construction;
process development; production operations; quality control;
and initial logistics support requirements (e.g., customer
life cycle support, the manufacture of spare parts, etc.)

3. Operation and support (O & S) cost -- consumer or user
operations of the system/product in the field; product
distribution (marketing and sales, transportation, and traffic
management); and sustaining logistic support throughout the
system/product life cycle (e.g., customer service, supply
support, test and support equipment, transportation and
handling, technical data, facilities, system modifications,
etc.).

4. Retirement and disposal cost -- disposal of nonrepairable items throughout the life cycle; system/product
retirement; material recycling; and applicable logistic
support requirements.

Life cycle cost is basically determined by identifying
functions in each phase of the life cycle; costing those
functions; applying the appropriate costs by function on a
year-to-year schedule; and ultimately accumulating the costs
for the entire span of the life cycle. Life cycle cost
includes all direct producer and consumer costs.[5]

---

[5] It should be noted here that all life cycle costs may be
difficult (if not impossible) to predict and measure. For
instance, some indirect costs caused by the interaction
effects of one system or another, social costs, etc., may
be impossible to quantify. Thus, the emphasis here relates
primarily to those costs that can be directly attributed to
a given system or product.

1.2.3 Life Cycle Cost Analysis

A life cycle cost analysis may be defined as the systematic analytical process of evaluating various alternative courses of action with the objective of choosing the best way to employ scarce resources. In other words, life cycle costing is employed in the evaluation of alternative system design configurations, alternative production schemes, alternative logistics support policies, and so on. The analysis constitutes the step-by-step approach, employing life cycle cost figures-of-merit as criteria, utilized in arriving at a cost-effective solution to a given problem. The analysis process is iterative in nature, can be applied to any phase of the system/product life cycle, and is discussed further in Chapter 3.

1.2.4 Cost Effectiveness

Cost effectiveness relates to the measure of a system or product in terms of technical performance (i.e., system effectiveness) and total life cycle cost. The performance parameter, or system effectiveness, addresses the aspect of "meeting the need" and may be expressed by one or a combination of figures-of-merit such as miles per gallon (for a vehicle), availability or the probability of system success, capacity in forms of units processed, speed, accuracy, size, weight, and so on. Life cycle cost constitutes those factors described earlier.

In the evaluation of alternatives through analysis, the criteria used in the selection of a preferred approach should not only include life cycle cost but must consider some aspect(s) of performance. The proper balance, presented as a cost effectiveness figure-of-merit, is desired. Figure 1-6 depicts the basic ingredients as defined here.

Referring to the figure, cost effectiveness is highly influenced by the inherent characteristics of system/product design and by the effectiveness of the logistic support

capability. An automobile may be an excellent performer when
it is operating in a satisfactory manner; however, unless
there is adequate logistic support available when it fails
its overall usefulness is questionable. In addition, the
design of the automobile and its support should be relatively
cost effective. Thus, life cycle cost is a significant facet
in the cost effectiveness equation.

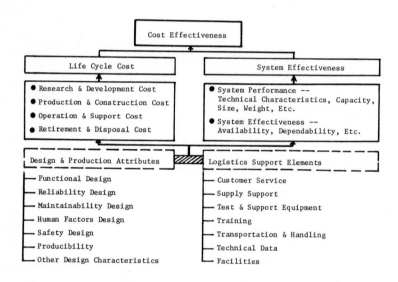

Figure 1-6 Basic Ingredients of Cost Effectiveness

1.2.5 Design to Cost (DTC)

The Design To Cost (DTC) concept establishes life cycle cost
as a system/product design parameter along with performance,
effectiveness, capacity, accuracy, size, weight, reliability,
maintainability, etc. Cost is assumed to be an active rather
than a resultant factor throughout the design process. Cost
targets or goals are initially established at program
inception as input criteria, and subsequent activities and

design decisions are directed toward compliance with these
targets.

Design to cost figures-of-merit should be in terms of life
cycle cost as the ultimate; however, sometimes DTC parameters
are established at a lower level to facilitate improved
visibility and closer cost control throughout the life cycle.
Several examples are:

1. Design to unit acquisition cost -- a factor which
includes only research and development cost and production
or construction cost.

2. Design to unit operation and support (O & S) cost -- a
factor which includes only O & S cost (and not acquisition
cost).

When sub-optimizing by considering only a single segment of
life cycle cost, the analyst must take care that decisions
are not based on that one segment alone without considering
the overall effects on total life cycle cost. For instance,
one can propose a given design configuration on the basis of
a low unit acquisition cost; however, the projected O & S
cost and life cycle cost for that configuration may be
considerably higher as compared to an alternative. Optimally,
acquisition cost should not be addressed without consideration
for O & S cost and vice versa, and both segments of cost must
be viewed in terms of life cycle cost.

1.2.6 Economic Life

In performing cost analyses one may assume a time period of
a shorter duration than the total physical life cycle of an
item. This period, identified as the "economic life", is the
time which is considered directly relevant to the objectives
of the analysis in question. For instance, a period of 15
years may constitute the projected physical life cycle of a
system or product but 10 years may be feasible in terms of
acquiring enough economic data for decision-making purposes.
When the economic life and the physical life cycle are

different, this fact must be noted and the associated costs
identified accordingly. In any event, care must be exercised
when defining the life cycle.

1.3 COST EMPHASIS IN THE SYSTEM/PRODUCT LIFE CYCLE

Experience has indicated that a major portion of the
projected life cycle costs for a given system or product
stems from the consequences of decisions made during the
early product planning function and as part of system
conceptual design. Such decisions deal with system
performance and effectiveness requirements, system
configuration, quantity of items to be produced, consumer
utilization factors, logistic support policies, and so on.
These decisions, made as a result of a market analysis or a
design feasibility study, actually guide subsequent design
and production activities, product distribution functions,
and the various aspects of sustaining product logistic
support. Thus, if ultimate life cycle costs are to be
optimized,it is essential that a high degree of cost
emphasis be stressed at the early stages of system/product
development. Figure 1-7 reflects a characteristic life cycle
cost trend curve as related to actions occurring during the
various phases of the life cycle.

Referring to the figure, the basic system/product life
cycle phases presented in Figure 1-4 are translated to
reflect emphasis in the early planning and design stages of
a program. The functions noted here are included in the
activities in Figure 1-4.

When applying cost emphasis in the system/product life
cycle, the initial step is to establish cost targets or firm
goals; i.e., one or more quantitative figures-of-merit to
which the system or product should be designed, produced (or
constructed), and supported for a designated period of time.
Secondly, these targets may be allocated to specific sub-
systems or elements as design constraints or criteria. With

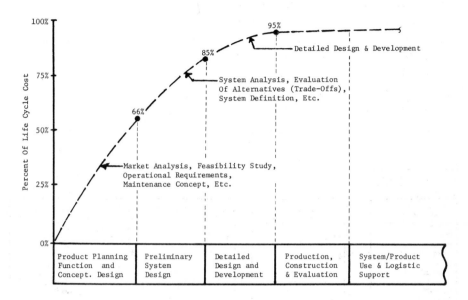

Figure 1-7   Actions Affecting Life Cycle Cost

the progression of design, various alternative configurations are evaluated in terms of compliance with the allocated factors and a preferred approach is selected. As the system/ product continues to evolve through the different stages of development, life cycle cost estimates are made and the results are compared against the initially specified requirements. Areas of non-compliance are noted and corrective action is initiated where appropriate. Cost emphasis throughout the system/product life cycle is illustrated in Figure 1-8 and discussed further.

1.3.1   Product Planning Function and Conceptual Design (Reference Figure 1.8, Block 1)

At the early stages of product planning and conceptual design, quantitative DTC figures-of-merit should be established as requirements to which the system or product is to be designed, tested, produced (or constructed), and supported. Such requirements may be stated in terms of "design to unit life cycle cost, where LCC includes. . ."; "design to unit acquisition cost, where acquisition cost includes . . ."; "design to unit operation and support cost, where O & S cost includes . . ."; or a combination thereof. These cost criteria, or constraints, usually evolve from an identified consumer need and are based on the results of a market analysis of some type.

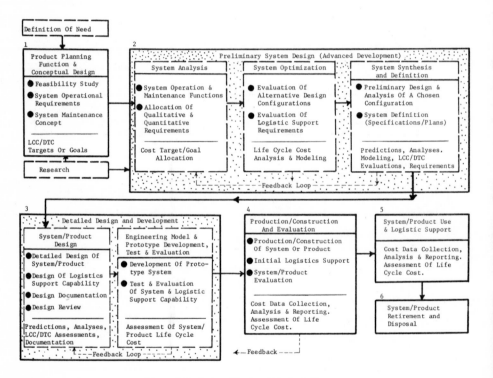

Figure 1-8 System/Product Life Cycle Process

1.3.2 Preliminary System Design (Reference Figure 1.9, Block 2)

With the quantitative requirements established, the next step constitutes the iterative process of analysis (i.e.,

optimization, synthesis, and system/product definition). The
criteria defined in Block 1 are initially allocated, or
apportioned, to various segments of the system to establish
guidelines for the design and/or the procurement of the
applicable element(s). As illustrated in Figure 1-9,
allocation is accomplished from the system level down to the
depth necessary to provide adequate cost control.

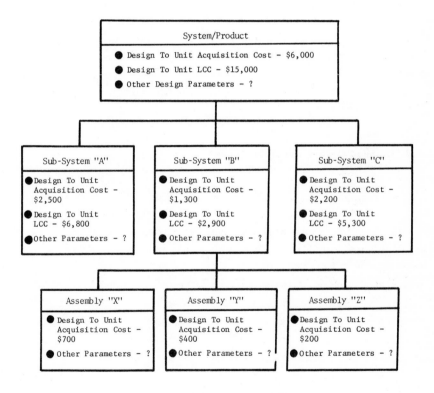

Figure 1-9   System / Product Cost Allocation

The factors projected in Figure 1-9 reflect the target cost
per individual unit (i.e., a single system or product in a
total population), and are based on system operational

requirements, the preliminary maintenance concept, and so on.[6]

   As the design process evolves, various alternative
approaches are considered in arriving at a preferred system
configuration. Life cycle cost analyses are accomplished in
evaluating each possible candidate with the objective of:
(1) ensuring that the candidate selected is compatible with
the established cost targets; and (2) determining which of
the various candidates being considered is preferred from an
overall cost effectiveness standpoint. Numerous trade-off
studies are accomplished, using life cycle cost analysis as
an evaluation tool, until a preferred design configuration is
chosen. Areas of compliance are justified, and non-compliant
approaches are discarded. This is an iterative process with
the necessary feedback and corrective action loop as
illustrated within Block 2 of Figure 1-8.

1.3.3   Detailed Design and Development
(Reference Figure 1.8, Block 3)

   As system/product design is further refined and design data
become available, the life cycle cost analysis effort
constitutes the evaluation of specific design characteristics
(as reflected by design documentation and engineering or
prototype models), the prediction of cost generating
variables, the estimation of costs, and the projection of
life cycle cost in terms of a cost profile. The results are
compared with the initial requirement and corrective action
is accomplished as necessary. Once again, this is an
iterative process, but at a lower level than what is

---

[6] Operational requirements cover system/product use,
   distribution, geographical location, effectiveness
   characteristics, environment, etc. The maintenance concept
   refers to the concept of system/product support throughout
   the life cycle. These requirements are initially identified
   through the activity represented in Figure 1-8, Block 1.
   Further discussion of operational requirements and
   maintenance concepts is included in subsequent chapters
   of this text.

accomplished during preliminary system design.

1.3.4 Production, Construction, Product Use, and Logistics Support
(Reference Figure 1.8, Blocks 4 and 5)

Cost emphasis in these latter stages of the system or product life cycle basically involves a data collection, analysis, and assessment function. Hopefully, valuable information is gained and utilized for the purposes of product improvement and from the standpoint of acquiring good historical data for future applications.

In summary, the process illustrated in Figure 1-8 is representative for a typical system or large scale product. The activities identified are not intended to infer an extensive level of effort, but constitute a "thought process". In some cases where large systems are being developed, requiring a significant amount of new design, all of the steps indicated in the figure may be appropriate and a large project organization is necessary. For products of a smaller nature involving primarily the utilization of "off-the-shelf" items, the basic process may still be applicable but the steps are simplified considerably and the level of effort is relatively small. In any event, the conceptual approach in Figure 1-8 is appropriate regardless of the system or product; however, the specific activities required are "tailored" in each application to meet the need.

Finally, life cycle costing is applicable in all phases of system design and development, production, construction, operational use and logistic support. Cost emphasis is created early in the life cycle by establishing quantita — tive cost factors as <u>requirements</u>. As the life cycle progresses, cost is employed as a major parameter in the evaluation of alternative design configurations and in the selection of a preferred approach. Subsequently, cost data are generated based on established design and production characteristics and are utilized in the development of life

cycle cost projections. These projections are in turn
compared with the initial requirements to determine degree of
compliance and the ultimate necessity for corrective action.
In essence, life cycle costing evolves from a series of rough
estimates to a relatively refined methodology, and is
employed as a management tool for decision making purposes.

1.4 THE CHALLENGES OF THE FUTURE

The major challenge for the future is to develop a degree
of cost consciousness both in the planning and design of new
systems (or products) and in the management of systems already
in the field. Cost must be considered as a design parameter
and cost emphasis must be applied at the appropriate time in
the system/product life cycle. Engineers, managers, and
support personnel alike must "think" cost! Further, cost
must be addressed on a total integrated life cycle basis.
With life cycle cost as a prime consideration, it is felt
that:

A. Cost growth for various systems and products will
intuitively decrease.

B. Cost estimates and projections will improve relative to
accuracy and completeness.

C. Accounting systems and the collection of cost data
will improve.

D. Budgeting procedures for new systems/products will
improve with the availability of better data.

In general, greater cost visibility is required which in
turn should result in the improved utilization of our
resources; i.e., increased productivity through the efficient
and effective use of personnel, materials, equipment,
facilities, and capital.

Chapter 2

SOME FUNDAMENTAL PRINCIPLES OF COSTING

The previous chapter introduces the concept of life cycle costing and its applications. Applications primarily include the accomplishment of cost analyses for the purposes of decision making. A cost analysis may be defined as the systematic analytical process of evaluating various alternative courses of action with the objective of choosing the best way to employ scarce resources. The cost analysis process is covered further in Chapter 3; however, prior to discussing the subject of analysis it is essential that we cover a few terms and definitions involving classifications of cost, cost categories and cost breakdown structure, cost estimating, the development of cost profiles, and the treatment of cost in the system/product life cycle. This chapter is dedicated to this purpose.

2.1 CLASSIFICATION OF COST[1]

The term "cost" is often used differently by different people in a variety of situations. Some people define cost

---

[1] B. Blanchard, <u>Engineering Organization And Management</u>, Prentice-Hall, Inc., 1976, Chapter 12.

in specific detail while others employ the term somewhat
loosely. Thus, it is necessary to establish some terminology
at this point with the objective of avoiding possible
confusion later on.

When evaluating certain activities there are obvious costs
which are identified with those activities and which can be
directly related to the expenditure of dollars. These costs
are identified herein as "economic costs". On the other hand,
there are non-economic costs of a more indirect nature and
difficult to convert into dollars, i.e., psychological costs,
political costs, social costs, etc. Discussion throughout
this text deals with economic costs.

As a second point, some costs are considered by the
decision maker as being relevant and some are identified as
irrelevant. Actually, all costs are relevant to some decision
or other and should be considered in life cycle costing if
one is to produce a high quality output. In solving specific
problems at the subsystem level, or when dealing with small
elements of a system, certain costs may be considered as
being irrelevant to the problem at hand. However, in each
instance the analyst should ensure that such costs are indeed
irrelevant prior to discarding them and treating them as such.

Finally, the analyst when dealing with life cycle cost may
tend to separate producer costs and consumer costs and
address either one or the other, not both; i.e., costs to you
as compared to costs to other people. As a consequence, the
definition of the life cycle tends to shift from the total
life cycle (as defined in Paragraph 1.2, Chapter 1) to a
small segment of the life cycle such as the portion that
deals with producer activities and producer costs. Actually,
all costs must be considered in the accomplishment of life
cycle cost analyses.

2.1.1 Past Costs and Future Costs

Costs that already have been incurred are the consequences

of past decisions, and are known as "sunk costs". Sunk costs are significant when assessing the actual cost of some past activity or product, and when determining whether a function was accomplished efficiently. Sunk costs are also beneficial in serving as a basis for predicting future costs, even though they cannot be recovered.

On the other hand, the day-to-day aspects of decision making affecting the future rely on all relevant costs from here on! Sunk costs are already expended, do not represent meaningful alternatives, and are no longer real costs. The important issue lies in the future cost of a given alternative. Life cycle cost analyses as discussed herein deal with future costs.

2.1.2 Total Cost and Unit Cost

When dealing with cost, the total cost concept should serve as a starting point to ensure that all relevant cost factors are appropriately considered. The analyst can easily overlook a significant facet of cost unless he (or she) intuitively addresses the overall cost spectrum prior to selecting the specific elements of cost that are pertinent to the problem at hand. Total cost includes all life cycle costs associated with the system or product, as defined earlier.

Unit cost, on the other hand, is the total cost divided by some related base and may be expressed in terms of cost per item produced, cost per person, cost per increment of effectiveness (e.g., reliability), cost per capacity output, cost per interval of time, and so on. Actually, unit costs should be expressed in measures that are the most meaningful for the purpose(s) at hand, and there must be a complete understanding as to what is included in both the numerator and denominator of the unit cost figure-of-merit used. Further, caution must be exercised since unit cost often represents an average that may change with the magnitude of the numerator, denominator, or both.[2]

2.1.3   Direct Cost and Indirect Cost

Within the overall total cost spectrum, some costs are
identified as being <u>direct</u> and others as being <u>indirect</u>. The
basic difference relates to traceability, where "direct"
pertains to costs that can be easily traced to a given cost
object. An attempt to identify some of the key factors in
each of these categories is presented below:

Direct Labor

All labor that is obviously identified with a given system
or product is classified as direct labor. This includes
management, engineering and production labor assigned to the
planning, design, development, manufacture, test and logistics
support of a system. Planners, researchers, engineers,
designers, draftsmen, technicians, machine operators,
assemblers, inspectors, and all other personnel whose efforts
are chargeable to a specific system are usually included in
the direct labor pool. For projects contracted with outside
agencies, all agency personnel charging their time against
project funds represent direct labor. Direct labor includes
the manhours associated with the life cycle functions
identified in Figure 1-4.

Direct Material

All materials that are included as an integral part and/or

---

[2] In certain instances, unit cost may be expressed using
some value less than total cost, such as system development
cost or product manufacturing cost. Again, the analyst
must be knowledgeable relative to what is and is not
included.

are traceable to the finished system or product constitute
direct material. This includes units, assemblies, sub-
assemblies, modules, and component parts of a system. Also,
any associated software is included.

Indirect or Overhead

Indirect labor or overhead constitutes personnel costs
that are not readily and directly traceable to a specific
product output, but are expended in the process of doing
business. Some examples are the costs of top level and
middle level management; certain engineering support
functions where basic research is being pursued in a staff
capacity; and organizations including finance and accounting,
legal, marketing, personnel administration and industrial
relations, engineering and production laboratories, material
handling, and so on. In addition, personnel fringe benefits
are often covered in this category (e.g., life and health
insurance, disability insurance, retirement, pension, social
security, etc.). Other indirect costs include facility
operation and maintenance, the cost of utilities, property
taxes and maintenance, and certain capital equipment.

At times it is difficult to determine which costs fall into
what category, since there are many areas that are not well
defined. Further, the allocation of costs may differ from
company to company (or agency to agency). One organization
may treat a certain cost element as direct where a different
organization will include the same type of cost in the
indirect pool. In life cycle costing, where all costs should
be considered, it is essential that the analyst identify
which costs are included in each category.

When relating direct and indirect costs, usually an
indirect overhead factor is applied to direct labor to cover

all labor expenses.[3] In addition, an indirect general and
administrative expense is sometimes applied to the total
estimated labor and material costs on a given project. Some
corporations or businesses employ a fixed percentage of the
direct cost to establish indirect cost, while others use a
variable factor to cover indirect costs. Also, the time
element relative to the application of a fixed or variable
factor may vary from organization to organization.

2.1.4 Variable Cost and Fixed Cost

Variable and fixed costs are sometimes defined in terms of
how the cost changes in relation to fluctuations in the
activity associated with a given cost allocation base. A cost
which is uniform on a per unit basis, but which fluctuates in
total in direct proportion to changes in the related total
activity or volume is <u>variable</u>. A typical example is the
variation of total cost when producing different quantities
of an item at "x" dollars per unit. In this instance, cost
variations occur with variations in volume.

On the other hand, a cost that remains constant in total
despite fluctuations in activity for a given period of time,
referred to as the relevant period, is considered as <u>fixed</u>.
A fixed cost does not change in <u>total</u> but may become
progressively smaller on a <u>per unit</u> basis as volume increases.
Property taxes, insurance, certain personnel expenses, some
capital equipment costs, and depreciation are examples of
fixed cost. However, it should be noted that these costs are

---

[3] The overhead or burden factor within a given organization
(when allocated) will often vary from one activity area
to another. Engineering overhead may constitute a given
percentage, manufacturing a different percentage, customer
service another percentage, and so on. The overhead for
an activity area is sometimes directly related to a
combination of personnel expenses, required support from
other organizations, facility usage, etc., and often
varies from one type of activity to another.

fixed only within the designated relevant period of time, since they may ultimately vary in the long term with overall economy shifts; i.e., inflation, cost of capital, etc. Different methods commonly used in projecting variable and fixed costs are illustrated in Figure 2-1.[4]

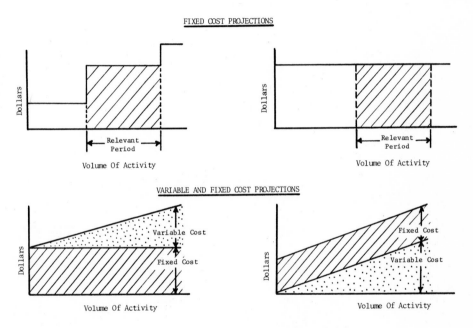

FIXED COST PROJECTIONS

VARIABLE AND FIXED COST PROJECTIONS

Figure 2-1   Variable and Fixed Cost Relationships

---

[4] Source: B. Blanchard, Engineering Organization And Management, Prentice-Hall, Inc., 1976, Chapter 12, Page 342. It is realized that the straight line representations of cost presented in Figure 2-1 are an oversimplification of real world conditions, particularly from the economist's point of view, where non-linear relationships are considered more valid. However, for the purposes of life cycle costing, the variable and fixed cost relationships presented herein are considered adequate.

Basically, all costs can be classified as either variable
or fixed, even though it may be difficult to assign some costs
clearly in one category or the other. In any event, whatever
the classification, the analyst must be aware of what is
included and what is not included.

2.1.5 Recurring and Nonrecurring Cost

Another approach in classifying cost involves the terms of
recurring and nonrecurring. Recurring cost refers to those
costs which occur again and again (from one period to the
next) or at specified intervals. Examples include the cost
of ongoing program management activities, continuing
engineering support required throughout the production/
construction phase of a program, repetitive activities
associated with assembly labor and material in producing a
given quantity of items, and sustaining customer service
activity for a system or product throughout its programmed
life cycle.

Nonrecurring cost, on the other hand, is usually a "one-
time" cost not of a repetitive nature. Examples are
engineering design and development, system/product
qualification testing, the acquisition and installation of
manufacturing tools and test equipment, the construction of
a new facility, and so on.

When evaluating changes in program schedules, different
quantities of products, alternative production schemes and
the like, it is often beneficial to classify costs as either
recurring or nonrecurring.

2.1.6 Incremental Cost

Incremental cost as defined herein refers to the difference
in total cost between two alternatives. Often in the
accomplishment of analyses, incremental or delta cost factors
are used to facilitate the decision making process.
Figure 2-2 illustrates this cost element.

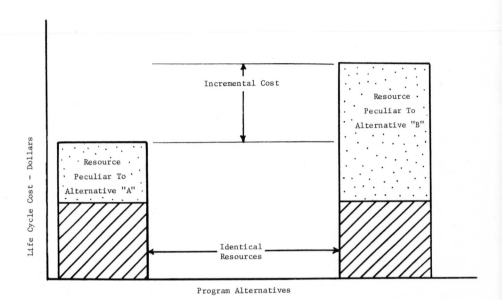

Figure 2-2 Incremental Cost Model

2.1.7 Functional Cost

The classification and allocation of costs by program functions such as engineering design, manufacturing, supply support, warehousing, distribution, etc., constitutes functional costing. Functional costing ties directly into the cost breakdown structure discussed in Paragraph 2.2.

2.2 COST BREAKDOWN STRUCTURE (CBS)

As the various major functions in the system/product life cycle are identified, work packages and specific tasks are developed, scheduled, and budgeted. Budgets for each program are allocated to various functions and to individual cost

centers.[5] The basic mechanism used initially for cost
allocation and subsequently for cost monitoring and control

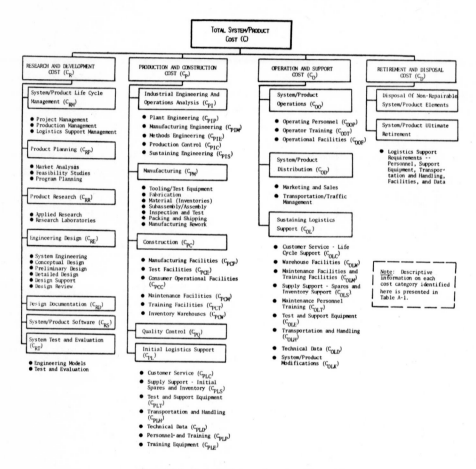

Figure 2-3   Cost Breakdown Structure (Example)

---

[5] These allocated factors may take the form of normal
cost estimates (working from the bottom up) or may
constitute design to cost goals/targets as described
in paragraphs 1.2 and 1.3, Chapter 1 (working from the
top down).

is the cost breakdown structure (CBS).[6] An example of a cost breakdown structure is presented in Figure 2-3.

The cost breakdown structure links objectives and activities with resources, and constitutes a logical subdivision of cost by functional activity area, major element of a system, and/or one or more discrete classes of common or like items. The cost breakdown structure, which is usually adapted or tailored to meet the needs of each individual program, should exhibit the following characteristics:

A. All life cycle costs should be considered and identified in the cost breakdown structure. This includes research and development cost, production and construction cost, operation and logistics support cost, and retirement and disposal cost. Refer to Paragraph 1.2, Chapter 1.[7]

B. Cost categories are generally identified with a significant level of activity or with a major item of material. Cost categories in the CBS must be well defined, and managers, engineers, accountants, and others must have the same understanding of what is included in a given cost category and what is not! Cost omissions and doubling (i.e., counting the same cost in two or more categories) must be precluded.

C. Costs must be broken down to the depth necessary to provide management the sensitivity required in evaluating various facets of system design and development, production, operational use and support. Management must be able to identify high cost areas and the cause and effect relationships.

D. The CBS and the categories defined should be coded in

---

[6] The cost breakdown structure (CBS) and work breakdown structure (WBS), although often treated on an individual basis, should be synonymous relative to application.

[7] This does not mean to imply that all cost categories are relevant to all analyses. The objective here is to include all life cycle costs and then identify those categories that are considered significant relative to the problem at hand. It is important that all identifiable costs be addressed.

such a manner as to facilitate the analysis of specific areas of interest while virtually ignoring other areas. For example, the analyst may wish to investigate supply support costs as a function of engineering design or distribution costs as a function of manufacturing, independent from other aspects of the system. The CBS should be designed with this objective in mind.

E. The CBS and the categories defined should be coded in such a manner as to enable the separation of producer costs, supplier costs, and consumer costs in an expeditious manner.

F. When related to a particular program, the cost structure should be directly compatible (through cross-indexing, coding, etc.) with planning documentation, the work breakdown structure, work packages, the organization structure, PERT/CPM and PERT/COST scheduling networks, Gantt charts, and so on. Costs that are reported through various management information systems must be compatible and consistent with those comparable cost factors in the CBS.

Referring to Figure 2-3, the cost categories identified are obviously too broad to ensure any degree of accountability and control. The analyst can not readily determine what is and what is not included, nor can he (or she) validate that the proper relationships of parameters have been utilized in determining the specific cost factors that are inputed into the illustrated cost structure. In other words, the analyst requires much more information than what is presented in the figure.

In response, Appendix A is included to illustrate an expansion of the CBS in Figure 2-3. Figure A-1 is identical, while Table A-1 includes a description of each cost category (in the order presented in the CBS), along with the symbology and quantitative relationships used to derive costs. Thus, by a thorough review of Table A-1, the analyst can acquire a more indepth knowledge of the assumptions made in determining life cycle cost employing this structure.

Whatever the application may be, the analyst must define the cost relationships in enough depth to provide a clear understanding as to what is happening throughout the cost analysis process.

In summary, establishing the cost breakdown structure is one of the initial steps in life cycle costing. The CBS constitutes the "framework" for defining life cycle costs and provides the communications link for cost reporting, analysis, and ultimate cost control. The CBS is the basic reference point for much of the material presented in subsequent sections of this text.

2.3 COST ESTIMATING [8]

With the cost breakdown structure established, it is now necessary to generate the cost data which are required as an input to the detailed relationships defined for the various cost categories (refer to the elements identified in Table A-1, Appendix A). The estimation of future costs is probably one of the most difficult tasks in the accomplishment of a life cycle cost analysis. In order to develop meaningful cost estimating relationships (CERs), the analyst must use a combination of historical data, bids and proposals from suppliers, analogies through experience with similar systems, and forecasting by the application of selected statistical techniques. Also, different methods for predicting costs

---

[8] The author appreciates the fact that cost estimating per se is a rather comprehensive subject, and that the material coverage presented herein is somewhat broad and general. Actually, there are many studies currently underway which are directed to developing cost factors and estimating relationships; however, the majority of these are peculiar to a given system or product in a particular environment. The discussion here is intended only to convey a conceptual approach to the subject matter. A more indepth coverage of cost estimating is included in: P. F. Oswald, Cost Estimating For Engineering And Management, Prentice-Hall, Inc., 1974.

are applied at different phases in the system/product life
cycle. During the early phases of the life cycle when little
information is available, cost predictions are more apt to
be derived through parametric costing, the application of
statistical forecasting techniques, and/or analogies of one
kind or another. As system design and development progresses,
formal cost quotes are usually available to support final
design and production activities. Also, enough design data
are available to enable relatively good predictions of future
actions associated with the operation and sustaining support
of that system during the latter phases of the life cycle.
Cost estimation as it applies to various phases of the life
cycle is discussed further in Chapter 4.

In determining the cost estimating needs for a given
program, the analyst must review the life cycle requirements,
identify the parameters in the CBS that are cost related,
and attempt to define the cause and effect relationships.
The objective is to determine the dependence of one parameter
on another and/or the interdependence of two or more
parameters on each other. Some research and development costs
for example, are largely independent of the quantity of items
produced and the length of time that a system is in
operational use. Production costs are highly dependent on
the consumer demand for the product, but are basically
independent of the number of years that the product is in use.
System logistics support costs are highly dependent on the
inherent reliability and maintainability characteristics of
the design. Actually, the analyst must not only address the
relationships of major cost categories but must deal with
specific cost-related parameters such as the product size and
weight, reliability (mean time between failure), product
inventory size, and so on.

For the purposes of further discussion, cost estimation is
addressed from the standpoint of discrete cost factors, cost
distributions, and the utilization of cost estimating
relationships (CERs).

2.3.1 The Application of Standard Cost Factors

By standard factors the author is referring to separate
and distinct individual costs such as:

1. The cost of engineering labor -- dollars/manhour for
principal engineer, senior engineer, technician, etc.

2. The cost of manufacturing labor by classification --
dollars/manhour/classification.

3. Overhead rate -- dollars/direct labor cost or percent.

4. Training cost -- dollars/student week.

5. Shipping cost -- dollars/pound/mile.

6. The cost of fuel -- dollars/gallon.

7. The cost of maintaining inventory -- percent of the
inventory value per year.

8. The cost of facilities -- dollars/cubic foot of
occupancy.

9. The cost of material "x" -- dollars/pound.

These and comparable factors, where actual quantitative
values can be directly applied, are usually established from
known rates and costs in the market place, and are a direct
input into the analysis. Care must be exercised to ensure
that the necessary inflationary and deflationary adjustments
are incorporated on a year-to-year basis.

2.3.2 Cost Distributions

Sometimes when analyzing historical cost data, one will
find that the actual cost of a given activity when completed
on a number of occasions will vary from time to time. This
variance may assume any form of distribution such as
illustrated in Figure 2-4.

In the prediction of future costs for comparable activities
on a new program, the analyst may wish to assume a
distribution and determine the median or mean value, variance,
standard deviation, etc., in order to assess risk in terms of
possible cost variations and probabilities. The distributions
associated with historical costs will facilitate this task.

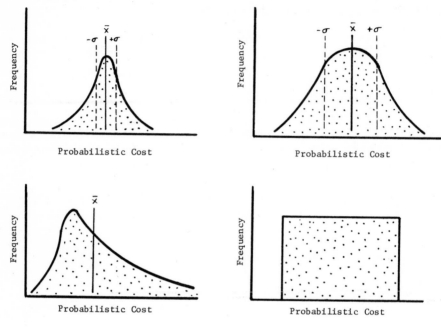

Figure 2-4   Cost Distributions

2.3.3   Cost Estimating Relationships (CERs)

Cost estimating relationships are basically "rules-of-thumb" which relate various categories of cost to cost generating or explanatory variables of one form or another. These explanatory variables usually represent characteristics of system/product performance, physical features, effectiveness factors, or even other cost elements. Estimating relationships may take different forms; i.e., continuous or discontinuous, mathematical or nonmathematical, linear or nonlinear, etc. A few examples are noted below.

Simple Linear Functions

A simple linear estimate may be expressed as:

$$y = a + bx \qquad (1)$$

where "y" and "x" are two variables and "a" and "b" are
numerical constants.

Linear equations are useful because many cost relationships
are of this form. Sometimes linear relationships are
developed employing curve fitting techniques (i.e., least
squares) or normal regression analysis using available
historical data. Such linear functions are utilized for
forecasting purposes and may relate a cost parameter to
another cost parameter, a cost parameter to a non-cost
parameter, and/or a non-cost parameter to another non-cost
parameter. Several illustrations are presented in Figure 2-5.

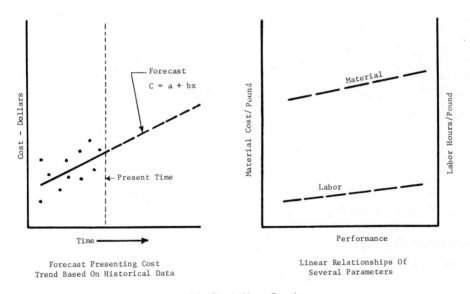

Forecast Presenting Cost   Linear Relationships Of
Trend Based On Historical Data   Several Parameters

Figure 2-5   Simple Linear Functions

Simple Nonlinear Functions

Obviously not all cost functions can be related directly to
a simple linear function. Some cost relationships may be
exponential in nature, hyperbolic, or may fit some other
curve. Examples of nonlinear forms involving a single

explanatory variable are:

$$y = ab^x \qquad \text{(exponential)} \qquad (2)$$

$$y = a+bX=cs^2 \qquad \text{(parabolic)} \qquad (3)$$

$$y = \frac{1}{a+bx} \qquad \text{(hyperbolic)} \qquad (4)$$

Figure 2-6 illustrates several nonlinear applications.

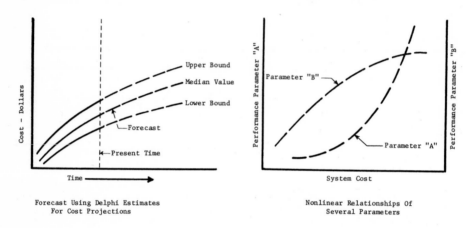

Forecast Using Delphi Estimates
For Cost Projections

Nonlinear Relationships Of
Several Parameters

Figure 2-6   Simple Nonlinear Functions

Discontinuous Step Functions

The estimating relationships introduced thus far imply a continuous function involving cost and other variables. However, in many instances cost can be constant over a specific range of the explanatory variable, then suddenly jump to a higher level at some point in time, remain constant for awhile, then jump to another level, and so on. This type of relationship is known as a "step function", and is illustrated in Figure 2-7. These kinds of functions are useful in illustrating the cost behavior of quantity procurements in production, support activities which are represented in small non-continuous increments, etc.

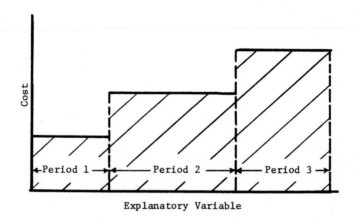

Figure 2-7   Discontinuous Step Function

Other Forms of Estimating

Of a more general nature, the analyst may use analogies as
a form of estimating.   In other words, historical data from
events in the past may be employed in terms of future
estimates on the basis of similarity.   Such estimates may be
used directly, or may be factored to some extent to
compensate for slight differences.   This is often known as
analogous cost estimating.

A somewhat different approach may constitute rank order
cost estimation.   A series of comparable activities are
evaluated in terms of cost and then ranked on the basis of
the magnitude of the cost; i.e., the highest cost activity on
down to the lowest cost activity.   After the ranking is
accomplished, the different activities are viewed in relation
to each other and the initial cost values may be adjusted if
the specific relationships appear to be unrealistic.   This is
basically an iterative process.

The estimation of costs in a life cycle cost analysis is
obviously a critical step in the process.   The proper
relationships should be established and realistic cost

factors must be derived for use in the analysis. In most
instances, the major constraint is the data base which may be
deficient in one way or another. Historical information may
be presented in the wrong format, lack of definition as to
what is included in the data may be a problem, inconsistencies
may be present, gaps in content may exist in critical areas,
and the depth of data included may be questionable in terms
of the sample size available for deriving cost estimates.
The analyst needs to exercise caution in the application of
a given technique (or relationship), must be thorough to
ensure that all available information is used in the correct
manner, and should adequately document all assumptions that
are made in the cost estimating process.

2.4 TREATMENT OF COST IN THE SYSTEM/PRODUCT LIFE CYCLE

2.4.1 Development of Cost Profiles

With the system/product life cycle defined and cost
estimating approaches established, it is now appropriate to
develop a cost profile (or cost projection) illustrating the
distribution of costs over the life cycle. In developing
a cost profile, there are several different procedures that
may be followed; however, the steps noted below are
suggested as a start.

1. Identify all activities throughout the life cycle that
will generate costs of one type or another. This includes
functions associated with planning, research and development,
test and evaluation, production, construction, product
distribution, system/product operational use, logistics
support, and so on.

2. Relate each activity identified in Step 1 to a specific
cost category in the cost breakdown structure (refer to
Figure 2-3). All program activities should fall into one or
more of the categories in the CBS. The cost category
descriptions in Appendix A should provide assistance in the
accomplishment of this step.

3. Establish the appropriate cost factors in <u>constant</u> dollars for each activity in the CBS. Constant dollars reflect the general purchasing power of the dollar at the time of decision; i.e., today. At this point, it is felt that relating costs in terms of constant dollars will allow for a direct comparison of activity levels from year to year prior to the introduction of variable inflationary cost factors, changes in price levels, economic effects of contractual agreements with suppliers, etc., which in turn often cause some confusion in the evaluation of alternatives. Also, using constant dollars tends to assure consistency in accomplishing comparative studies.

4. Within each cost category in the CBS, project the individual cost elements into the future on a year-to-year basis through the life cycle as applicable. The results should constitute a cost stream in constant dollars for these activities that are included.

5. For each cost category in the CBS and for each applicable year in the life cycle, introduce the appropriate inflationary factors, economic effects of learning curves, changes in price levels, and so on.[9] The modified values, in the form of a new cost stream, reflect realistic costs as they are anticipated for each year of the life cycle; i.e., expected 1980 costs in 1980, 1981 costs in 1981, etc. These costs may be used directly in the preparation of future budget requests since they reflect the actual dollar needs anticipated for each year in the life cycle.

6. Summarize the individual cost streams by major categories in the CBS and develop a top level cost profile.

Figure 2-8 reflects the output of Item 3 above, where constant dollar estimates are summarized under the major categories in the CBS, which is illustrated in Figure 2-3. A comparison of costs can be made in terms of the percent

---

[9] The various aspects of inflation and learning curves are discussed further in subsequent paragraphs of this chapter.

contribution of each major category to the total. Categories
where the percent contribution is relatively high should be
broken down into the different sub-categories included
therein, and the high cost areas should be investigated
further in order to determine the cause(s). The breakout of
costs in this fashion not only allows for a comparison of
different activities for a given system/product configuration,
but also facilitates the direct comparison with other systems
wher' costs are presented in a like manner.

Cost Category (Refer to Figure 2-3)	Constant Dollars	Percent Contribution (%)
Research & Development Cost (C_R)	$130,579	10.3
System/Product Life Cycle Management (C_{RM})	19,016	1.5
Product Planning (C_{RP})	2,536	0.2
Product Research (C_{RR})	6,339	0.5
Engineering Design (C_{RE})	68,459	5.4
Design Documentation (C_{RD})	10,142	0.8
System/Product Software (C_{RS})	8,874	0.7
System Test & Evaluation (C_{RT})	15,213	1.2
Production & Construction Cost (C_P)	574,296	45.3
Industrial Engineering & Operations Analysis (C_{PI})	13,945	1.1
Manufacturing (C_{PM})	458,929	36.2
Construction (C_{PC})	67,191	5.3
Quality Control (C_{PQ})	11,411	0.9
Initial Logistics Support (C_{PL})	22,820	1.8
Operation & Support (C_O)	505,836	39.9
System/Product Operations (C_{OO})	83,672	6.6
System/Product Distribution (C_{OD})	64,656	5.1
Sustaining Logistics Support (C_{OL})	357,508	28.2
Retirement & Disposal Cost (C_D)	57,049	4.5
GRAND TOTAL	$1,267,760	100.0%

Figure 2-8 Life Cycle Cost Breakdown

The results from the above sequence of steps are presented
in Figure 2-9. First, it is possible and often beneficial
to evaluate the cost stream for individual activities of the
life cycle such as research and development, production,
operation and support, and so on. Second, these individual
cost streams may be shown in the context of the total cost
spectrum. Finally, the total cost profile may be viewed
from the standpoint of the logical flow of activities and the
proper level and timely expenditure of dollars. Additional
discussion of cost profiles is presented later.

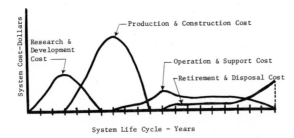

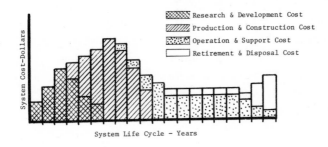

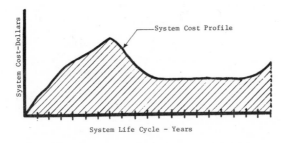

Figure 2-9 Development of a Cost Profile

2.4.2 Dealing with Inflation

When developing time-phased cost profiles, the aspect of
inflation should be considered for each future year in the
life cycle. During the past several decades, inflation has
been a significant factor in the rising costs of products and
services and in the reduction of the purchasing power of the
dollar. Inflation is a rather broad term covering the
general increase(s) in the unit cost of an item or activity,
and is primarily related to labor and material costs.

1. Inflation factors applied to <u>labor</u> -- increased labor
costs due to salary and wage increases; cost of living
increases; and increases in overhead rates due to the rising
costs of personnel fringe benefits, retirement benefits,
insurance, etc. Inflation factors should be determined for
different categories of labor (i.e., engineering labor,
technician labor, manufacturing labor, construction labor,
customer service personnel labor, management labor, and so
on), and should be estimated for each year in the life cycle.

2. Inflation factors applied to <u>material</u> -- increased
costs due to material availability, supply and demand
characteristics; the increased costs of material processing;
and increases in material handling and transportation costs.
Inflation factors will often vary with each type of material,
and should be estimated for each year in the life cycle.
These factors are usually different from those applied to
labor.

Increasing costs of an inflationary nature often occur as a
result of new contract provisions with suppliers, new labor
agreements and union contracts, revisions in procurement
policies, shifts in sources of supply, the introduction of
engineering changes, program schedule shifts, changes in
productivity levels, changes in item quantities, and for other
comparable reasons. Further, inflation factors are influenced
to some extent by geographical location and competition.
When reviewing the various causes of inflation, one must be

extremely careful to avoid overestimating and double counting
for the effects of inflation. For instance, a supplier's
proposal may include provisions for inflation and, unless
this fact is noted, there is a good chance that an additional
estimate for inflation will be included for the same item.

Inflation factors should be estimated on a year-to-year
basis if at all possible. Since inflation estimates may
change considerably with general economic conditions at the
national level, cost estimates far out in the future (i.e.,
five years and greater) should be reviewed at least annually
and adjusted as required. Inflation factors may be
established by using price indices, or as a last resort, by
the application of a uniform inflation rate.

2.4.3 Application of Learning Curves

When accomplishing an activity or process on a repetitive
basis, learning takes place and the experience gained often
results in reduced cost. Although learning and the
associated cost variations occur at different activity points
throughout the life cycle, the greatest impact of learning on
cost is realized in the production of large quantities of a
given item. In such instances, the cost of the first unit
produced is generally higher than the cost of the 25th unit,
which may be higher than the cost of the 50th unit, and so on.
This is primarily due to job familiarization by the workers
in the production facility, development of more efficient
methods for item fabrication and assembly, the use of more
efficient tools, and improvement in overall management. The
effects of learning generally results in the largest portion
of any cost savings taking place relatively early in a
uniform production run, with a leveling off taking place
later on.

In the development of life cycle cost projections, the
analyst must review all activities to evaluate the effects of
learning on cost. Where the effects are significant, it may
be appropriate to apply a learning curve in order to develop

a more realistic cost profile. Learning curves are commonly
derived on the basis of assuming a constant percentage cost
savings for each doubling of the quantity of production units.
For example, an eighty percent (80%) <u>unit</u> learning curve
implies that the second unit costs eighty percent of the
first, the fourth unit costs eighty percent of the second,
the eighth unit costs eighty percent of the fourth, and so
on. This learning curve is then applied to the production
cost profile.

In actuality, unit learning curves may vary considerably
depending on the expected magnitude of the cost savings
estimated for the second unit, the 10th unit, the 20th unit,
etc. Because of the product complexity, an 80% unit cost
reduction may not be realized until the production of the 10th
unit. In this case, an 80% learning curve will be based on
the 10th, 20th, 40th and 80th units as being the major
milestones for cost measurement. Thus, we still may utilize
an 80% learning curve, but the cost factors will be different.
The analyst should evaluate the complexity of tasks in the
production process and attempt to determine the type of unit
learning curve that is most appropriate for the situation at
hand. An example of a variety of unit learning curves is
presented in Figure 2-10.

Sometimes in the application of learning curves it may be
more appropriate to use a cumulative average learning curve.
If it turns out that the projected average cost of producing
the first 20 units is 80% of the average cost of producing
the first 10 units, then the process follows an 80%
<u>cumulative average</u> learning curve.

The application of learning curves must not only consider
labor cost but should also cover material cost, although the
percentages in each case may be different. While labor costs
relate to both the required personnel skill levels and manhours to accomplish a given function, material costs may vary
as a function of factory tooling, material scrapage rates
(or percent of raw material utilized after the fabrication
process), procurement methods, and inventory policies. Again,

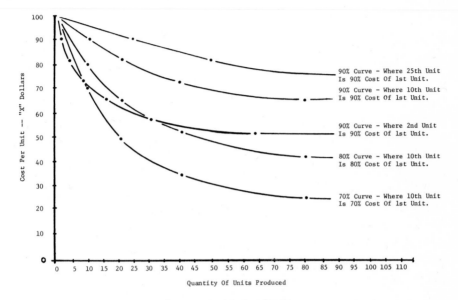

Figure 2-10 Unit Learning Curves

there are many factors involved and different learning curves may be applied depending on the specific situation.

Finally, in the application of learning curves the analyst must ensure that the production process is indeed continuous and relatively void of design changes, manufacturing changes in producing the product, and/or organization changes that will ultimately cancel out the effects of a learning curve altogether, if not create a negative learning curve where producing the 10th unit is more costly than the first.

The proper application of learning curves is considered significant in life cycle costing. Although the effects of learning curves may be minimal for research and development activities, they may be significant in determining production costs and follow-on system/product operation and maintenance support costs. In order to gain more insight on the subject, the review of additional material is recommended.[10]

2.4.4 Time Value of Money[11]

It should be recognized that a dollar today is worth more than a dollar in the future, primarily due to the fact that the investment of money can earn interest over time. Since the dollar in hand can be invested and accumulate interest each year, one's preference should be to receive the dollar now. In essence, money has time value and the relationship between interest and time leads to the concept of "time value of money".

Throughout the development of a given system or product there are many decisions required, and such decisions evolve through the evaluation of alternative proposals of one type or another. Each proposal considered in the evaluation process, representing a potential investment, is viewed from the standpoint of anticipated receipts and disbursements that will occur over the designated life cycle; i.e., revenues and costs at dispersed points in time. Alternatives such as the investment in Configuration "A", Configuration "B", or the investment of money in a bank, are evaluated in a like manner. Since revenues and costs are related to different activities at different times in the life cycle, a common point of reference must be assumed such that all alternatives can be compared on an equivalent basis. In other words, the flow of revenues and costs (having time value) for each alternative being considered must be equated to a common reference point. This point is generally the "present time" or "now", when decisions that have a

[10] W. J. Fabrycky, P. M. Ghare, P. E. Torgersen, Industrial Operations Research, Prentice-Hall, Inc., 1972.

[11] A good source for further discussion on the subject of time value of money is: W. J. Fabrycky and G. J. Thuesen, Economic Decision Analysis, Prentice-Hall, Inc., Englewood Cliffs, N.J., 1974.

significant impact on the future are made; thus, all future revenues and costs for each year in the life cycle are discounted to the present value.

The aspect of discounting refers to the application of a selected rate of interest to measure the difference in importance of preference between dollars at the present time and anticipated dollars in the future. Discounting allows for the evaluation of the time-phased profiles of money streams for various alternatives as if they occurred at one point in time (the only fair method of evaluation if one is to make a decision today) rather than spread over the project life cycle. "Interest" is the rent paid for the use of money or the gain received from an investment, depending on whether you are the borrower or the lender. An "interest rate" is the ratio of this value over time, usually expressed annually. For example, if one were to invest $1,000 at a simple interest rate of six percent per annum, the interest (I) at the end of one year would be:

$$I = 1,000 \ (0.06) \ (1) = \$60$$

The principle amount plus the interest received at the end of the year would be $1,060.

Interest rates will vary with the market conditions and the overall economy. Such rates applied to individual investments are usually based on the "prime rate", which is the lowest rate generally charged on business loans to large, well-established, financially-sound corporations. This rate is usually specified by high volume money market banks and is relatively uniform throughout the nation. In essence, the rate used in comparing future dollars with today's dollars depends on the alternative opportunities available to exchange one for the other.[12]

---

[12] Interest rates and their application to loans and investments are discussed in depth in textbooks on finance and financial management. One source is J. C. Van Horne, Financial Management And Policy, 3rd Edition, Prentice-Hall, Inc., Englewood Cliffs, N.J., 1974.

The established interest rate(s) is employed in discounting and discounting is a technique for converting different money flows occurring over time to an equivalent amount at a specified point. For the purposes of illustration, assume that a five-year project is undertaken, resulting in a series of money transactions, as illustrated in Figure 2-11.

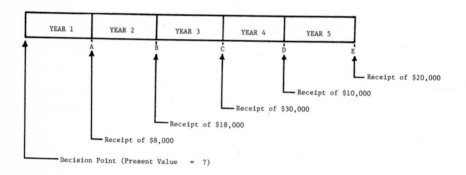

Figure 2-11 Present Value of Money Transactions

Although revenues and costs usually occur at discrete points throughout any given year (i.e., January, April, June, September, etc.), they are generally treated either at the beginning or at the end of the applicable time period. In this instance, the revenue receipts are related to the end of each year throughout the project life cycle. The objective here is to convert these receipts to the present value. For Year 1, the sum of all estimated receipts is represented at Point "A". The question is: What is the value of these receipts in terms of the decision point in Figure 2-11? This can be determined from Equation (5), representing a single payment present value expression.

$$P = F \left[\frac{1}{(1+i)^n} \right] \qquad (5)$$

where "P" is the present value or present principle sum, "F" is the future sum at some interest point, "i" is the annual interest rate, and "n" is the interest period.

Assuming an interest rate of 10 percent, the present value of the receipts at Point "A" in Figure 2-11 is:

$$P = 8,000 \left[\frac{1}{(1+0.1)} \right] = (8,000)(0.9091) = \$7,272.80$$

For Point "B", this becomes:

$$P = 18,000 \left[\frac{1}{(1+0.1)^2} \right] = (18,000)(0.8264) = \$14,875.20$$

Now, consider the present value of the combined receipts at Points "A" and "B". This can be calculated from Equation (6).

$$P = F_A \left[\frac{1}{(1+i)} \right] + F_B \left[\frac{1}{(1+i)^2} \right] \qquad (6)$$

Assuming the undiscounted estimates of $8,000 and $18,000 at Points "A" and "B" respectively, the present value is:

$$P = 8,000 \left[\frac{1}{(1+0.0)} \right] + 18,000 \left[\frac{1}{(1+0.1)^2} \right] = \$22,148$$

This process continues until the receipts for each year in the life cycle are discounted to the present value and totaled. The total present value of receipts for the project represented in Figure 2-11 is $63,635 (note that the undiscounted total value is $86,000). When the receipts or costs are different for each year in the life cycle, the present value expression is a continuation of Equation (6), or:

$$P = F_A \left[\frac{1}{(1+i)} \right] + F_B \left[\frac{1}{(1+i)^2} \right] \qquad (7)$$

$$+ F_C \left[\frac{1}{(1+i)^3} \right] + \ldots + F_n \left[\frac{1}{(1+i)^n} \right]$$

Present value calculations can be simplified by using standard interest tables and by multiplying the future sum

by the appropriate factor.[13] Figure 2-12 presents an
abbreviated sample of present-value factors, and Appendix B
includes some additional tables.

n \ i	2%	4%	6%	8%	10%	15%	20%	25%
1	0.9804	0.9615	0.9434	0.9259	0.9091	0.8696	0.8333	0.8000
2	0.9612	0.9246	0.8900	0.8573	0.8264	0.7561	0.6944	0.6400
3	0.9423	0.8890	0.8396	0.7938	0.7513	0.6575	0.5787	0.5120
4	0.9238	0.8548	0.7921	0.7350	0.6830	0.5718	0.4823	0.4096
5	0.9057	0.8219	0.7473	0.6806	0.6209	0.4972	0.4019	0.3277
6	0.8880	0.7903	0.7050	0.6302	0.5645	0.4323	0.3349	0.2621
7	0.8706	0.7599	0.6651	0.5835	0.5130	0.3759	0.2791	0.2097
8	0.8535	0.7307	0.6274	0.5403	0.4665	0.3269	0.2326	0.1678
9	0.8368	0.7026	0.5919	0.5002	0.4241	0.2843	0.1938	0.1342
10	0.8203	0.6756	0.5584	0.4632	0.3855	0.2472	0.1615	0.1074
11	0.8043	0.6496	0.5268	0.4289	0.3505	0.2149	0.1346	0.0859
12	0.7885	0.6246	0.4970	0.3971	0.3186	0.1869	0.1122	0.0687
13	0.7730	0.6006	0.4688	0.3677	0.2897	0.1625	0.0935	0.0550
14	0.7579	0.5775	0.4423	0.3405	0.2633	0.1413	0.0779	0.0440
15	0.7430	0.5553	0.4173	0.3152	0.2394	0.1229	0.0649	0.0352
16	0.7284	0.5339	0.3936	0.2919	0.2176	0.1069	0.0541	0.0281
17	0.7142	0.5134	0.3714	0.2703	0.1978	0.0929	0.0451	0.0225
18	0.7002	0.4936	0.3503	0.2502	0.1799	0.0808	0.0376	0.0180
19	0.6864	0.4746	0.3305	0.2317	0.1635	0.0703	0.0313	0.0144
20	0.6730	0.4564	0.3118	0.2145	0.1486	0.0611	0.0261	0.0115
25	0.6095	0.3751	0.2330	0.1460	0.0923	0.0304	0.0105	0.0038
30	0.5521	0.3083	0.1741	0.0994	0.0573	0.0151	0.0042	0.0012
40	0.4529	0.2083	0.0972	0.0460	0.0221	0.0037	0.0007	0.0001
50	0.3715	0.1407	0.0543	0.0213	0.0085	0.0009	0.0001	....
100	0.1380	0.0198	0.0029	0.0005	0.0001	....	....	....

Figure 2-12   **Present Value Factors (Typical)**
(Source: B. S. Blanchard, *Engineering Organization
and Management,* Prentice-Hall, Inc. 1976.
By Permission.)

[13] The appropriate interest factors are included in most
textbooks on the subject of economic analysis.

In cases where cash flows in each future period are identical, the present value of the series, representing an annuity, can be determined by multiplying the value of the cash flow by a compound discount factor. For example, the present value of a future stream of $1,000 receipts for a five-year period using a 10 percent discount rate is:

$$\overset{\cdot}{P} = 1,000 \ (3.7908) + \$3,790.80$$

The compound discount rate is the summation of the individual factors for the first five periods indicated under the 10 percent column in Figure 2-12 (i.e., 0.9091, 0.8264, 0.7513, 0.6830, and 0.6209). An example of some typical compound factors is presented in Figure 2-13.

Where Figure 2-11 illustrates a continuous flow of money transactions over a five-year period, it is now appropriate

Present Value of One Dollar per Year "n" at Interest Rate "i"

Year	10%	11%	12%	13%	14%	15%	16%	17%	18%	19%	20%
1	0.9091	0.9009	0.8929	0.8850	0.8772	0.8696	0.8621	0.8547	0.8475	0.8403	0.8333
2	1.7355	1.7125	1.6901	1.6681	1.6467	1.6257	1.6052	1.5852	1.5656	1.5465	1.5278
3	2.4868	2.4437	2.4018	2.3612	2.3216	2.2832	2.2459	2.2096	2.1743	2.1399	2.1065
4	3.1699	3.1024	3.0373	2.9745	2.9137	2.8550	2.7982	2.7432	2.6901	2.6386	2.5887
5	3.7908	3.6959	3.6048	3.5172	3.4331	3.3522	3.2743	3.1993	3.1272	3.0576	2.9906
6	4.3553	4.2305	4.1114	3.9976	3.8887	3.7845	3.6847	3.5892	3.4976	3.4098	3.3255
7	4.8684	4.7122	4.5638	4.4226	4.2883	4.1604	4.0386	3.9224	3.8115	3.7057	3.6046
8	5.3349	5.1461	4.9676	4.7988	4.6389	4.4873	4.3436	4.2072	4.0776	3.9544	3.8372
9	5.7590	5.5370	5.3282	5.1317	4.9464	4.7716	4.6065	4.4506	4.3030	4.1633	4.0310
10	6.1446	5.8892	5.6502	5.4262	5.2161	5.0188	4.8332	4.6586	4.4941	4.3389	4.1925
11	6.4951	6.2065	5.9377	5.6869	5.4527	5.2337	5.0286	4.8364	4.6560	4.4865	4.3271
12	6.8137	6.4924	6.1944	5.9176	5.6603	5.4206	5.1971	4.9884	4.7932	4.6105	4.4392
13	7.1034	6.7499	6.4235	6.1218	5.8424	5.5831	5.3423	5.1183	4.9095	4.7147	4.5327
14	7.3667	6.9819	6.6282	6.3025	6.0021	5.7245	5.4675	5.2293	5.0081	4.8023	4.6106
15	7.6061	7.1909	6.8109	6.4624	6.1422	5.8474	5.5755	5.3242	5.0916	4.8759	4.6755
16	7.8237	7.3792	6.9740	6.6039	6.2651	5.9542	5.6685	5.4053	5.1624	4.9377	4.7296
17	8.0215	7.5488	7.1196	6.7291	6.3729	6.0472	5.7487	5.4746	5.2223	4.9897	4.7746
18	8.2014	7.7016	7.2497	6.8399	6.4674	6.1280	5.8178	5.5339	5.2732	5.0333	4.8122
19	8.3649	7.8393	7.3658	6.9380	6.5504	6.1982	5.8775	5.5845	5.3162	5.0700	4.8435
20	8.5136	7.9633	7.4694	7.0248	6.6231	6.2593	5.9288	5.6278	5.3527	5.1009	4.8696
21	8.6487	8.0751	7.5620	7.1016	6.6870	6.3125	5.9731	5.6648	5.3837	5.1268	4.8913
22	8.7715	8.1757	7.6446	7.1695	6.7429	6.3587	6.0113	5.6964	5.4099	5.1486	4.9094
23	8.8832	8.2664	7.7184	7.2297	6.7921	6.3988	6.0442	5.7234	5.4321	5.1668	4.9245
24	8.9847	8.3481	7.7843	7.7829	6.8351	6.4338	6.0726	5.7465	5.4509	5.1822	4.9371
25	9.0770	8.4217	7.8431	7.3300	6.8729	6.4641	6.0971	5.7662	5.4669	5.1951	4.9476

Figure 2-13 **Compound Present Value Factors (Typical)**
(Source: B. S. Blanchard, *Engineering Organization and Management*, Prentice-Hall, Inc. 1976. By Permission.)

to show a discontinuous flow of cash receipts. Figure 2-14
illustrates a nine-year life cycle with cash receipts
indicated at the end of Years 1, 4, 5, 6, 7, and 9. Note
that there is a series of identical receipts at the end of
Years 4, 5, 6, and 7, which can be discounted by using a
compound factor to relate the series back to the end of
Year 3 and then a single discount factor to convert this
value to the present time. The total present value of the
money flow in Figure 2-14 is $11,168.05 (versus an
undiscounted total of $19,000).

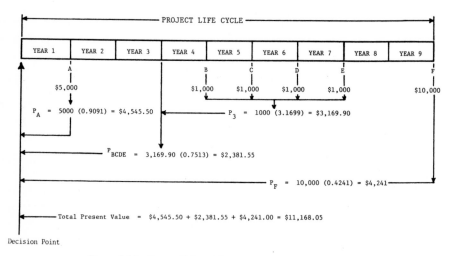

Figure 2-14   Present Value of Discontinuous Money Transactions

The above discussion should now be carried one step further
to illustrate the evaluation of alternative cost streams. As
stated earlier, the present value approach is required when
comparing alternatives and in evaluating two (or more)
different cost streams on a comparable basis. Figure 2-15
presents a simplified version of two alternative projects,
and the objective is to select a preferred approach using a
discount rate of eight percent. Referring to the figure,
Design "B" is preferred on the basis of the comparison
between the two cost streams.

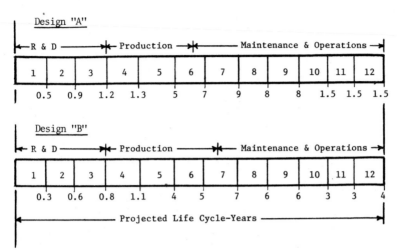

Decision Point

Year	Undiscounted Cost-M$		Discount Factor	Present Value Cost - M$	
	Design "A"	Design "B"		Design "A"	Design "B"
1	0.5	0.3	0.9259	0.4629	0.2542
2	0.9	0.6	0.8573	0.7716	0.5144
3	1.2	0.8	0.7938	0.9526	0.6350
4	1.3	1.1	0.7350	0.9555	0.8085
5	5	4	0.6806	3.4030	2.7224
6	7	5	0.6302	4.4114	3.1510
7	9	7	0.5835	5.2515	4.0845
8	8	6	0.5403	4.3224	3.2418
9	8	6	0.5002	4.0016	3.0012
10	1.5	3	0.4632	0.6948	1.3896
11	1.5	3	0.4289	0.6434	1.2867
12	1.5	4	0.3971	0.5957	1.5884
			Total	$ 26.4664M	$ 22.6777M

Choice - Design "B"

Figure 2-15 Evaluation of Alternatives

The discussion thus far deals with the conversion of anticipated future revenues and costs to the present value. This is necessary for the evaluation of proposals in terms of the present time. However, one may wish to relate money transactions to some future point in time, assuming this point to be at a time when a major investment decision will be made. In such instances, the single payment present value equation (Equation 5) can be transposed to:

$$F = P \left[(1 + i)^n \right] \qquad (8)$$

This equation can be used to determine the results of various investments. For instance, assume that \$6,000 is invested today in some venture and the annual interest rate is eight percent, the compound amount at the end of Year 2 is:[14]

$$F = 6,000 \left[(1 + 0.08)^2 \right] = \$6,998.40$$

With the application of present value and future value concepts, the analyst can relate these to the life cycle and convert revenues and costs to any designated decision point. Figure 2-16 illustrates this, where the anticipated decision point is at the end of Year 2. The discounted value of the cost stream at the decision point is \$53,724.80. Likewise, these principles can be extended to the evaluation of alternative cost streams as illustrated in Figure 2-15.

In summary, revenues and costs may be treated differently, depending on the problem at hand. Money has time value and discounting is appropriate in the direct comparison of alternative cost profiles. Discounting is employed to relate

---

[14] For simplicity purposes, Appendix B includes interest tables covering present value and future value factors, and may be used to facilitate the numerical process used in arriving at an answer. The future value factor in this instance is 1.1664.

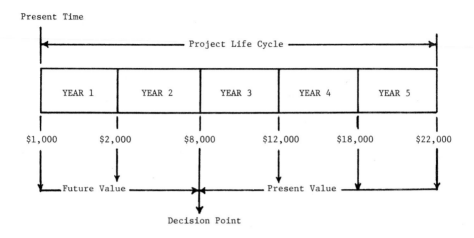

$$\text{Value At Decision Point (10\%)} = 8,000 + 2,000 \ (1.100) + 1,000 \ (1.210)$$
$$+ \ 12,000 \ (0.9091) + 18,000 \ (0.8265) + 22,000 \ (0.7513) = \$53,724.80$$

Figure 2-16   Present Value/Future Value Cost Projection

all revenues and costs to a specific decision point, whether now or in the future.[15]

2.4.5   Use of Cost Profiles in Analysis

Figure 2-9 (Paragraph 2.4) illustrates the steps required in developing an undiscounted cost profile for a specific project. In the evaluation of alternatives a similar profile may be developed for each project being considered, and the various alternative projects in question are then reviewed in terms of selecting a preferred approach. When reviewing different profiles the analyst should not only

---

[15] If the analyst wishes to evaluate a preferred cost profile on the basis of future budget requirements, then he (or she) may wish to convert the discounted values back to the inflated yearly values discussed in Paragraph 2.4.

look at the quantitative life cycle cost figures-of-merit developed by summing the costs reported through the cost breakdown structure (refer to Figure 2-8), but the analyst should also address the time impacts of costs.

To illustrate this point, Figure 2-17 shows two different undiscounted cost profiles where the ultimate quantitative figures-of-merit are identical. In this situation, the decision maker would be indifferent regarding the choice of Configuration "A" or "B". However, the time impact of costs for "A" and "B" are considerably different. Configuration "A" requires lower initial acquisition costs (i.e., research and development, production) and relatively high operating and support costs. On the other hand, Configuration "B" requires higher acquisition costs and lower operating and support costs. The costs for "A" are definitely higher during the later years.

Undiscounted Cost Profiles (Costs In Millions Of Dollars)

Year	1	2	3	4	5	6	7	8	Total
Cost Profile "A"	0.9	1.7	2.8	2.6	2.4	2.4	2.4	1.9	17.1
Cost Profile "B"	1.1	2.9	3.6	2.4	2.1	1.8	1.7	1.5	17.1

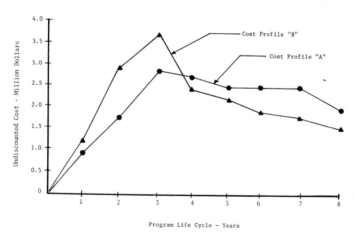

Figure 2-17 Alternative Cost Profiles (Undiscounted)

In view of the differences in the time impact of costs
for Configuration "A" and "B", the question arises as to
whether the analyst would still be indifferent regarding the
choice of "A" or "B" if the time preference assumptions
were adjusted to reflect present value costs. Figure 2-18
converts the undiscounted profiles illustrated in
Figure 2-17 to discounted profiles using first a six percent
discount factor and then a 15 percent discount factor. In
both instances, Configuration "A" assumes a slight advantage;
i.e., a difference of approximately $400,000 with a six per
cent discount rate and $700,000 with a 15 percent discount
rate. This is a significant difference if the analyst
considers that absolute cost values are important. In any
event, when comparing alternatives the time value of money
concept must be addressed.

2.4.6 Breakeven Analysis (Payback)[16]

In the evaluation of alternatives, consideration must not
only be given to which alternative is preferred from the
standpoint of overall life cycle cost, but also to the point
in time in the life cycle when that alternative actually
assumes a favorable position. In some instances, a given
alternative may be preferable on the basis of the
quantitative life cycle cost figure-of-merit; however, the
time preference of the cost profile may not be favorable when
compared to other opportunities, particularly if the
perceived advantage is not realized until a point far out in
the life cycle.

A breakeven analysis should be accomplished prior to
arriving at a final decision in connection with the selection

---

[16] The coverage of breakeven analysis in this text is
basically limited to revenues and costs as a function of
time. The author appreciates the fact that there are
many additional applications employing a variety of
indices.

Life Cycle Cost

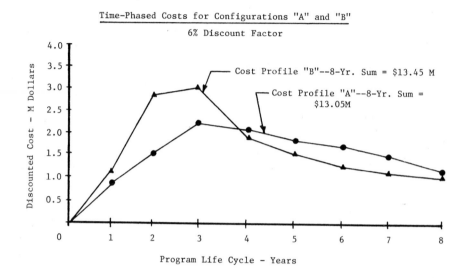

Time-Phased Costs for Configurations "A" and "B"

6% Discount Factor

Cost Profile "B"--8-Yr. Sum = $13.45 M

Cost Profile "A"--8-Yr. Sum = $13.05M

Discounted Cost – M Dollars

Program Life Cycle – Years

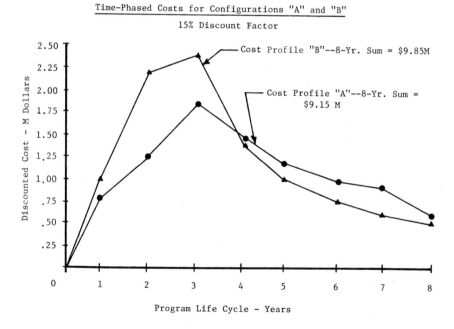

Time-Phased Costs for Configurations "A" and "B"

15% Discount Factor

Cost Profile "B"--8-Yr. Sum = $9.85M

Cost Profile "A"--8-Yr. Sum = $9.15 M

Discounted Cost – M Dollars

Program Life Cycle – Years

Figure 2-18 Alternative Cost Profiles (Discounted)

of a preferred approach. Such an analysis may assume a
variety of forms. Relative to life cycle cost, it may be
desirable to determine when the cumulative cost of one
alternative exceeds the cumulative cost of another. In this
instance, the analysis aids in selecting the least costly
approach in terms of life cycle cost. The curves projected
in Figure 2-19 indicate that Configuration "A" is preferable
to "B" on the basis of lowest overall life cycle cost, and
"A" assumes a preferable position at the designated
"breakeven point". The shaded area represents benefits
derived based on cost avoidance.

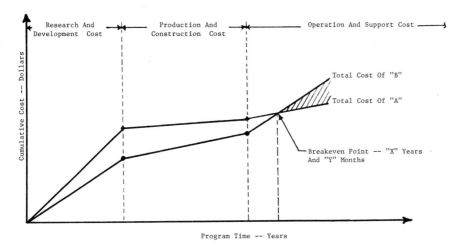

Figure 2-19 **Breakeven Analysis**

Referring to the figure, the analyst must ask the
question: Is the breakeven point reasonable in terms of
possible system/product obsolescence, competition, and
business risk and uncertainty? If the breakeven point is
too far out in time, it may appear to be more feasible to
select Configuration "B" in lieu of "A" due to possible
obsolescence of the system or competition resulting in the
introduction of a better product. Also, if the magnitude

of the benefits derived are small by accepting "A" (i.e., limited cost savings), then "B" may be preferable when considering all program risks.

When considering the various aspects of risk the projections illustrated in Figure 2-19 may assume the profile depicted in Figure 2-20. If variable cost estimates are used as an input to the life cycle cost analysis (e.g., an upper bound value and a lower bound value shown in Figure 2-6, or a distribution of cost estimates as presented in Figure 2-4), then the output may result in a narrow band effect as indicated. In evaluating the two alternatives as shown in Figure 2-20, there is a specific point in time when Configuration "A" is obviously preferred and a time when "B" is definitely preferred; however, there is a period of uncertainty when there is a risk associated with the selection of either configuration (between Points "X" and "Y" in the figure). The occurrence of such should direct the analyst to review the input cost factors, relative to

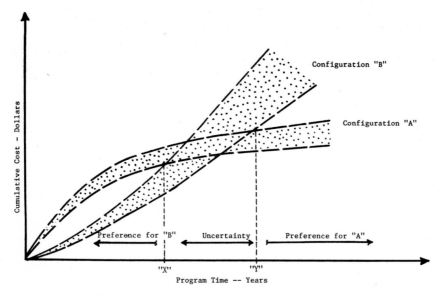

Figure 2-20 Range of Cost Estimates for Alternatives

improved estimates, with the objective of further narrowing
the band and reducing the period of uncertainty.

Figure 2-21 illustrates the cash flows for two projects
being considered (note that both revenues and costs are
included).[17] Referring to the profile for Project "A", the

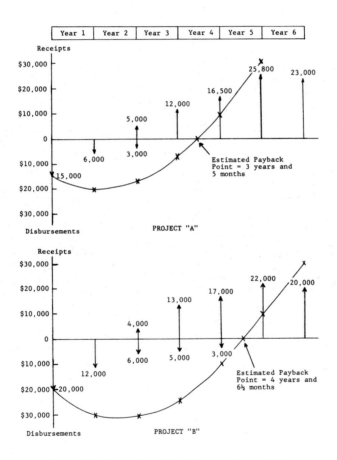

**Figure 2-21 Comparison of Cash Flows and Payback Points
(Source: B. S. Blanchard, *Engineering Organization
and Management,* Prentice-Hall, Inc. 1976.
By Permission.)**

---

[17] B. Blanchard, <u>Engineering Organization And Management</u>,
Prentice-Hall, Inc., 1976, Chapter 11.

initial investment of $15,000 and the added cost factors of
$6,000 at the end of Year 1 and $3,000 at the end of Year 2
represent a $24,000 total cost. The revenue values of
$5,000 in Year 2, $12,000 in Year 3, and a proportion of the
$16,500 in Year 4 are added and compared to the cost. The
point in time when the incremental amount of revenue
accumulated during Year 4 is equivalent to the total cost is
the breakeven or payback point, which is approximately
three years and five months after project initiation. This,

PROJECT "A"

Year	Cash Flow		Discount Factor	Net Present Value	
	Benefits	Costs		Benefits	Costs
0		$15,000	0.0000		$15,000.00
1		6,000	0.9091		5,454.60
2	$5,000	3,000	0.8264	$ 4,132.00	2,479.20
3	12,000		0.7513	9,015.60	
4	16,500		0.6830	11,269.50	
5	25,800		0.6209	16,019.22	
6	23,000		0.5645	12,983.50	
Total	$62,300	$24.000		$53,419.82	$22,933.80

PROJECT "B"

Year	Cash Flow		Discount Factor	Net Present Value	
	Benefits	Costs		Benefits	Costs
0		$20,000	0.0000		$20,000.00
1		12,000	0.9091		10,909.20
2	$ 4,000	6,000	0.8264	$ 3,305.60	4,958.40
3	13,000	5,000	0.7513	9,766.90	3,756.50
4	17,000	3,000	0.6830	11,611.00	2,049.00
5	22,000		0.6209	13,659.80	
6	20,000		0.5645	11,290.00	
Total	$76,000	$46,000		$49,633.30	$41,673.10

Note: These values represent the cash flows in
Figure 2-21. A 10% discount rate is assumed.

Figure 2-22 Present Value of Cash Flows (Two Projects)
(Source: B. S. Blanchard, *Engineering Organization
and Management,* Prentice-Hall, Inc. 1976.
By Permission.)

when compared to the payback point of four years and six
months for Project "B", results in the selection of
Project "A" as the preferred approach.

Prior to making a final decision, however, the analyst may
wish to proceed one step further and determine net present
value of money transactions for both projects and make a
comparison on the basis of benefits and costs. The results
should support Project "A", considering the time phased
profiles. Figure 2-22 presents the present value of the
cash flows for each project.

Referring to the figure, the net present value for
Project "A" (using a 10 percent discount rate) is $30,486.02,
and the net present value for Project "B" is $7,960.20.
Thus, Project "A" is preferred.

QUESTIONS AND PROBLEMS

1. Define in your own words the following: total cost; unit
    cost; indirect cost; variable cost; fixed cost; recurring
    cost; nonrecurring cost; incremental cost; functional cost;
    and marginal cost.
2. What characteristics should be incorporated in a cost
    breakdown structure?
3. How does the cost breakdown structure relate to the work
    breakdown structure?
4. Define what is meant by a cost estimating relationship.
    Give some examples.
5. Identify the steps required in developing a cost profile.
    Select a system of your choice and develop a life cycle
    cost profile.
6. What is meant by "constant" dollars? Inflated dollars?
    Present value?
7. Refer to Figure 2-8. What do the relative costs indicate?
    Discuss the various cause and effect relationships.

8. Discuss how you would treat inflation in determining life cycle costs.

9. How would you apply learning curves in the system/product life cycle?

10.

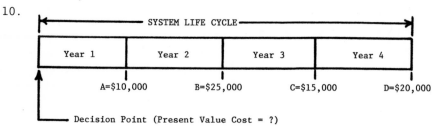

    What is the present value of the cost stream illustrated above using an 8% discount rate?

11. What is the present value of a future stream of $1,000 for a four-year period, using an eight per cent discount rate?

12. Find the compound amount of $1,000 four years from now at a nominal annual interest rate of six per cent compounded semi-annually.

13. Two alternatives below are being evaluated in terms of present cost in millions of dollars. Which one would you select? Why? Assume a 9% constant interest rate.

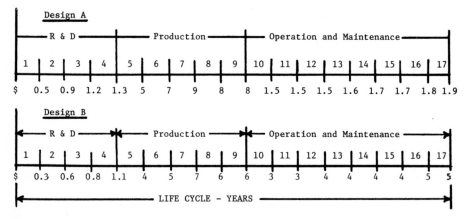

14. Compare the two design alternatives below in terms of equivalent costs at the designate decision point. Which alternative would you select?

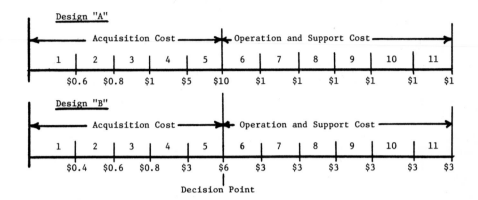

15. What is a breakeven analysis? Why is it important?

Chapter 3

THE ELEMENTS OF COST ANALYSIS

Thus far, the material presented covers an introduction to life cycle costing along with some of the principles involved in treating and applying costs. The intent of this chapter is to discuss the requirements for analyses and the steps involved in the basic life cycle cost analysis process.

3.1 REQUIREMENTS OF LIFE CYCLE COST ANALYSIS

Throughout the system/product life cycle, as illustrated in Figure 1-8, there are many decisions required of both a technical and non-technical nature. The majority of these decisions, particularly those at the earlier stages of a program, have life cycle implications and definitely impact life cycle cost. It may appear initially that a specific problem will not directly impact life cycle cost; however, the indirect effects on cost may turn out to be significant. Thus, engineers and managers alike should consider life cycle costs in their decision making process.

For each specific problem where there are possible alternative solutions and a decision is required in the selection of a preferred approach, there is an overall analysis process that one usually follows, either intuitively

or on a more formal basis.[1] The problem must be well defined;
an evaluation approach must be established; a model of some
type is developed to facilitate the evaluation process; data
are generated on each alternative and analyzed; and a
recommendation for a proposed solution is made. This is an
iterative process (with the necessary feedback provisions),
and is "tailored" to the specific problem at hand. Figure 3-1
illustrates this process in a simplified manner.

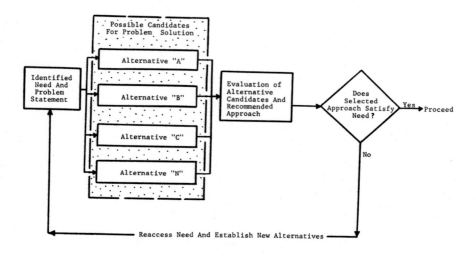

Figure 3-1 The Basic Evaluation Process

The steps identified above may be expanded to better
illustrate the life cycle cost analysis process and to relate
this approach to specific applications. Figure 3-2 reflects
a typical step-by-step sequence of activities that may be
generally applied to any given problem in any phase of the
life cycle. Again, the steps shown, although applicable in

---

[1] The term "preferred" does not necessarily infer "optimal"
as the goals and the constraints of the analysis may not
permit true optimization. "Preferred" does imply the best
among a number of available alternatives within the given
constraints.

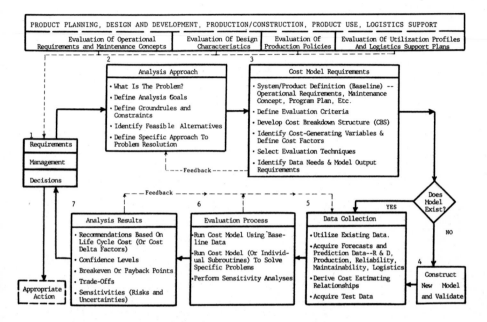

Figure 3-2 Life Cycle Cost Analysis Process

each instance, are tailored to the specific problem at hand and the overall process is iterative in nature. A detailed discussion of significant points dealing with this process is included in Paragraph 3.2.

Relative to applications in the system/product life cycle, a few problem oriented examples where life cycle cost analysis is appropriate to support the decision making process are noted. Specifically, life cycle cost analysis should be employed in the evaluation of:

A. Alternative system/product operational, utilization, and environmental profiles.

B. Alternative system maintenance concepts and logistics support policies.

C. Alternative system/product design configurations-- packaging schemes, diagnostic routines, built in test versus external test, manual functions versus automation, hardware versus software approaches, component selection and

standardization, reliability versus maintainability, levels
of repair versus discard decisions, etc.

D. Alternative procurement sources and the selection of
a supplier for a given item.

E. Alternative production approaches -- continuous versus
discontinuous production, quantity of production lines,
number of inventory points and levels of inventory, levels
of product quality, inspection and test alternatives, and so
on.

F. Alternative product distribution channels, transportation and handling methods, warehouse locations, etc.

G. Alternative logistics support plans -- customer
service levels, sustaining supply support levels, maintenance
functions and tasks, etc.

H. Alternative product disposal and recycling methods.

I. Alternative management policies and their impact on
the system.

The above concerns are characteristic for any system or
product. However, the point to be made here is that life
cycle cost (and not R & D cost or production cost only)
constitutes the evaluation criterion for selecting a
preferred approach. Each decision has life cycle cost
implications. For instance; an equipment packaging
configuration will directly effect the test equipment and
spare parts required for the follow-on sustaining support
of that equipment; product reliability will effect both
production requirements and maintenance and logistics support
policies; product utilization will effect design requirements;
and so on. The interactions are many and varied, a point
which is supported further in subsequent sections of this text.

3.2 THE ANALYSIS APPROACH

The analysis process commences with the identification of
a need for analysis supported by the necessary management
action to initiate the tasks required in fulfilling analysis
objectives. The basic steps in a typical life cycle cost

analysis are illustrated in Figure 3-2, although the extent
of effort and depth of coverage will vary depending on the
problem situation. In essence, the figure conveys a
"thought process" stemming from the identification of a
problem and ending with a recommended approach for problem
resolution.

3.2.1 Definition of the Problem

  The initial step constitutes the clarification of
objectives, defining the issues of concern, and bounding
the problem such that it can be studied in an efficient and
timely manner. In many cases, the nature of the problem
appears to be obvious whereas the precise definition of the
problem may be the most difficult part of the entire process.
The problem at hand must be defined clearly, precisely, and
presented in such a manner as to be easily understood by all
concerned. Otherwise, it is highly doubtful whether an
analysis of any type will be meaningful.

3.2.2 Goals of the Analysis

  From the problem statement the analyst needs to identify
the specific goals of the analysis. For instance; is the
objective to evaluate two alternatives on the basis of life
cycle cost? Is there a requirement to determine the life
cycle cost of System "XYZ" for budgetary purposes? Does the
evaluation need to show system performance in terms of
design to unit acquisition cost? Is it necessary to evaluate
supply support costs as a function of the equipment design
packaging configuration?
  Actually, there are many such questions that the decision
maker might wish to address. There may be a single overall
analysis goal (e.g., design to minimum life cycle cost), and
any number of sub-goals. The primary question is -- what
is the purpose of the analysis and what do you need to learn
through the analysis effort?

Identifying the goals of the analysis is extremely important and may seem rather elementary. However, it is not uncommon to find instances where the analysis effort becomes the <u>driving force</u> and the original goals are lost in the process; or the goals have unintentionally shifted as a result of the analyst becoming too involved in the details and losing sight of the "big picture". The analyst must take care to ensure that realistic goals are established at the start of the analysis process (refer to Figure 3-2, Block 2), and that these goals remain insight throughout the process.

3.2.3 Groundrules and Constraints

In support of the problem definition and the goals, the analyst must define the groundrules and constraints (or bounds) within which the analysis effort is to be accomplished. By groundrules, the author is referring to information concerning such factors as the resources available for conducting the analysis (i.e., necessary manpower skills, availability of a computer if required, etc.), the time schedule allowed for completion of the analysis, and/or related management policy or direction that in any way will effect the analysis. In many instances, a manager may not completely understand the problem or the analysis process and direct that certain tasks be accomplished in a prescribed manner and at a designated time, which in turn may not be compatible with the analysis objectives. On other occasions, a manager may have a preconceived idea as to a given decision outcome and direct that the analysis must support <u>that</u> decision, whether realistic or not. In any event, at times there are external inhibiting factors that may impact on the validity of the analysis effort. In such cases, the analyst should make every effort to alleviate the problem through education. Should any unresolved problems exist, the analyst should document such as part of the analysis report and relate the impact effects of the problem on the analysis results.

Relative to the technical characteristics of a system or product, the analysis output may be constrained by bounds (or limits) that are established through the definition of system performance features, operational requirements, the maintenance concept, and/or through advanced program planning. For instance, there may be a maximum weight requirement for a given product, a minimum reliability requirement, a maximum allowable unit life cycle cost goal, a minimum capacity output for a plant, and so on. These various bounds, or constraints, must be defined in terms of the trade-off areas allowable in the evaluation of alternatives. Figure 3-3 illustrates this point.

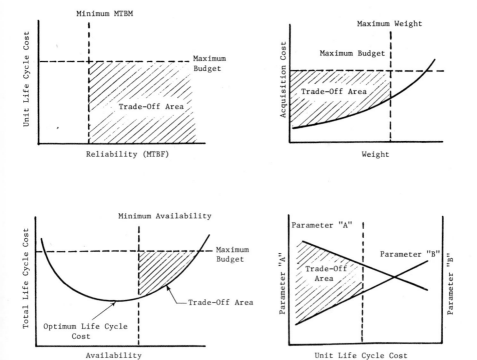

Figure 3-3 Trade-Off Areas (Showing Bounds)

Referring to the figure, all alternative candidates which fall within the trade-off area are eligible for consideration, while those which fall outside of this area are not -- even though one of these alternatives may turn out to be more cost effective in the long term.

3.2.4 Identification of Feasible Alternatives

Within the established groundrules and constraints, the analyst should identify alternative solutions to the problem at hand. Initially, all possible candidates should be considered, even though the more alternatives that are considered the more complex the problem becomes. However, it is desirable to list all possible candidates to ensure against inadvertent omissions, and then eliminate those candidates which are clearly unattractive, leaving only a few for evaluation. Those few candidates are then analyzed with the intent of selecting a preferred approach.

It is realized that there may be many top level candidates for consideration, many different configurations of each major candidate, numerous variations within each configuration, and so on. Initially, major candidates are considered and a preferred approach is selected. Then, different configurations of the selected approach are evaluated and a specific configuration is chosen from that group of alternatives. This is an iterative process working from the top level down to the depth necessary to support a given decision. The process described above is applicable for each iteration.

3.2.5 Selection of Evaluation Criteria

The criteria employed in the evaluation process may vary considerably depending on the stated problem, the groundrules and constraints, and the complexity of the analysis. For instance, at the system level, parameters of primary

importance include cost effectiveness, life cycle cost,
system effectiveness, operation and support cost,
availability, capacity, and so on. At the detailed level,
significant parameters may include accessibility,
standardization of components, inventory costs, etc. The
order of parameters will vary at different levels as
illustrated in Figure 3-4.

Reference: Figure 1-6

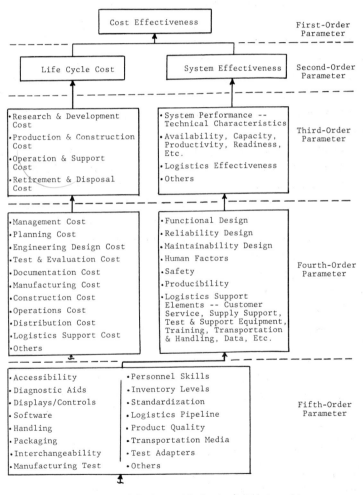

Figure 3-4 Order of Evaluation Parameters

As stated earlier, the parameters selected as evaluation
criteria should relate directly to the problem statement
and the goals of the analysis. For example, the problem
may be to design a system or product that will perform a
certain mission with a specific degree of effectiveness at
minimum life cycle cost. There may be several possible
candidates, each of which is evaluated in terms of system
effectiveness and life cycle cost. On the other hand, the
problem may entail the selection of the best among several
alternative off-the-shelf equipment items using design
supportability characteristics as criteria (e.g.,
accessibility, diagnostic aids, standardization of
components, etc.). In this instance, there are a number of
evaluation factors.

In the event that there are many evaluation parameters
involved in any given analysis effort, each parameter should
be reviewed from the standpoint of relevancy or degree of
importance. The degree of importance may be realized by
applying parameter weighting factors (the most important
items receiving the heaviest weighting). Each parameter,
with its appropriate weighting factor, should then be related
to life cycle cost. In essence, all parameters are related
to cost in some manner, and the life cycle cost implications
must be assessed regardless of the criteria employed for
evaluation purposes.

3.2.6 Selection of a Cost Model

The next step in the process involves the analytical phase.
This entails the selection and combining of various analytical
techniques in the form of a model or a series of models.[2]

---

[2] There are many categories of models to include physical
models, abstract models, symbolic models, mathematical
models, etc. A model, as defined here, refers to an
analytical or mathematical model. B. Blanchard,
Logistics Engineering And Management, Prentice-Hall, Inc.,
1974, Page 120, includes discussion on model characteristics
and selection criteria.

A model, in principle, is a simplified representation of the real world which abstracts certain features of the situation relative to the problem being analyzed. A model can be used as a tool to gain knowledge through analysis and as a means of conveying information. It is employed by the analyst to assess the likely consequences of various alternative courses of action being examined. A model is relatively economical (as it costs less to derive knowledge from a model than from the real thing) and is generally available far in advance of the entity or situation that it is intended to represent.

The model may be quite simple or highly complex, very mathematical or not at all, computerized or manually implemented, and so on. The extensiveness of the model will depend on the nature of the problem relative to the type and quantity of variables, input parameter relationships, number of alternatives being evaluated, and the overall complexity of operation. The ultimate objective in the selection or development of a model is simplicity, usefulness, and reliability. A model used for analysis purposes should incorporate the following features:

1. The model should represent the dynamic characteristics of the system or entity being evaluated. Situations change constantly and the model should incorporate the necessary provisions to reflect such changes in a manner simple enough to understand and manipulate, and yet close enough to reality to yield beneficial results.

2. The model should highlight those factors that are most relevant to the problem being analyzed, and suppress (with discretion) those that are not as important. Anticipated high cost contributors in a life cycle cost analysis must be highly visible.

3. The model should be comprehensive by including all relevant factors and reliable in terms of the repeatability of results.

4. The design of the model should be simple enough to allow for its timely implementation in problem solving. It

should be available when needed and incorporate the necessary
characteristics such that it can be utilized in an efficient
manner by the analyst or manager involved in the analysis
process.

  5. The model should be designed in such a manner as to
enable the evaluation of specific elements of the system
independent from other elements. Often times the analyst is
interested in evaluating the total system initially, then
concentrating on a specific element of the system (perhaps
making some changes here and there), and finally looking at
other related elements or the system as an entity. The model
must incorporate the necessary flexibility, through the
proper design of sub-routine packages of one type or another,
to allow for the evaluation of the system, its elements, and
the interaction effects between elements. Further, the
analyst needs to know what is going on within the model at
all times. If the model is large and highly complex, the
analyst may input data at one end and receive an elaborate
report at the output which has little meaning in terms of
analyzing cause and effect relationships and having any
confidence in the analysis results.

  6. The model design should incorporate the necessary
provisions for easy modification and/or expansion to permit
the evaluation of additional factors as may be required.
The model development process often includes a series of
trial runs before the overall objective is met. Initial
attempts may suggest information gaps that are not
immediately apparent; hence, changes must be incorporated to
cover the deficiencies. Also, the analyst may decide to
change the groundrules of the problem somewhat and evaluate
a broader range of opportunities. Hopefully, the model
design will allow for such variations.

  When reviewing the requirements for a life cycle cost
analysis, the needs of the analyst may vary somewhat
depending on the specific phase in the life cycle in which
the analysis is being accomplished. Early in the life

cycle, when precise data are limited and the information required is likely to be of a general nature, the analyst may choose to derive life cycle costs manually or through the use of a simple model with a few input factors. The process may employ basic accounting techniques and the model requirements may constitute a series of simple arithmetic calculations. Later during preliminary system design, detailed design and development, and in the subsequent phases (refer to Figure 1-8, Blocks 2, 3, 4, and 5), the analysis process becomes a little more complex requiring a series of models (or sub-routines).[3] In order to cover the broad spectrum, the more complex situation is discussed, with the understanding that almost any segment of the overall model requirements can be employed in a more simplified manner as appropriate.

In addressing the indepth analysis approach with the desired model design features in mind, experience indicates that a series of models (or a single model with a series of sub-routines) is required. Life cycle costing itself constitutes a compilation of a variety of cost factors representing many different types of activities. One might assume that a single model is necessary for the purposes of collecting costs only.[4] If the objective is to evaluate a system in terms of total life cycle cost as well as the various individual segments of cost, then the life cycle cost model should be composed of various sub-routines which address the major areas where high cost visibility is desired,

---

[4] At this point, reference to the single model refers only to the function of summarizing costs at a top level through the use of accounting techniques. The more detailed aspects of determining costs at the lower level are discussed later.

[3] The terminology associated with "model" and "sub-routine" may vary depending on the analyst and his experience. The point discussed here relates to the design of an analytical tool in such a manner as to incorporate manageable segments through which one can maintain the flexibility required in the analysis.

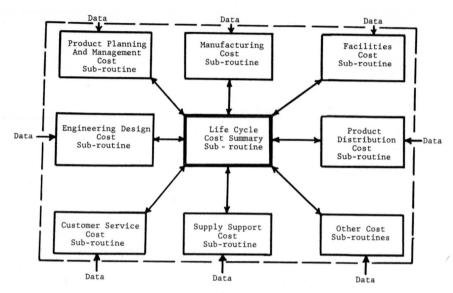

Note: Although not shown here, many of the sub-routines actually interact with each other in terms of data input and output.

Figure 3-5   Life Cycle Cost Model Configuration (Sample)

plus the sub-routine which summarizes these costs for the overall system. Figure 3-5 illustrates this point.

An example of a life cycle cost of this type, which employs basic accounting techniques, is included in Appendix A. Cost categories are identified in Figures 2-3 and A-1, quantitative relationships are presented in Table A-1, and these relationships are combined into an expression for life cycle cost. The cost model in Appendix A is directly compatible with the concept presented in Figure 3-5. Not only can the analyst review the total life cycle cost figure-of-merit of a system or product, but he (or she) can assess individual segments of cost such as engineering design cost (C_{RE}), test and evaluation (C_{RT}), manufacturing cost (C_{PM}), sustaining logistics support (C_{OL}), and so on.

The next step is to investigate further into the data

requirements for a model such as the one presented in
Appendix A. Review of the individual categories in the
appendix indicates that there are many different parameter
relationships, and in some instances the data required to
determine costs are derived using such analytical techniques
as simulation, dynamic and/or linear programming, queueing
theory, probabilistic concepts, network and sequential
analysis, and so on. For instance, in predicting future
engineering design costs one may derive costs from some form
of a management oriented probabilistic network. In
determining inventory requirements for costing purposes, one
becomes heavily involved in the probabilities of demand,
stockout, and so on. When predicting future system/product
maintenance requirements, the analyst may wish to use
simulation techniques to determine anticipated failure
patterns. Thus, the task of acquiring and manipulating data
for life cycle costing purposes assumes significant
proportions, and a series of additional models are often
developed to provide the data that serves as an input to the
life cycle cost model. Such a conglomerate of models and
their relationships are illustrated in Figure 3-5.[5]

Referring to the figure, there are a variety of
independent and yet interrelated functions required in life
cycle costing. The significant functions may be handled in
a manageable form through the development of individual
models (or sub-routines) that can be employed for analyses
at the sub-system or element level and yet provide the
necessary data into the life cycle cost model.[6] In

---

[5] Referring to Figure 3-6, the analyst may wish to consider
the group of individual models shown as being one LCC
model with a number of different sub-routines. This is
optional as long as the modular approach is used that will
allow for the analysis of individual segments of the
system.

[6] The individual model design and the functions represented
will of course vary depending on the goals and objectives
of the analysis effort.

accomplishing a life cycle cost analysis, the desired cost
factors for the system and for various categories in the
cost breakdown structure are an output of the life cycle
cost model (Figure 3-6, Block 6). However, if the costs

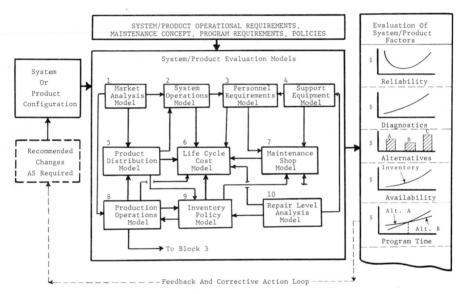

Figure 3-6   Application of Models

associated with personnel are unusually high, then the
analyst may wish to exercise the personnel requirements
model independently. This in turn may require output data
from another model. In any event, the flexibility is built
in such that the analyst may evaluate the system or product
as an entity, or any major segment thereof. Further, the
analyst should be familiar with what is going on within the
analytical process since he (or she) is able to evaluate the
input/output data of the various models shown.

  Referring to Figure 3-2 (Block 3), cost model requirements
are initially based on the problem definition, the analysis
goals and objectives, etc. In addition, there needs to be
some description of system/product operational requirements,
the maintenance concept, and the basic program plan
identifying major functions and the applicable life cycle

phases. This does not mean to infer that a <u>final</u> system
configuration should be defined at this point, but the
analyst must assume a "baseline" from which to commence with
the analysis process. The baseline is then employed in the
development of the cost breakdown structure and the specific
cost factors discussed in Chapter 2. With this information
at hand combined with knowledge of the desired model
characteristics, the analyst is ready to select an analytical
model for use as a tool in the analysis process.

In selecting a model for evaluation purposes, it is
desirable to first investigate those tools that are currently
available.[7] If a model already exists and is proven, then
it may be feasible to adopt that model. In this case,
extreme caution must be exercised to ensure that the model
being considered will adequately address the problem and
that it incorporates the necessary characteristics for an
indepth analysis with the desired sensitivities. Many
analytical models have been developed and reviewing the
descriptions of some would initially indicate an excellent
match (i.e., the appropriate analytical technique for the
problem at hand); however, when it comes to application, the
model may turn out to be inappropriate. Improper application
may not provide the results desired and may be costly.

On the other hand, it may be necessary to construct a new
model. If this is the case, the analyst should generate a
comprehensive list of system/product parameters that will
describe the situation being simulated. Next, it is
necessary to develop a matrix of some type showing parameter
relationships, each parameter being analyzed with respect to
every other parameter to determine the magnitude of the
relationship. Model input/output factors and parameter
feedback requirements must be established. A cost breakdown
structure is developed reflecting these various parameter
relationships, along with cost factors and cost generating

---

[7] A representative sample of some currently available models
and their application is included in Appendix C.

variables. The model is then constructed considering the
design characteristics described earlier, and testing is
conducted to ensure validity. Testing is usually difficult
since the model is designed to simulate future activities
which are impossible to verify. However, it may be possible
to select a known system or product which has been in use
for a number of years and exercise the model using established
parameters. Data and parameter relationships are known and
the results can be compared with actual historical
experience.

Model development is an art and not a science, and quite
often turns out to be an experimental process. Sometimes
the analyst goes through a number of iterations prior to
accomplishing his (or her) objectives of providing a
satisfactory analytical tool. However, when the ultimate
objective is met the model should provide a number of
benefits to include the following.

1. In accomplishing a life cycle cost analysis, there are
many interrelated elements that must be integrated as a
system and not treated on an individual basis. The model
makes it possible to evaluate the system as an entity, and
allows for consideration of all significant variables of the
problem on a simultaneous basis. Often the model will
uncover relations between various aspects of a problem which
are not readily apparent in the verbal description.

2. The analytical model enables a comparison of many
possible alternative solutions and aids in selecting the
best among them rapidly and efficiently. Accomplishing the
same objective manually would be time consuming and costly.

3. The analytical model can often be employed to explain
situations that have been left unexplained in the past by
indicating cause and effect relationships.

4. The analytical model readily identifies the type and
complexity of the data that is required for the analysis
per se.

5. The analytical model can be employed to facilitate the
prediction or forecasting of future events such as effective-

ness factors, cost estimates, reliability and maintainability
parameters, logistics requirements, etc.

6. The analytical model aids in identifying areas of risk
and uncertainty.

These benefits should become more obvious through the
presentation of the case study examples in Chapter 4.

3.2.7 Data Requirements

Definition of the analysis goals and groundrules, combined
with the identification of evaluation criteria, will in
essence dictate the data output requirements for the life
cycle cost analysis; i.e., the type of data desired from the
analysis and the preferred format in which the data are to
be presented. With the analysis output requirements defined,
the analyst develops the methodologies and relationships
necessary to produce the desired results. This basically
is accomplished through the model selection and/or
development process described in Paragraph 3.2 where system
parameters, estimating relationships, and cost factors are
identified (refer to the detailed relationships presented
in Appendix A). The completion of these steps leads to the
identification of the input data necessary for accomplishing
the analysis itself.

The acquisition of the right type of input data in a
timely manner and presented in a manageable format is one of
the most important steps in the overall life cycle cost
analysis process. The requirements for data must be
carefully defined since the application of too little data,
too much data, the wrong type of data, etc., can invalidate
the overall analysis resulting in poor decisions which may
be quite costly in the long term. Further, every effort
should be made to avoid the unnecessary expenditure of
valuable resources in generating data which may turn out not
to be required at all for the given analysis effort.
Unfortunately, there is a tendency to undertake elaborate
analytical exercises to develop meaningless precise

quantitative factors at times when only top system-level
estimates are required to satisfy the immediate need.

The requirements for input data may vary considerably
depending on the type and depth of analysis being performed,
which is often a function of the program phase in which the
analysis is accomplished. During the early conceptual
design stages of system/product development, available data
are limited, and the analyst must depend primarily on the use
of various cost estimating relationships, projections based
on past experience covering similar type systems, and
intuition. As system design progresses, improved data (e.g.,
drawings, parts lists, analyses, predictions, etc.) are
available and the analyst is able to accomplish a more
indepth analysis. Ultimately, when hardware is produced and
in the field, test and field data are collected for
assessment purposes; thus, the analyst is able to develop
a fairly realistic estimate of life cycle costs utilizing
this "real world" experience as an input into the analysis.

In essence, the analysis process is iterative and applied
throughout the life cycle, and the analyst utilizes the best
data available for the purpose(s) intended. In the absence
of what appears to be valid input data, the analyst should
employ the best techniques or methods available to generate
such data through forecasts and predictions. In any event,
the analyst should investigate all possible data sources
for appropriate application. The major sources of data are
highlighted below.

Existing Data Banks

Actual historical information on existing systems/products,
similar in configuration and function to the item(s) being
developed, may be used when applicable. Often it is feasible
to employ such data and apply complexity factors as necessary
to compensate for any differences in technology, configuration,
projected operational environment, and the time frame.
Information in this category may be available in the form of

documented case studies on other related items, analyses and reports from different programs, and field data covering products already in operational use.

Early System/Product Planning Data

Advanced planning information for the system or product being evaluated often includes market analysis data, definition of system operational requirements and the maintenance concept, the results of technical feasibility studies, and program management data (e.g., definition of the life cycle, identification of major life cycle functions, schedules, etc.), The analyst should review this data to determine the following system/product characteristics:

a.   Physical configuration and major performance features (e.g., approximate size, weight, output, packaging approach, etc.).

b.   The mission that is to be performed or the need that is to be fulfilled. This includes: a scenario of some type; utilization factors (hours or cycles of use per day or month); effectiveness requirements (availability, reliability, maintainability goals); cost targets or goals; and so on.

c.   The geographical location where the system or product is to be distributed and used, and the anticipated calendar time period of use. An overall inventory profile is desirable.

d.   The maintenance concept and logistics support philosophy (as applicable to sustaining life cycle support).

e.   The environment in which the system or product is to be distributed, utilized, and supported. This includes an environmental profile identifying temperature extremes, vibration and shock conditions, humidity, etc., covering the various states in which the system will exist -- operating mode, storage mode, transportation mode, maintenance and support mode, etc.

The analyst requires the above data in order to commence

with the life cycle cost analysis.[8] This information serves
as the baseline upon which all subsequent program activities
evolve. If the basic information is not available, then the
analyst must make some assumptions along these lines and
proceed accordingly. All assumptions must be thoroughly
documented.

Supplier Documentation

Proposals, catalogs, design data, and reports covering
special studies conducted by suppliers (or potential
suppliers) are used as a data source when appropriate.
Quite often major elements of a system are either procurred
as "of-the-shelf" items or developed through a sub-
contracting arrangement of some type. Various potential
suppliers will submit proposals for consideration, and these
proposals may include not only acquisition cost factors but
(in some instances) life cycle cost projections. If
supplier cost data are used, the analyst must become
completely knowledgeable as to what is and is not included.
Omissions and/or the double counting of costs must be
precluded.

Individual Cost Estimates [9]

Throughout the early Phases of a program, cost estimates
are usually being generated on a somewhat continuing basis.
These estimates may cover research and development (R & D)
activities, production or construction activities, and/or
system operating and support activities. Research and
development activities, which are basically nonrecurring in

---

[8] Specific examples of the types of data required are
included in the case studies presented in Chapter 4.

[9] An excellent source for cost estimating is: P. R. Oswald,
Cost Estimating For Engineering And Management,
Prentice-Hall, Inc., 1974.

nature, are usually covered by initial engineering cost
estimates or by "cost-to-complete" projections. Such
projections primarily reflect labor costs and include
inflationary factors, cost growth due to design changes, and
so on.

Production cost estimates are often presented in terms of
both nonrecurring costs and recurring costs. Nonrecurring
costs are handled in a manner similar to R & D costs. On
the other hand, recurring costs are frequently based on
individual manufacturing cost standards, value engineering
data, industrial engineering standards, etc. Quite often,
the individual cost standard factors that are used in
estimating recurring manufacturing costs are documented
separately, and are revised periodically to reflect labor
and material inflationary effects, supplier price changes,
effects of learning curves, etc. System/product operating
and support (O & S) costs are based on the projected
activities throughout the operational use and logistics
support phase of the life cycle, and are undoubtedly the
most difficult to estimate. Operating costs are a function
of the system/product mission requirements and utilization
factors. Support costs are basically a function of the
inherent reliability and maintainability characteristics in
the system design, and the logistics requirements necessary
to support all scheduled and unscheduled maintenance
actions throughout the programmed life cycle. Logistics
support requirements include: maintenance personnel and
training; supply support (spares, repair parts, and
inventories); test and support equipment; transportation and
handling; facilities; and certain facets of technical data.
Thus, individual O & S cost estimates are based on the
predicted frequency of maintenance or the mean time between
maintenance (MTBM) factor, and on the logistics support
resources required when maintenance actions occur. These
factors are derived from reliability and maintainability
prediction data, logistics support analysis (LSA) data, and

other supporting information, all of which is supported by
system/product engineering design data.[10]

The analyst must be cognizant of the sources from which
the various individual cost estimates are derived, the
numerous assumptions upon which these estimates are based,
and the specific cost related factors that are inherent in
each estimate. In addition, the analyst must ensure that
the estimates are current and that a maximum degree of
consistency exists from one estimate to the next (where
applicable). Given these requisites, the resultant
individual cost estimates constitute an input into the cost
breakdown structure in Appendix A and the life cycle cost
analysis. In the absence of such cost data, the analyst
will be required to generate the necessary costs using the
estimating techniques discussed in Paragraph 2.3, Chapter 2.

Engineering Test Data and Field Data

During the latter phases of system development and
production, and when the system/product is in operational
use, the experience gained represents the best source of
data for actual analysis and assessment purposes. Such data
are collected and used as an input to the life cycle cost
analysis. Also, field data are utilized to the extent
possible in assessing the life cycle cost impact that may
result from any proposed modifications on prime equipment,
software, and/or the elements of logistics support.

---

[10] The Logistics Support Analysis (LSA) constitutes the
on-going iterative analytical process that is employed
to (a) assess a given or assumed configuration in terms
of its inherent supportability characteristics, and (b)
to identify the ultimate logistics support requirements
for that configuration. The LSA is discussed further in:
B. Blanchard, Logistics Engineering And Management,
Prentice-Hall, Inc., 1974, Chapter 6 and Appendix B.

These five main sources of data identified for life cycle
costing purposes are presented in a summary manner to
provide one with an overview as to what the analyst should
look for when completing an analysis. Examples of specific
data needs (and the various possible available sources) are
presented through the case studies described in Chapter 4.
In pursuing the data requirements further, the analyst will
find that a great deal of experience has been gained in
determining R & D and production/construction costs; however,
very little historical cost data are currently available in
the 'operations and support area. The accounting of O & S
costs has been somewhat lacking in the past, but this
situation should ultimately rectify itself as the current
emphasis on life cycle costing continues to grow in the
future.

3.2.8   Validation of Analytical Approach

Prior to applying the model directly to the problem at
hand, the analyst should make every reasonable effort to
ensure that the selected model does indeed incorporate the
necessary characteristics to satisfy the desired objectives.
One approach is to select a "reference" system or product
that is currently in use and which is similar or analogous
to the proposed system. Existing data covering the
reference system is' used as an input to the analysis, and
the output results are compared with actual demonstrated
experience associated with that system. These results can be
assessed at the system level, subsystem level, or for a
particular element of the system. A close correlation
between the analysis results and actual experience would
indicate that the analytical technique is valid in terms of
the intended application. On the other hand, if the data
results are significantly different the analyst should
investigate the specific areas of incompatibility and the
reasons for such.

3.2.9 Sensitivity Analysis

When completing a life cycle cost analysis, there may be
a few key parameters about which the analyst is very
uncertain due to inadequate input data, initial assumptions,
pushing the state-of-the-art, or any combination of factors.
The basic questions are -- How sensitive are the results of
the analysis to variations of these uncertain parameters?
Will these variations tend to justify the selection of an
alternative configuration not currently being considered?
How much variation of a given parameter is required to shift
the decision from selecting Alternative "B" in lieu of
Alternative "A"? The intent is to (1) determine the
sensitivity of certain input parameters to the analysis
results, and (2) to assess the risk and uncertainty
associated with a given decision; i.e., the probability of
making a wrong decision (refer to the discussion pertaining
to Figure 2-20). In essence, the engineer or manager needs
to address the "what if" questions in an attempt to minimize
the risk associated with given decisions.

In accomplishing a sensitivity analysis, the analyst may
wish to employ the model using a "baseline" system
configuration, and then rerun the model while varying
different key input parameters to determine the impact on
the results.[11] Variation may be accomplished by applying
different multiple factors to the input parameter being
tested. For instance, the analyst may wish to investigate
the:

1. Variation of the frequency of maintenance factor
(1/MTBM) as a function of 0 & S cost and life cycle cost.
Since MTBM is a significant parameter in determining 0 & S
costs (plus ultimate life cycle cost) and is derived through

---

[11] A "baseline" configuration refers to an <u>assumed</u> configuration of the system or product being evaluated. It is
a <u>starting point</u> utilized for analysis purposes, and
does not necessarily reflect the final configuration
selected.

a combination of assumptions and predictions, it would be
worthwhile to test the effect of MTBM on life cycle cost.
For instance, multiple factors of 0.5 and 1.5 may be applied
to the MTBM figure and the model is run once for each
factor. Through the application of a series of multiple
factors, the analyst is able to assess the delta effects
between MTBM and any individual category of cost and/or
total life cycle cost.

2. Variation of system utilization or operating time as a
function of the quantity of maintenance actions, test and
support equipment utilization, and facility usage. Since
system utilization varies considerably from one location to
the next, or with different user organizations, it would be
worthwhile to test this parameter in terms of O & S costs
and life cycle cost. Again, the quantity of maintenance
actions is a significant factor in determining O & S cost,
and support equipment and facilities may be high cost
contributors.

3. Variation of the system diagnostic capability as a
function of supply support costs and O & S cost. The depth
and accuracy of incorporated diagnostics directly impact the
extent to which possible equipment malfunctions can be
traced and the resulting requirements for spare parts. Since
there is a significant concern as to how much diagnostic
capability should be incorporated in the equipment design,
particularly with regard to electronic equipment, the
analyst may wish to test this parameter.

4. Variation of the corrective maintenance manhours per
operating hour (MMH/OH) factor as a function of direct
personnel costs and O & S cost. Since MMH/OH is a function
of the quantity of corrective maintenance actions and the
personnel skill levels required for the accomplishment of
maintenance (which are predicted), it would be worthwhile to
determine the sensitivities in this area. This is
particularly true when personnel costs are a relatively high
contributor to life cycle cost.

5. Variation of the product demand rate (i.e., quantity

of items demanded per year) as a function of production cost and life cycle cost.

6. Variation of the logistics pipeline (e.g., product distribution time) as a function of supply support costs and life cycle cost.

7. Variation of the assumed discount rate as a function of life cycle cost.

Actually, there are many input parameters that can be evaluated in a like manner. The selection process as to which parameters should be tested for sensitivity purposes relates directly to the high cost categories and the major cost drivers (i.e., the parameters that have the greatest impact on cost). In each instance, the analyst should be concerned not only with the delta effects of these variations on total life cycle cost, but the degree of variation that can occur without introducing any unnecessary risk in decisions pertaining to the selection of alternatives. The degree of variation that can be tolerated will relate directly to the accuracy of the input data requirements necessary for the life cycle cost analysis (refer to Paragraph 3.2). If the allowable output variation is relatively small and the input data factors vary over a wide range, then the analyst may wish to expend some additional effort to acquire better input data.

The sensitivity analysis can be extremely beneficial to the decision maker, and often conveys more information than any other single aspect of the overall life cycle cost analysis process. The analyst can readily identify cause and effect relationships, is able to predict trends, and is better prepared to respond to the "what if" questions.

3.2.10 Analysis Results

The analysis results may constitute a life cycle cost profile for a single system configuration, a total life cycle cost comparison of two or more configurations, a comparison of breakeven or payback points for various options, and/or delta incremental cost comparison of a series of alternatives. Again, the output relates back to the problem definition, the goals of the analysis, and the system or product being evaluated. In any event, the analyst follows the basic steps illustrated in Figure 3-2 and arrives at a recommendation for management consideration.

In making a final recommendation as to a proposed course of action, the analyst should review the overall analysis process in terms of problem definition, validity of stated assumptions, model parameter relationships, inclusions/ exclusions, adequacy of data input, and stated conclusions. The main question is -- Is the recommended approach valid and does the preferred configuration <u>clearly</u> have the advantage over other alternative considerations? In response, the analyst may wish to pose a number of specific questions in the form of a checklist as an aid in assessing the final output results. Figure 3-7 presents a sample checklist including some rather basic but significant questions that may pertain to any type of analysis effort.

3.3 THE ASPECTS OF RISK AND UNCERTAINTY

The process of analysis leads to decisions that may have a significant impact on the future. Inherent in this process are the aspects of risk and uncertainty since the future is of course, unknown.[12] In accomplishing a life cycle cost analysis, there are many areas where risk and uncertainty

---

[12] Quite often the terms "risk" and "uncertainty" are used jointly in the interests of simplicity. Actually, risk implies the availability of discrete data in the form of a probability distribution around one or more parameters. Uncertainty implies a situation that may be probabilistic in nature, but one which is not supported by discrete data. Some factors may be measured in terms of risk or may be stated under conditions of uncertainty.

A. GENERAL

   1. Has the problem been adequately defined?
   2. Have the analysis goals and objectives been defined?
   3. Have the evaluation criteria been identified?
   4. Has the analysis effort followed the process identified in Figure 3-2?

B. SYSTEM/PRODUCT REQUIREMENTS

   1. Have the system/product configuration and major performance features been defined?
   2. Has the mission of the system been defined?
   3. Have the distribution and system utilization factors been defined?
   4. Has the maintenance concept been defined?
   5. Have the environmental requirements been defined?
   6. Has the system life cycle been defined?

C. ALTERNATIVES

   1. Are all current capabilities adequately considered among alternatives?
   2. Have all feasible alternatives been considered?
   3. Have the selected alternatives been justified on the basis of life cycle cost?
   4. Have the inadequacies of those alternatives which are rejected been justified and documented?

D. MODEL RELATIONSHIPS

   1. Does the model adequately address the problem?
   2. Does the model reflect the dynamic characteristics of the system/product being evaluated?
   3. Is the model sensitive to the requirements of the analysis?
   4. Is the model designed in such a manner as to allow for the evaluation of specific elements of the system independent from other elements?
   5. Can the model be easily modified to permit the evaluation of additional cost factors?
   6. Does the model allow for a timely response?
   7. Does the model provide valid (comprehensive) and reliable (repeatable) results?

E. COST

   1. Has the overall cost breakdown structure been defined?

   2. Are all cost categories in the cost breakdown structure adequately defined?
   3. Are the cost breakdown structure and work breakdown structure compatible?
   4. Are all life cycle costs being considered?
   5. Are all cost estimating relationships relevant?
   6. Are all cost factors realistic?
   7. Are variable and fixed costs separately identifiable?
   8. Are recurring and nonrecurring costs separately identifiable?
   9. Are direct and indirect costs separately identifiable?
  10. Are the proper inflationary factors included?
  11. Is the discount rate specified and employed in the evaluation of alternatives?
  12. Are incremental and marginal costs considered where appropriate?
  13. Are the effects of learning curves considered in the costs of repetitive functions?
  14. Are the cost aspects of all alternatives treated in a consistent and comparable manner?
  15. Is the cost amortization employed where applicable?
  16. Has the sensitivity of cost estimates been properly addressed through a sensitivity analysis?
  17. Has a breakeven analysis been accomplished in the evaluation of alternatives? Does it support the alternative selected?

F. DATA

   1. Have all data requirements been identified?
   2. Have all data sources been identified?
   3. Has the best source of data been utilized?

G. ANALYSIS RESULTS

   1. Are all assumptions adequately documented?
   2. Are all major assumptions reasonable?
   3. Are the conclusions and recommendations logically derived from the material presented in the analysis?
   4. Are the conclusions and recommendations really feasible in light of political, social, ecological, policy, or other considerations?
   5. Are the conclusions and recommendations based on insignificant differences?

*The questions are so designed that the answer to each item (as applicable) should be "yes".

Figure 3-7 Analysis Checklist (Sample)

can be introduced, and the more that this occurs the less valid the analysis becomes. Hence, although the various aspects of risk and uncertainty can not be eliminated altogether, it is the intent to minimize such to the greatest extent possible. With this in mind, the author has chosen to identify a few significant areas where the introduction of risk and uncertainty are likely to be most prevalent, and where the analyst should proceed with caution.[13]

------

[13] The author does not consider that the list of items discussed herein is all inclusive by any means.

3.3.1   Selection of Evaluation Criteria

The selection of evaluation criteria described in
Paragraph 3.2 is one of the most formidable areas of
concern in the analysis process. The problem is the
greatest for large systems where comparisons are frequently
made between alternatives which fulfill a specific need but
by different means (e.g., a train versus an airplane used in
fulfilling a transportation need). In such instances,
evaluation criteria should include system performance
features, effectiveness characteristics, political and
social factors, and economic considerations. For each
alternative the factors may be different and hence, difficult
to compare on a direct basis, Also, some of the system
features are impossible to quantify realistically and are
conveniently left out of the analysis. Other factors that
are quantifiable are sometimes combined as a single criterion
figure-of-merit, creating an "apple-orange" mixing effect
and introducing bias into the analysis.

For small systems or products, the problem of selecting
criteria is considerably reduced although not entirely
eliminated. Many of the large scale system interaction
effects drop out in the analysis process. Although there is
still the danger associated with quantifying factors
improperly and combining multiple criteria, the magnitude
of the risk and uncertainty introduced is somewhat less.

In the interest of minimizing the introduction of risk and
uncertainty in the analysis, the analyst must select
evaluation criteria judiciously in order to capture as many
of the relevant system/product characteristics as possible.
The inappropriate mixing of criteria should be avoided, and
those features that cannot be adequately expressed must be
identified and all related assumptions must be stated.

3.3.2   The Treatment of System Parameters in the Analysis

When accomplishing a life cycle cost analysis, the analyst
assigns discrete quantitative values to the various

parameters identified in the cost breakdown structure. In
this capacity, the <u>expected</u> (or mean) value is often
selected without consideration for measures of dispersion.
In some instances, the expected value may be the best figure
to use; however, in many cases experience indicates that a
range of values would be more appropriate since variations
do occur for one reason or another. Although variances in
the precise statistical sense are often difficult (if not
impossible) to calculate in most analysis efforts,
dispersion can be determined by introducing ranges of values
to reflect anticipated real world conditions. The question
then relates to the implications of various assumptions,
using ranges of input values, in terms of the cost analysis
results.

   For illustration purposes, Figure 3-8 shows two
alternatives where the overall costs are equal when
considering the probability distributions reflecting the
dispersion of each. If the analyst were to use expected
values only (i.e., $\overline{X}_A$ and $\overline{X}_B$), the selection would
undoubtedly lead to Factor "A" with the lowest expected cost.
However, if measures of dispersion were available, the

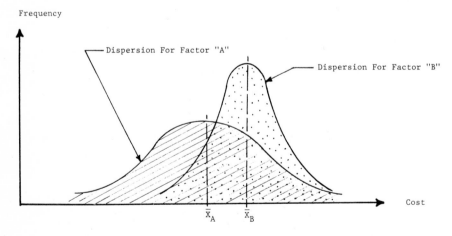

Figure 3-8 Dispersion of Costs

analyst may decide to choose Factor "B" with a higher
expected cost but at the same time having a much lower
degree of risk associated with the outcome since the spread
in the probability distribution is considerably less.

The treatment of risk and uncertainty in a life cycle cost
analysis is accomplished through individual parametric type
analyses where ranges of values for cost generating variables
can be evaluated to determine what impact they have on the
final outcome. Cost sensitivities can be explored, which in
turn will address the problem of risk and uncertainty. In
other words, areas and magnitude of risk and conditions of
uncertainty should become more visible, minimized if possible,
and managers will be in a better situation when addressing
the "what if" questions that arise on a day-to-day basis.

3.3.3 Application of Input Data

The requirements and sources of data are covered briefly
in Paragraph 3.2. From these sources, the analyst must
identify system operating features, maintenance and logistics
support parameters, reliability and maintainability values,
production and O & S cost factors, and so on. Many of these
data elements are represented by a discrete expected value
and a probability distribution indicating the range of
values around the expected value. The analyst in applying
these data elements must be cognizant of not only the
sources of data available, but knowledgeable of the various
data elements and the distributions associated with each.
By not being familiar with the characteristic behavior of the
many different data input values, the analyst is likely to
introduce unnecessary risk and uncertainty into the analysis
through:

1. Using data directly from other analyses without the
assurance that it is indeed applicable to the problem at
hand.

2. Making errors in data interpretation and extrapolations.

3. Making errors in the development and application of

cost estimating relationships, and in applying the wrong
techniques.

4. Making unrealistic or invalid assumptions.

Unless particular care is taken in the development and
application of data, there is likely to be a wide range of
cost values (i.e., much wider than the range of costs
illustrated in Figure 2-20), the cost trends may be highly
inaccurate, and the degree of risk and uncertainty is likely
to be greater than anticipated. This, in turn, will increase
the probability of making the wrong decision.

3.3.4 Summary

Since the aspects of risk and uncertainty can be
introduced in any phase of the life cycle cost analysis
process, the analyst should make every effort to become
thoroughly familiar with the specific steps presented in
Figure 3-2. Understanding the process, the requirements for
life cycle costing, the characteristics of model design and
utilization, the sources and application of data, and the
interpretation and analysis of results is considered
essential. In many instances, the sensitivity analysis can
be effectively used to assist in understanding the behavior
characteristics of the system/product being evaluated and
in determining cost trends. Finally, by accomplishing life
cycle cost analyses on a continuing basis and through the
application of such analyses to various varieties of systems
and products, the analyst can gain significantly in
improving his (or her) abilities in management decision
making.

QUESTIONS AND PROBLEMS

1. Identify and define a specific problem of your choice. Develop a flow diagram and describe (in detail) the process of accomplishing a life cycle cost analysis based on the problem that you have defined.

2. Identify some of the applications for life cycle cost analyses.

3. Why is it important to initially define the problem before undertaking a life cycle cost analysis?

4. What is a model? List the desired characteristics of a model.

5. Identify some of the necessary requisites in the selection and/or development of a model. What cautions should be followed?

6. What are the benefits associated with the use of analytical models?

7. What is a sensitivity analysis? Name some of the benefits derived from a sensitivity analysis?

8. Refer to Problem 1. Identify and describe a model of your choice for application in solving the problem as defined. Identify the data input requirements and data sources necessary for the successful implementation of your model.

9. Define "risk" and "uncertainty". How are they related to each other?

10. How is risk and uncertainty introduced into a life cycle cost analysis? Be specific.

11. What steps would you initiate to minimize or reduce the risk and uncertainty in a given analysis?

12. If you were assigned the task to review and assess the results of a specific life cycle cost analysis, what would you look for in the evaluation process? You may wish to develop a checklist of some type to facilitate the review.

Chapter 4

COST ANALYSIS APPLICATIONS IN THE SYSTEM / PRODUCT LIFE CYCLE

The previous chapters deal primarily with the principles and concepts necessary as an introduction to life cycle costing. Although this information is an essential prerequisite, it is believed that a good understanding of the subject area can only be acquired by delving into some of the details of establishing a cost breakdown structure, defining cost estimating relationships, and determining specific segments of cost. Unless one actually gets <u>involved</u> at the detailed level, it is difficult (if not impossible) to adequately understand various system/product parameters and the interactions that occur. It is not sufficient to merely feed data into a computer model and observe the output without thoroughly understanding what takes place in the process. Once that this understanding is attained, then the computer model can be useful in facilitating the analysis effort.

With the objective of illustrating some of the detailed steps required in a life cycle analysis, four individual case study examples have been introduced in this chapter. In presenting each case study, only enough detail is included to provide an understanding of the requirements involved in such an analysis and to promote further discussion. A

complete step-by-step procedure covering each element of the
system or product in question would be too comprehensive
within the confines of this text. However, the highlights
and critical areas are addressed.

The case study examples discussed herein are varied in
nature and presented in different levels of detail. As
every life cycle cost analysis is somewhat unique unto
itself, the case studies will not in all instances completely
respond to one's specific problem; however, by reviewing
these cases, one will hopefully acquire enough insight to
assist in the resolution of the many unique problems that
arise on a day-to-day basis. It is hoped that the reader
will review each case study in detail; that a self-analysis
will take place, stimulating additional interest in the
approach suggested; and that the knowledge gained will
enhance the reader's understanding of the life cycle cost
process.

4.1   LIFE CYCLE COST ANALYSIS APPLICATIONS

The applications of life cycle cost analysis are numerous
and varied. During the early stages of product planning and
conceptual design, life cycle cost analyses can be employed
to aid in defining system operational requirements, the
maintenance concept, and major program planning objectives.
The following questions may arise, and life cycle costing
is an appropriate technique to employ in determining a
response that will reflect an efficient use of resources:

A.   How should the system or product be distributed and
effectively utilized? What is the most cost-efficient
approach?

B.   How many product distribution centers are required and
where should they be geographically located? What is the
most cost-efficient approach?

C.   How should the system/product be supported throughout
its planned life cycle? How many levels of maintenance
are necessary, and what logistics support resources are

required at each level? What is the most cost-effective
approach?

D. What type of program plan is required to satisfy the
identified consumer need(s)? What is the most cost-
effective approach?

Life cycle cost becomes a significant parameter in the
early decision process relative to both management and
engineering functions, and realistic LCC/DTC targets can be
established with the intent of imparting a high degree of
cost consciousness in system/product design.

During preliminary and detailed system/product design,
life cycle costing continues as an iterative process in
supporting decisions at a lower level in the system
hierarchy. A few typical questions that may arise are noted
as follows:

A. Is there an existing design that will fulfill the
need? If so, what supplier sources are available, and
which source should be selected? What is the most cost-
effective approach?

B. If new design is required, which configuration is the
most cost-effective in terms of life cycle cost? Design
decisions involving equipment packaging schemes, automatic
versus manual functions, diagnostic provisions, etc., have
a significant impact on life cycle cost.

C. Does the selected design configuration incorporate the
necessary supportability characteristics to reflect the
lowest life cycle cost (i.e., reliability, maintainability,
human factors, etc.)?

D. Are the logistics support requirements identified for
the selected design configuration optimal in terms of life
cycle cost? Do the analysis and planning data reflect the
correct items of support, at the proper level, and at the
right time?

As the system/product design progresses, alternatives may
be evaluated using the life cycle cost technique as a tool
to facilitate the decision-making process.

During the production/construction phase of the life cycle,

major questions that arise pertain to production rates,
production flow, inventory and distribution policies, quality
control practices, etc. Since production decisions can
significantly impact follow-on system or product operation
and support functions, the life cycle costing technique
should be employed in the evaluation of alternatives.

Finally, life cycle cost analyses are accomplished
throughout the operational use and logistics support phase
when the system/product is being used in the field by the
consumer. The analysis at this stage constitutes an
assessment of actual costs based on experience, and use of
the life cycle cost technique serves to identify major
problem areas and high cost contributors. Further, life
cycle costing is employed to evaluate the economic impact of
potential modifications proposed for the system or product.

In summary, life cycle cost analysis applications are
appropriate in all phases of the system/product life cycle
as illustrated in Figure 1-8 (Chapter 1). Whenever major
decisions are being considered, the impact of such decisions
should be assessed in terms of life cycle cost.

4.2   SELECTED CASE STUDY EXAMPLES

In an attempt to illustrate some of the specifics
pertaining to the life cycle cost analysis process, four
individual case study examples are covered herein. A brief
description of each is noted.

Case Study Number 1. This example covers the life cycle
cost analysis of a new communication system required for
use in a large metropolitan/county area. The system
constitutes a network incorporating aircraft, helicopter,
patrol vehicle, and ground facility applications. Several
alternative design configurations are evaluated in terms
of total life cycle cost.

Case Study Number 2. This example covers a level of repair
analysis involving a number of computer system assemblies.
A decision is required as to whether to design the

assemblies such that repair can be accomplished when failures occur, or whether the assemblies should be discarded at failure.

Case Study Number 3. This example illustrates the life cycle cost considerations in the selection of a private automobile from inventory. The case presented pertains directly to our personal family experiences relative to purchasing a car.

Case Study Number 4. This example addresses the major life cycle cost considerations related to the acquisition of a new machine by a corporation desiring to manufacture a new product.

Although there are as many examples of life cycle cost applications as one may wish to include, it is hoped that the four case studies presented herein will accomplish the objectives stated earlier.

4.2.1 Case Study Number 1

This example illustrates a life cycle cost analysis involving the evaluation of two alternative system configurations. The approach is to define system operational requirements, the maintenance concept, the required program planning information, and then translate these into life cycle cost figures. The application presented relates to the early design stages of the life cycle.

Definition of the Problem [1]

A large metropolitan area is in need to upgrade its overall communications capability by acquiring a new communication system for installation in county patrol aircraft,

---

[1] Definition of the problem in this instance implies all of the steps in Block 2 of Figure 3-2 plus a description of system operational requirements, the maintenance concept, and the program plan.

helicopters, ground vehicles, designated facilities, and in the central communications control facility. The new communication system should be adaptable for use in all designated applications (i.e., airborne and ground), and the only configuration differences should constitute the inter-face connections, mounting fixtures, etc. In addition, the communication system must accomplish the following basic objectives:

A. Objective Number 1

The system is to be installed in three low flying light aircraft (10,000 feet or less) in quantities of one per aircraft. The system shall enable communication with loitering helicopters dispersed within a 200-mile radius, and with the central communications control facility. It is anticipated that each aircraft will fly 15 times per month with an average flight duration of three hours. The system utilization requirement is 1.1 hours of system operation for every hour of aircraft operation, which includes air time plus some ground time. It is assumed that all functions of the system are fully operational throughout this time period. The system must exhibit a MTBM of at least 500 hours and a $\overline{\text{M}}$ct not to exceed 15 minutes.[2]

B. Objective Number 2

The system is to be installed in each of five helicopters, and shall enable communication with patrol aircraft through a 200-mile range, other helicopters within a 50-mile radius, and with the central communications control facility. It is anticipated that each helicopter will fly 25 times per month with an average flight duration of two hours. The utilization requirement is 0.9 hours of system operation for

---

[2] Refer to Appendix D for a definition of such terms as MTBM, MTBF, $\overline{\text{M}}$ct, etc.

every flight hour of helicopter operation. The system must
meet a 500 hour MTBM requirement and a $\overline{M}ct$ of 15 minutes or
less.

C. Objective Number 3

The system is to be installed in each of 50 police patrol
vehicles (one per vehicle), and shall enable communication
with other vehicles within a 10-mile radius, with any one of
the five fixed communications facilities at a range of 25
miles, and with the central communications control facility
at a range of 50 miles or more. Each vehicle will be in
operation on the average of five hours per day, five days
per week, and will be utilized 100% during that time. The
required MTBM is 400 hours, and the $\overline{M}ct$ is 30 minutes.

D. Objective Number 4

Two systems are to be installed in each of five fixed
communications facilities optimally located throughout the
metropolitan geographical area. Each system shall enable
communication with patrol vehicles at a range of 25 miles,
and with the central communications control facility at a
range of 50 miles. System utilization requirements are 120
hours per month; the required MTBM is 200 hours; and the $\overline{M}ct$
should not exceed 60 minutes.

E. Objective Number 5

Ten systems are to be installed in the central
communications control facility, and shall enable
communication with patrol aircraft and loitering helicopters
at a range of 200 miles, the five fixed communication
facilities at a range of 50 miles, and with patrol vehicles
within a 10-mile radius. In addition, each system shall be
able to communicate with the intermediate maintenance
facilities. The average utilization requirement for each
system is three hours per day for 360 days per year. The

MTBM requirement is 200 hours, and the $\overline{M}ct$ shall not exceed 45 minutes.

F. Objective Number 6

Two mobile vans shall be used to support intermediate level maintenance at the five fixed communication facilities. Each van shall incorporate one communication system which will be used on the average of two hours per day for a 360-day year. The required MTBM is 400 hours, and the $\overline{M}ct$ is 15 minutes.

These six objectives are illustrated in the communications network shown in Figure 4-1. Note that the requirements for 80 communication systems are shown along with the proposed maintenance support facilities. This information serves as the baseline required to commence with the analysis.

In line with the stated operational objectives, there is a need to acquire a new communication system that will meet the performance and effectiveness requirements (e.g. voice transmission range, clarity of message, MTBM, $\overline{M}ct$, etc.). Further, budget limitations suggest that the unit life cycle cost of the system should not exceed \$35,000.[3] Advanced program planning indicates that a full complement of systems must be in operation five years after the start of the program, and that this capability must be maintained through the 11th year of the program. The significant program milestones and projected number of systems in operational use are presented in Figure 4-2.[4]

Based on a review of the available sources of supply, there is no existing system that will completely fulfill the need;

---

[3] Unit life cycle cost in this instance is determined by dividing the total life cycle cost figure-of-merit by the number of operating systems (i.e., 80).

[4] The profile in Figure 4-2 forms the basis for defining the system life cycle, the major life cycle functions, and life cycle costs by year. In essence, a 13-year life cycle is assumed.

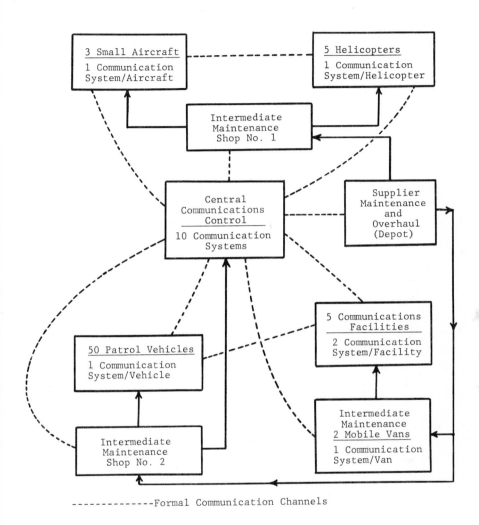

Figure 4-1 Communications Network

however, there are two new candidate design configurations that should suffice assuming that all design goals are met. The objective here is to evaluate each configuration in terms of life cycle cost and to recommend a preferred approach.

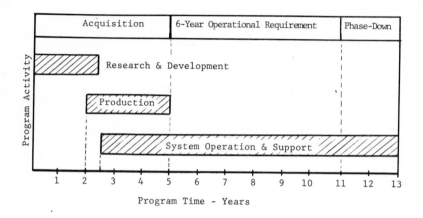

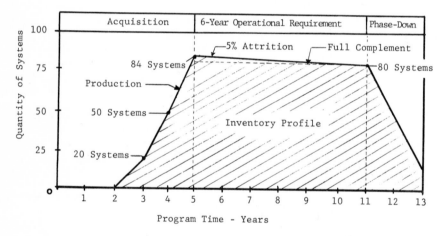

Figure 4-2   Program Plan

Analysis Approach

The analysis approach generally follows the steps illustrated in Figure 3-2. However, prior to the identification of a cost breakdown structure (CBS) and the development of cost factors, the analyst needs to further expand the description of the baseline system configuration and the maintenance concept. As a start, an assumed

packaging scheme is developed and shown in Figure 4-3. This
configuration (including units, assemblies, and modules) is
developed from conceptual design information, and is fairly
representative of each of the candidates being considered.[5]

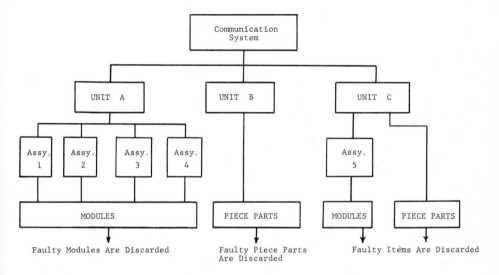

Figure 4-3 System Packaging Scheme (Baseline Configuration)

The maintenance concept can be defined as a series of
statements and/or illustrations that include criteria
covering maintenance levels, support policies, effectiveness
factors (e.g., maintenance time constraints, turnaround times,
transportation times), and basic logistic support
requirements.[6] The maintenance concept is a prerequisite to

---

[5] The configuration reflected in Figure 4-3 obviously does
not represent <u>final</u> design, but is close enough for life
cycle costing purposes (particularly for analyses
accomplished in the early stages of a program). Further
design definition will occur as the program progresses.

[6] Refer to: B. Blanchard, <u>Logistics Engineering And
Management</u>, Prentice-Hall, Inc., 1974, Chapter 4.

the system or product design, whereas a detailed maintenance
plan reflects the results of design and is used for the
acquisition of those logistics elements required for the
sustaining life cycle support of the system in the field.
The maintenance concept can best be conveyed through the
illustration in Figure 4-4.[7]

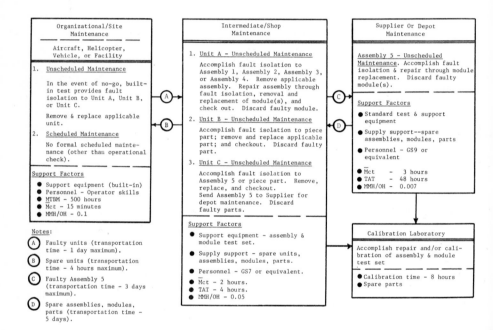

Figure 4-4 System Maintenance Concept Flow (Repair Policy)

[7] The quantitative support factors presented in the figure
are considered as minimum design requirements. For each
alternative configuration being evaluated in a life cycle
cost analysis, the support factors may vary somewhat as a
function of the specific design characteristics. However,
the minimum requirements still must be met.

Referring to the figure, there are three levels of maintenance to consider. "Organizational" maintenance is performed in the aircraft or helicopters, in the patrol vehicles, or in the various communication facilities (as applicable) by user or operator personnel. "Intermediate" maintenance, or the second level of maintenance, is accomplished in a remote shop facility by trained personnel possessing the skills necessary to perform the assigned functions. "Depot" maintenance, the highest level of maintenance, constitutes the specialized repair or overhaul of complex components at the supplier's facility by highly skilled supplier maintenance personnel.

The specific functions scheduled to be accomplished on the communication system at each level of maintenance are noted. In the event of a malfunction, fault isolation is performed to the applicable unit by using the built-in test capability (i.e., Unit "A", "B", or "C"). Units are removed and replaced at the organizational level and sent to the intermediate maintenance shop for corrective maintenance. At the intermediate shop, units are repaired through assembly and/or part replacement; assemblies are repaired through module replacement; and so on.

The illustrated maintenance concept in Figure 4-4 indicates the functions that are anticipated for each level of maintenance; the effectiveness requirements in terms of maintenance frequency and times; and the major elements of logistics support to include personnel skill levels, test and support equipment, supply support requirements, and facilities. This information is not only required as an input to the system design process, but serves as the basis for determining O & S costs in the total life cycle cost spectrum.

With the problem (or need) defined, combined with a description of system operation requirements and the maintenance concept, it is now appropriate to proceed with the specific steps involved in the life cycle cost analysis

of the two proposed alternative configurations. These steps,
leading to the generation of cost data, are noted below.

A. Development of the Cost Breakdown Structure (CBS)

The CBS assumed for the purposes of this evaluation is
presented in Figures 2-3 and A-1, and the cost categories
for the CBS are described in Table A-1, Appendix A. Although
all of the cost categories may turn out not to be relevant
or highly significant in terms of the magnitude of cost as
a function of total life cycle cost, this CBS does serve as
a good starting point. Initially, all costs must be
considered, with the subsequent objective of concentrating
on those cost categories reflecting the high contributors.

B. Identification of Cost-Generating Activities

The problem statement deals with the evaluation of two
alternative communication system configurations, and the
selection of a preferred approach. In both instances there
will be required activities involving planning, management,
engineering design, test and evaluation, production,
distribution, system operations, maintenance and logistics
support, and ultimate equipment disposal. In an attempt to
be more specific for the life cycle cost analysis, the
analyst may wish to perform the following steps:

1. Identify all anticipated program activities that will
generate costs of one type or another in the life cycle for
each of the two alternatives.

2. Relate each identified activity to a specific cost
category in the CBS (refer to Figure A-1 and Table A-1,
Appendix A). Each activity should fall into one or more of
the categories in the CBS. If not, the CBS should be
expanded or revised as appropriate to cover the required
effort.

3. Develop a matrix-type worksheet for the purposes of
recording costs for each applicable category by year in the

life cycle.[8] Figure 4-5 illustrates an example of data
format presentation. The assumed life cycle and the major
activities are based on the program plan presented in
Figure 4-2.

4. Generate cost input data for each applicable activity
listed in matrix, and record the results in Figure 4-5.

The cost information may then be presented in various
forms (e.g., refer to Figure 2-8), analyzed, exercised
through a sensitivity analysis, etc.

C. Generation of Input Cost Data[9]

1. Research and development cost (C_R) includes those early
life cycle costs that will be incurred by the metropolitan
agency responsible for the acquisition of the communication
system (i.e., the customer or consumer), and those costs
incurred by the supplier in the development of the system
(i.e., the contractor). There will be some "common costs"
to the customer associated with both alternatives and
relating to initial program planning, the accomplishment of
feasibility studies, the development of operational
requirements and the maintenance concept, the preparation of
top-level system specifications, and general management
activities. Also, there will be supplier costs that are
peculiar to each alternative and that are included in the
supplier's proposal as submitted to the customer.

Although the analyst may ultimately wish to evaluate only

---

[8] The matrix desired could be a direct printout from the
life cycle cost model. Model design must consider the
various data output requirements in terms of both content
and format.

[9] The material covered here is presented in enough detail to
convey the overall approach used in the evaluation of the
two alternative communication system configurations. An
indepth discussion of each cost input factor would be
rather extensive and certainly prohibited within the
confines of this text.

Program Activity	Cost Category Designation	Cost By Program Year ($)													Total Cost (Constant) $	Total Cost (Actual $)	Percent Contribution (%)
		1	2	3	4	5	6	7	8	9	10	11	12	13			
Alternative "A"																	
1. Research & Development	C_R																
a. Life Cycle Management	C_{RM}																
b. Product Planning	C_{RP}																
(1) Feasibility Studies	--																
(2) Program Planning	--																
2. -----------------------																	
3. -----------------------																	
Others																	
Alternative "B"																	
1. Research & Development	C_R																
2. -----------------------																	

Figure 4-5   Cost Collection Worksheet (Example)

delta or incremental costs (i.e., those costs peculiar to
one alternative or the other--refer to Figure 2-2), the
approach here is to address total life cycle cost.[10]
Relative to research and development costs, the analyst uses
a combination of customer cost projections and the proposals
submitted by each of the two potential suppliers as source
data for the life cycle cost analysis. Figure 4-6 presents a
summary of research and development costs.

It should be noted that the costs presented here are
primarily nonrecurring costs, constituting management and
engineering labor with the proper inflationary factors
included. Labor costs are developed from manpower
projections indicating the class of labor (i.e., manager,
supervisor, senior engineer, engineer, technician, etc.) and
the manhours of effort required by class per month for each
functional activity. The manhours per month are then
converted to dollars by applying standard cost factors.

---

[10]It is important to look at total life cycle cost in order
to properly assess major cost drivers. The aspect of
delta cost can be reviewed at a later time.

Program Activity*	Cost Category Designator	Cost By Program Year (Inflated Dollars)			Total Actual Cost ($)
		Year 1	Year 2	Year 3	
A. Customer Costs – Alternative "A"					
1. System/Product Management	C_{RM}	40,248	44,273	48,700	133,221
2. Production Planning	C_{RP}	15,960	--	--	15,960
B. Supplier Costs – Alternative "A"					
1. System/Product Management	C_{RM}	35,604	38,165	40,081	113,850
2. Product Planning	C_{RP}	10,062	11,068	--	21,130
3. Engineering Design	C_{RE}	50,728	82,736	103,552	237,016
4. Design Documentation	C_{RD}	10,110	18,115	20,200	48,425
5. System Test & Evaluation	C_{RT}	--	--	67,648	67,648
Total Research & Development Cost For Alternative "A"	C_R	162,712	194,357	280,181	637,250
A. Customer Costs – Alternative "B"					
1. System/Product Management	C_{RM}	40,248	44,273	48,700	133,221
2. Product Planning	C_{RP}	15,960	--	--	15,960
B. Supplier Costs – Alternative "B"					
1. System/Product Management	C_{RM}	32,508	35,759	39,335	107,602
2. Product Planning	C_{RP}	--	--	--	--
3. Engineering Design	C_{RE}	65,194	81,175	91,750	238,119
4. Design Documentation	C_{RD}	12,214	12,110	15,300	39,624
5. System Test & Evaluation	C_{RT}	--	--	60,531	60,531
Total Research & Development Cost For Alternative "B"	C_R	166,124	173,317	255,616	595,057

*Only applicable cost categories are listed. There are no costs associated with product research (C_{RR}) and system software (C_{RS}).

Figure 4-6   Research and Development Cost Summary

Both indirect and direct costs are included, along with a 10% per year inflation factor. Material costs are included in test and evaluation (Category C_{RT}) since engineering prototype models must be produced in order to verify the system performance, effectiveness, and supportability characteristics.

The supplier costs for Alternatives "A" and "B" in Figure 4-6 are derived directly from the two individual supplier proposals. Direct costs, indirect costs, inflation

factors for both labor and material, general and
administrative expenses, and projected supplier profits are
included.

2. <u>Production and construction cost</u> (C_p) includes the
recurring and nonrecurring costs associated with the
production of the required 80 operational systems plus the
four additional systems intended to compensate for possible
attrition. Referring to Figure 4-2, the leading edge of the
inventory profile represents the production requirements.
Obviously, the analyst must convert the projected smooth
line effect to a specific production profile as shown in
Figure 4-7. This profile becomes the basis for determining
production costs.

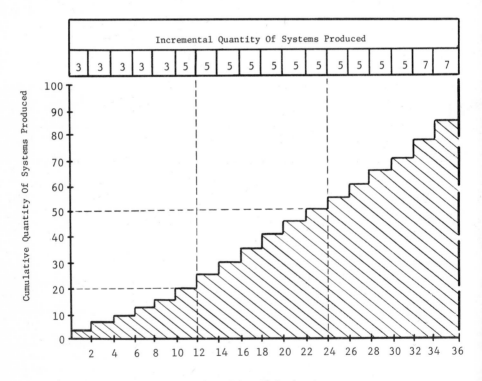

Months After Start Of Production

Figure 4-7 System Production Requirements

If permitted the option, each of the two potential suppliers may propose an entirely different production scheme while still meeting the inventory requirements illustrated in Figure 4-2. This, of course, would in all probability create a significant variation in the input planning factors and cost. However, in this instance the specified production scheme in Figure 4-7 is assumed for both alternatives.

Production and construction cost considers the appropriate factors indicated in Figure 2-3 and A-1, and the results are tabulated in Figure 4-8

a. System/product management cost (C_{RM}) includes the ongoing management activity required throughout the production phase. Costs in this category are a continuation of the system/product management cost stream reflected in the R & D cost summary in Figure 4-6.

b. Industrial engineering and operations analysis cost (C_{PI}) addresses the functions of production planning, manufacturing engineering, methods engineering, etc. A minimal level of effort is entered in Figure 4-8.

c. Manufacturing recurring cost (C_{PMR}) includes those activities related directly to the fabrication, assembly, inspection, and test of the 84 systems being produced. Each of the two potential suppliers submitted a proposal covering functions compatible with and in direct support of the production scheme illustrated in Figure 4-7. Since the majority of such activities are repetitive in nature, each supplier estimated the cost of the first system and then projected a learning curve to reflect the cost of subsequent systems. The proposed learning curves for Alternatives "A" and "B" are illustrated in Figure 4-9. These curves support the recurring manufacturing costs included in Figure 4-8.

d. Manufacturing nonrecurring cost (C_{PMN}) covers all costs associated with the acquisition and installation of special tooling, fixtures and jigs, and factory test equipment. These costs, included in the supplier's proposal, are basically a one-time expenditure during Year 2 in antic- ipation of the production requirements commencing in Year 3.

Program Activity *	Cost Category Designator	Cost By Program Year (Inflated Dollars)				Total Actual Cost ($)
		Year 2	Year 3	Year 4	Year 5	
A. Customer Costs - Alternative "A"						
1. System/Product Management	C_{RM}	--	--	53,570	58,927	112,497
B. Supplier Costs - Alternative "A"						
1. Industrial Engineering and Operations Analysis	C_{PI}	10,000	18,000	20,000	20,200	68,200
2. Manufacturing						
a. Recurring Cost	C_{PMR}	--	174,000	226,500	234,600	635,100
b. Nonrecurring Cost	C_{PMN}	48,900	--	--	--	48,900
3. Quality Control	C_{PQ}	--	25,400	26,000	27,102	78,502
4. Initial Logisitcs Support						
a. Supply Support	C_{PLS}	--	9,600	19,200	19,200	48,000
b. Test & Support Equipment	C_{PLT}	5,000	65,000	--	--	70,000
c. Technical Data	C_{PLD}	5,100	--	--	--	5,100
d. Personnel Training	C_{PLP}	16,400	15,000	15,000	--	46,400
Total Production & Construction Cost For Alternative "A"	C_P	85,400	307,000	360,270	360,029	1,112,699
A. Customer Costs - Alternative "B"						
1. System/Product Management	C_{RM}	--	--	53,570	58,927	112,497
B. Supplier Costs - Alternative "B"						
1. Industrial Engineering and Operations Analysis	C_{PI}	15,000	20,000	16,000	15,000	66,000
2. Manufacturing						
a. Recurring Cost	C_{PMR}	--	167,000	235,500	255,000	657,500
b. Nonrecurring Cost	C_{PMN}	55,100	--	--	--	55,100
3. Quality Control	C_{PQ}	--	19,800	22,100	31,090	72,990
4. Initial Logistics Support						
a. Supply Support	C_{PLS}	--	18,340	19,340	19,340	57,020
b. Test & Support Equipment	C_{PLT}	5,000	65,000	--	--	70,000
c. Technical Data	C_{PLD}	5,350	--	--	--	5,350
d. Personnel Training	C_{PLP}	16,400	15,000	15,000	--	46,400
Total Production & Construction Cost For Alternative "B"	C_P	96,850	305,140	361,510	379,357	1,142,857

* Only applicable cost categories are listed.

Figure 4-8 Production and Construction Cost Summary

    e. <u>Quality control cost</u> (C_{PQ}) includes the category of quality assurance which is a sustaining level of activity required to ensure that good overall product quality exists throughout the production process, and the category of

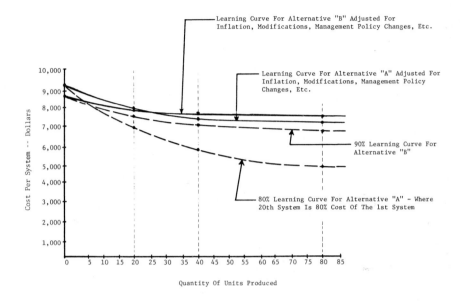

Learning Curve For Alternative "B" Adjusted For Inflation, Modifications, Management Policy Changes, Etc.

Learning Curve For Alternative "A" Adjusted For Inflation, Modifications, Management Policy Changes, Etc.

90% Learning Curve For Alternative "B"

80% Learning Curve For Alternative "A" - Where 20th System Is 80% Cost Of The 1st System

Cost Per System -- Dollars

Quantity Of Units Produced

Figure 4-9   Production Learning Curves

qualification testing which constitutes the testing of a representative sample of items to verify that the level of quality inherent in the items being produced is adequate. The costs from each supplier's proposal are included.

f.   Initial spares and inventory cost (C_{PLS}) covers the acquisition of major units to support organizational maintenance, and a few assemblies plus parts to provide support at the intermediate level of maintenance. These items represent the inventory safety stock factor, and are located at the intermediate maintenance shops and the supplier facility identified in Figure 4-1. Replenishment spares for the sustaining support of the system in operational use throughout the life cycle are covered in Category C_{OLS}. This category covers an initial limited procurement, whereas the replenishment spares are based on realistic consumption and demand factors.

The assumptions used in determining costs are as follows:

Alternative "A" -- one complete set of units (Unit A, Unit B, and Unit C) are required for Shop Number 1, Shop Number 2, each of the mobile vans, and for the supplier facility as a backup. The acquisition price for: Unit A is $3,800; Unit B is $2,150; and Unit C is $2,650. Five sets are equivalent to $43,000 with $8,600 in Year 3, $17,200 in Year 4, and $17,000 in Year 5. The cost of assemblies and parts is $5,000 ($1,000 in Year 3, $2,000 in Year 4, and $2,000 in Year 5).

Alternative "B" -- Six sets of units (Unit A, Unit B, and Unit C) are required. The additional unit (above and beyond the requirements for Alternative "A") is to be located at Shop Number 2 to cover the anticipated increased number of maintenance actions. The acquisition price for Unit A is $3,530; Unit B is $2,060; and Unit C is $2,580. Six sets are equivalent to $49,020 with $16,340 in each of Years 3, 4, and 5. The cost of assemblies and parts is $8,000 ($2,000 in Year 3, $3,000 in Year 4, and $3,000 in Year 5).

g. Test and support equipment acquisition cost (C_{PLT}) covers the "assembly and module test set" located in each intermediate maintenance facility, and several items of commercial and standard equipment located at the supplier facility to support depot maintenance (refer to Figures 4-1 and 4-4). The design cost associated with the test set is $5,000 expended in Year 2. The production acquisition price of each test set is $15,000 and there are four test sets required. Referring to Figure 4-10, there are systems being introduced into operational use in Year 3 at all locations; thus, the four test sets must be available in Year 3. The commercial and standard equipment needed for depot maintenance requires no additional design effort, and can be acquired at a price of $5,000. Thus, the costs for Year 3 are $65,000. The test and support equipment requirements for each alternative are considered to be comparable. The sustaining annual maintenance and logistics requirements for test equipment are included in cost category C_{OLE}.

h. <u>Technical data cost</u> (C_{PLD}) relates to the preparation and publication of system installation and test instructions operating procedures, and maintenance procedures. These data are required to operate and maintain the system in the field throughout its programmed life cycle. The acquisition cost of this data is $5,100 for Alternative "A" and $5,350 for Alternative "B". Data costs are applicable to Year 2.

i. <u>Personnel training cost</u> (C_{PLP}) covers the initial cost of training system operators and maintenance technicians. For operator training, it is assumed that 20 operators are trained in Year 2, 30 operators in Year 3, and 30 operators in Year 4. The cost of training is $500/student (for each alternative configuration). In the maintenance area, formal

CATEGORIES OF SYSTEMS	PROGRAM YEAR												
	1	2	3	4	5	6	7	8	9	10	11	12	13
Communication Systems In Use	--	--	20	50	80	80	80	80	80	80	80	30	10
1. Aircraft Application (3)	--	--											
a. Quantity Of Systems	--	--	1	3	3	3	3	3	3	3	3	3	1
b. System Operating Time (Hrs.)	--	--	594	1,782	1,782	1,782	1,782	1,782	1,782	1,782	1,782	1,782	594
2. Helicopter Application (5)													
a. Quantity Of Systems	--	--	2	5	5	5	5	5	5	5	5	5	3
b. System Operating Time (Hrs.)	--	--	1,080	2,700	2,700	2,700	2,700	2,700	2,700	2,700	2,700	2,700	1,620
3. Patrol Vehicles (50)													
a. Quantity Of Systems	--	--	7	22	50	50	50	50	50	50	50	10	2
b. System Operating Time (Hrs.)	--	--	9,100	28,600	65,000	65,000	65,000	65,000	65,000	65,000	65,000	13,000	2,600
4. Communications Facilities (5)													
a. Quantity Of Systems	--	--	5	10	10	10	10	10	10	10	10	5	--
b. System Operating Time (Hrs.)	--	--	7,200	14,400	14,400	14,400	14,400	14,400	14,400	14,400	14,400	7,200	--
5. Central Communications Control (1)													
a. Quantity Of Systems	--	--	4	8	10	10	10	10	10	10	10	4	3
b. System Operating Time (Hrs.)	--	--	4,320	8,640	10,800	10,800	10,800	10,800	10,800	10,800	10,800	5,400	3.240
6. Mobil Vans													
a. Quantity Of Systems	--	--	1	2	2	2	2	2	2	2	2	2	1
b. System Operating Time (Hrs.)	--	--	720	1,440	1,440	1,440	1,440	1,440	1,440	1,440	1,440	1,440	720

Figure 4-10 Quantity of Systems in Use and Operating Time

training will be given to two technicians assigned to each
of the four intermediate maintenance facilities. These
technicians will accomplish "on-the-job" training for the
additional personnel in the shops/vans. The cost of
maintenance training is $800/student week, or $6,400 in
Year 2.

   3. Operation and support cost (C_O) includes the cost of
operating and supporting the system throughout its programmed
life cycle. These costs primarily constitute user costs,
and are based on the program planning information in
Figure 4-2. The inventory profile in the figure is expanded
as shown in Figure 4-10 to indicate the specific quantity of
systems in use and the total operating time (in hours) for
all systems in each applicable year of the life cycle.

System utilization is based on the individual operating
times stated in the six objectives described as part of the
problem definition, and is determined from Equations (1)
through (6).

Operating time for aircraft application (hours) =
(quantity of system in aircraft)(15 flights/month)(12) x
(3 hours/flight)(1.1)   (1)

Operating time for helicopter application (hours) =
(quantity of systems in helicopters)(25 flights/month) x
(12 months)(2 hours/flight)(0.9)   (2)

Operating time for patrol vehicle application (hours) =
(quantity of systems in patrol vehicles)(5 hours/day) x
(5 days/week)(52 weeks/year)(1.0)   (3)

Operating time for communication facility application
(hours) = (quantity of systems in facilities) x
(120 hours/month)(12)   (4)

Operating time for central communication control
application (hours) = (quantity of systems) x
(3 hours/day)(360 days/year)   (5)

Operating time for mobile van application (hours) =
(quantity of systems in vans)(2 hours/day) x
(360 days/year)   (6)

Although the actual utilization of the system will vary
from operator to operator, from organization to organization,
from one geographical area to the next, etc., the factors
included in Figure 4-10 are average values and are employed
in the baseline example. Also, it is assumed that each
alternative configuration being evaluated will be operated
in the same manner.

Operation and support cost (C_O) includes those individual
costs associated with system operations, distribution, and
sustaining logistics support (refer to Appendix A). Only
those significant costs that are applicable to the
communication system are discussed herein.

a. Operating personnel cost (C_{OOP}) covers the total costs
of operating the communication system for the various
applications. Since the operator is charged with a number
of different duties, only that allocated portion of time
associated with the direct operation of the communication
system is counted. Operating personnel cost is determined
from Equation (7), using the data in Figure 4-10 as a base.

C_{OOP} = (cost of operator labor)(quantity of operators) x
(quantity of systems)(hours of system operation) x
(% allocation)   (7)

In determining operator costs, different hourly rates are
applied for the various applications (e.g., \$14.50/hour for
the aircraft and helicopter application, \$10.50/hour for the

facility application, etc.) and varied allocation factors
are applied because of a personnel workload difference from
one application to the next. The resulting costs are
included in Figure 4-11.

   b. <u>System distribution and transportation cost</u> (C_{ODT})
covers the initial transportation and installation cost;
i.e., the packing and shipping of systems from the supplier's
manufacturing facility to the point of application, and
installation of the system for operational use. Equation (8)
is used to determine total cost in this category.

C_{ODT} = (cost of transportation) + (cost of packing) +
(cost of system installation)   (8)

where transportation and packing costs are based on
dollars/cwt (i.e., \$30/cwt for transportation and
\$40/cwt for packing), and installation costs are a
function of labor cost in dollars/manhour and the
quantity of manhours required.

Costs in this category are based on the quantity of
systems indicated in Figure 4-10, and on the appropriate
transportation rate stuuctures. The analyst should review
the latest Interstate Commerce Commission (ICC) documentation
on rates in order to determine the proper transportation
costs. The figures used in this life cycle cost analysis
are presented in Figure 4-11.

   c. <u>Unscheduled maintenance cost</u> (C_{OLA}) covers the
personnel activity costs associated with the accomplishment
of unscheduled or corrective maintenance on the communication
system. Specifically, this includes: the direct and
indirect labor cost in the performance of maintenance actions
(a function of maintenance manhours and the cost/manhour);
the material handling cost associated with given maintenance
actions; and the cost of documentation for each maintenance
action. These costs for the two alternative communication
system configurations being evaluated are summarized in
Figure 4-12.

Program Activity	Cost Category Dsgnatn.	Cost By Program Year													Total Actual Cost ($)
		1	2	3	4	5	6	7	8	9	10	11	12	13	
A. <u>Alternative "A"</u>															
1. Operating Personnel	C_{OOP}	--	--	861	2,584	2,584	2,584	2,584	2,584	2,584	2,584	2,584	2,584	861	24,978
2. Transportation	C_{ODT}	--	--	8,000	20,000	32,000	32,000	32,000	32,000	32,000	32,000	32,000	12,000	4,000	268,000
3. Unscheduled Maintenance	C_{OLA}	--	--	3,715	8,886	14,871	14,871	14,871	14,871	14,871	14,871	14,871	4,896	1,536	123,130
4. Maintenance Facilities	C_{OLM}	--	--	139	334	559	559	559	559	559	559	559	184	56	4,626
5. Supply Support	C_{OLS}	--	--	8,880	21,360	35,760	35,760	35,760	35,760	35,760	35,760	35,760	11,760	3,600	295,920
6. Maintenance Personnel Training	C_{OLT}	--	--	--	--	1,300	1,300	1,300	1,300	1,300	1,300	1,300	--	--	9,100
7. Test & Support Equipment	C_{OLE}	--	--	1,625	3,250	3,250	3,250	3,250	3,250	3,250	3,250	3,250	3,250	1,625	32,500
8. Transportation & Handling	C_{OLH}	--	--	168	378	630	630	630	630	630	630	630	210	84	5,250
Total Operation & Support Cost For Alternative "A"	C_O	--	--	23,388	56,792	90,954	90,954	90,954	90,954	90,954	90,954	90,954	34,884	11,762	763,504
B. <u>Alternative "B"</u>															
1. Operating Personnel	C_{OOP}	--	--	861	2,584	2,584	2,584	2,584	2,584	2,584	2,584	2,584	2,584	861	24,978
2. Transportation	C_{ODT}	--	--	8,000	20,000	32,000	32,000	32,000	32,000	32,000	32,000	32,000	12,000	4,000	268,000
3. Unscheduled Maintenance	C_{OLA}	--	--	4,529	10,881	18,322	18,322	18,322	18,322	18,322	18,322	18,322	6,077	1,812	151,553
4. Maintenance Facilities	C_{OLM}	--	--	169	409	690	690	690	690	690	690	690	229	68	5,705
5. Supply Support	C_{OLS}	--	--	10,800	26,160	44,160	44,160	44,160	44,160	44,160	44,160	44,160	14,640	4,320	365,040
6. Maintenance Personnel Training	C_{OLT}	--	--	--	--	1,300	1,300	1,300	1,300	1,300	1,300	1,300	--	--	9,100
7. Test & Support Equipment	C_{OLE}	--	--	2,113	4,225	4,225	4,225	4,225	4,225	4,225	4,225	4,225	4,225	2,113	42,251
8. Transportation & Handling	C_{OLH}	--	--	210	462	756	756	756	756	756	756	756	252	84	6,300
Total Operation & Support Cost For Alternative "B"	C_O	--	--	26,682	64,721	104,037	104,037	104,037	104,037	104,037	104,037	104,037	40,007	13,258	872,927

* Only applicable cost categories are listed.

Figure 4-11 Operation and Support Cost Summary

Program Activity		1	2	3	4	5	6	7	8	9	10	11	12	13
A. Alternative "A"														
1. Organizational Maintenance (System Level)	Total Manhours	--	--	9.25	22.25	37.25	37.25	37.25	37.25	37.25	37.25	37.25	12.25	3.75
	Personnel Cost	--	--	102	245	410	410	410	410	410	410	410	135	41
	Material Handling Cost	--	--	370	890	1,490	1,490	1,490	1,490	1,490	1,490	1,490	490	150
	Documentation Cost	--	--	370	890	1,490	1,490	1,490	1,490	1,490	1,490	1,490	490	150
2. Intermediate Maintenance	Total Manhours	--	--	111	267	447	447	447	447	447	447	447	147	45
	Personnel Cost	--	--	1,443	3,471	5,811	5,811	5,811	5,811	5,811	5,811	5,811	1,911	585
	Material Handling Cost	--	--	370	890	1,490	1,490	1,490	1,490	1,490	1,490	1,490	490	150
	Documentation Cost	--	--	740	1,780	2,980	2,920	2,980	2,980	2,980	2,980	2,980	980	300
3. Depot Maintenance	Total Manhours	--	--	16	36	60	60	60	60	60	60	60	20	8
	Personnel Cost	--	--	240	540	900	900	900	900	900	900	900	300	120
	Material Handling Cost	--	--	40	90	150	150	150	150	150	150	150	50	20
	Documentation Cost	--	--	40	90	150	150	150	150	150	150	150	50	20
Total Unscheduled Maintenance Cost		--	--	3,715	8,886	14,871	14,871	14,871	14,871	14,871	14,871	14,871	4,896	1,536
B. Alternative "B"														
1. Organizational Maintenance	Total Manhours	--		11.25	27.25	46.00	46.00	46.00	46.00	46.00	46.00	46.00	15.25	4.50
	Personnel Cost	--		124	300	506	506	506	506	506	506	506	168	50
	Material Handling Cost	--		450	1,090	1,840	1,840	1,840	1,840	1,840	1,840	1,840	610	180
	Documentation Cost	--		450	1,090	1,340	1,840	1,840	1,840	1,840	1,840	1,840	610	180
2. Intermediate Maintenance	Total Manhours	--		135	327	552	552	552	552	552	552	552	183	54
	Personnel Cost	--		1,755	4,251	7,176	7,176	7,176	7,176	7,176	7,176	7,176	2,379	702
	Material Handling Cost	--		450	1,090	1,840	1,840	1,840	1,840	1,840	1,840	1,840	610	180
	Documentation Cost	--		900	2,180	3,680	3,680	3,680	3,680	3,680	3,680	3,680	1,220	360
3. Depot Maintenance	Total Manhours	--		20	44	72	72	72	72	72	72	72	24	8
	Personnel Cost	--		300	660	1,080	1,080	1,080	1,080	1,080	1,080	1,080	360	120
	Material Handling Cost	--		50	110	180	180	180	180	180	180	180	60	20
	Documentation Cost	--		50	110	180	180	180	180	180	180	180	60	20
Total Unscheduled Maintenance Cost		--		4,529	10,881	18,322	18,322	18,322	18,322	18,322	18,322	18,322	6,077	1,812

Program Year

Note: Costs are rounded off.

Figure 4-12   Unscheduled Maintenance Cost (Two Alternatives)

Determining unscheduled maintenance cost is dependent on predicting the number of anticipated maintenance actions that are likely to occur throughout the life cycle; i.e., the expected frequency of unscheduled maintenance, or the reciprocal of the MTBM. Since there is no scheduled maintenance permitted in this instance, the MTBM factor assumed here is directly equated with unscheduled maintenance actions. The frequency of maintenance is usually based on the reliability failure rates for individual components of the system, and is derived from reliability prediction data, logistics support analysis data, maintenance engineering analyses, or a combination thereof.

Review of the objectives in the problem definition indicates that the need relative to MTBM requirements differs from one application to the next. Since it is the goal to design a single system configuration for use in all applications (to the maximum extent practicable), the most stringent conditions must be met. Thus, the new system is required to exhibit a MTBM of 500 hours or greater. Response to this requirement by the two suppliers is illustrated in Figure 4-13. Note that the predicted MTBM for

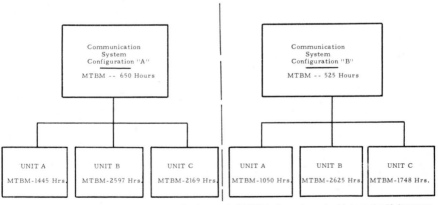

Note: The frequency of maintenance in this instance is 1/MTBM. It may be preferable to work with frequency factors rather than with MTBM values.

Figure 4-13 System Maintenance Factors

Alternative "A" is 650 hours and for Alternative "B" is 525
hours. These values are further broken down to unit level
compatible with the system packaging scheme in Figure 4-3
and the illustrated maintenance concept in Figure 4-4.
Although failures are randomly distributed in general, these
values are used to determine an average factor for the
frequency of maintenance.

Using the information in Figure 4-13, the next step is to
calculate the average number of maintenance actions for each
system (and unit-level) configuration by year throughout the
life cycle. This is accomplished by dividing the system
operating time in Figure 4-10 by the MTBM. The results
(rounded off to the nearest whole number) are presented in
Figure 4-14.[11]

Personnel labor cost covering the accomplishment of
unscheduled maintenance is a function of maintenance manhours
and the cost/manhour. Maintenance manhour and labor cost
factors in this instance are based on the number of
technicians (with specific skill levels) assigned to a given
maintenance action; and the length of time that the
technicians are assigned. The assumed factors are:

Organizational maintenance -- 0.25 M_{MHU}/maintenance
action at a cost of $11.00/$M_{MHU}$.

Intermediate maintenance -- 3 M_{MHU}/maintenance action
at a cost of $13.00/$M_{MHU}$.

Supplier (or depot) maintenance -- 4 M_{MHU}/maintenance
action at a cost of $15.00/$M_{MHU}$.

---

[11] A more precise method is to use a random number generator,
or accomplish a Monte Carlo analysis of some type, to
determine the number of maintenance actions; and then to
assess each individual anticipated maintenance action in
terms of expected logistics support resource requirements.
The analyst should adapt to the needs of the analysis. It
is felt that the approach used herein is adequate for the
purposes at hand.

Alternative	Application	System Or Unit	1	2	3	4	5	6	7	8	9	10	11	12	13
Alternative Configuration "A"	Aircraft Application	System	--	--	1	3	3	3	3	3	3	3	3	3	1
		Unit A	--	--	1	1	1	1	1	1	1	1	1	1	1
		Unit B	--	--	--	1	1	1	1	1	1	1	1	1	--
		Unit C	--	--	--	1	1	1	1	1	1	1	1	1	--
	Helicopter Application	System	--	--	2	4	4	4	4	4	4	4	4	4	3
		Unit A	--	--	1	2	2	2	2	2	2	2	2	2	1
		Unit B	--	--	--	1	1	1	1	1	1	1	1	1	1
		Unit C	--	--	1	1	1	1	1	1	1	1	1	1	1
	Patrol Vehicle Application	System	--	--	14	44	100	100	100	100	100	100	100	20	4
		Unit A	--	--	6	20	45	45	45	45	45	45	45	9	2
		Unit B	--	--	4	11	25	25	25	25	25	25	25	5	1
		Unit C	--	--	4	13	30	30	30	30	30	30	30	6	1
	Communications Facilities	System	--	--	11	22	22	22	22	22	22	22	22	11	--
		Unit A	--	--	5	10	10	10	10	10	10	10	10	5	--
		Unit B	--	--	2	5	5	5	5	5	5	5	5	2	--
		Unit C	--	--	4	7	7	7	7	7	7	7	7	4	--
	Central Communications Control	System	--	--	7	13	17	17	17	17	17	17	17	8	5
		Unit A	--	--	3	6	8	8	8	8	8	8	8	4	2
		Unit B	--	--	2	3	4	4	4	4	4	4	4	2	1
		Unit C	--	--	2	4	5	5	5	5	5	5	5	2	2
	Mobile Vans	System	--	--	2	3	3	3	3	3	3	3	3	3	2
		Unit A	--	--	1	1	1	1	1	1	1	1	1	1	1
		Unit B	--	--	--	1	1	1	1	1	1	1	1	1	--
		Unit C	--	--	1	1	1	1	1	1	1	1	1	1	1
Alternative Configuration "B"	Aircraft Application	System	--	--	2	4	4	4	4	4	4	4	4	4	2
		Unit A	--	--	1	2	2	2	2	2	2	2	2	2	1
		Unit B	--	--	--	1	1	1	1	1	1	1	1	1	--
		Unit C	--	--	1	1	1	1	1	1	1	1	1	1	1
	Helicopter Application	System	--	--	2	5	5	5	5	5	5	5	5	5	3
		Unit A	--	--	1	2	2	2	2	2	2	2	2	2	1
		Unit B	--	--	--	1	1	1	1	1	1	1	1	1	1
		Unit C	--	--	1	2	2	2	2	2	2	2	2	2	1
	Patrol Vehicle	System	--	--	17	54	124	124	124	124	124	124	124	25	5
		Unit A	--	--	9	27	62	62	62	62	62	62	62	12	2
		Unit B	--	--	3	11	25	25	25	25	25	25	25	5	1
		Unit C	--	--	5	16	37	37	37	37	37	37	37	8	2
	Communications Facilities	System	--	--	14	27	27	27	27	27	27	27	27	14	--
		Unit A	--	--	7	14	14	14	14	14	14	14	14	7	--
		Unit B	--	--	3	5	5	5	5	5	5	5	5	3	--
		Unit C	--	--	4	8	8	8	8	8	8	8	8	4	--
	Central Communications Control	System	--	--	8	16	21	21	21	21	21	21	21	10	6
		Unit A	--	--	4	8	11	11	11	11	11	11	11	5	3
		Unit B	--	--	2	3	4	4	4	4	4	4	4	2	1
		Unit C	--	--	2	5	6	6	6	6	6	6	6	3	2
	Mobile Vans	System	--	--	2	3	3	3	3	3	3	3	3	3	2
		Unit A	--	--	1	1	1	1	1	1	1	1	1	1	1
		Unit B	--	--	--	1	1	1	1	1	1	1	1	1	--
		Unit C	--	--	1	1	1	1	1	1	1	1	1	1	1

Note: The figures are rounded off to the nearest whole number.

Figure 4-14 Quantity of Unscheduled Maintenance Actions

The manhour factors used are related to personnel requirements for direct maintenance where the elapsed times are indicated by the $\overline{Mct}$ values. The hourly rates include direct dollars plus a burden or overhead rate. Manhour

calculations, personnel cost, material handling cost (i.e.,
$10/maintenance action), and documentation cost (i.e.,
$30/maintenance action, or $20 at the intermediate level and
$10 at the organizational level) are noted in Figure 4-12
for each of the configurations being evaluated. The total
cost factors are also included in Figure 4-11.

d. Maintenance facilities cost (C_{OLM}) is based on the
occupancy, utilities, and facility maintenance costs as
prorated to the communication system. Facilities cost in
this instance is primarily related to the intermediate level
of maintenance.

e. Supply support cost (C_{OLS}) includes the cost of:
spare parts required as a result of system failures; spare
parts required to fill the logistics pipeline to compensate
for delays due to active repair times, turnaround times, and
supplier lead times; spare parts required to replace
repairable items which are condemned or phased out of the
inventory for one reason or another (e.g., those items that
are damaged to the extent beyond which it is economically
feasible to accomplish repair); and the cost of maintaining
the inventory throughout the designated period of support.

Referring to the illustrated maintenance concept in
Figure 4-4, spare units are required in the intermediate
maintenance shops to support unit replacements at the
organizational level. Spare assemblies, modules, and certain
designated piece parts are required to support intermediate
maintenance actions, and some assemblies and parts are
required to support supplier repair activities or depot
maintenance. In other words, the maintenance concept
indicates the type of spares required at each level of
maintenance, and the system network in Figure 4-1 (with
specific geographical locations defined) conveys the quantity
of maintenance facilities providing overall system support.
A logistics support analysis is accomplished to provide
additional maintenance data as required.

The next step is to determine the quantity of spare parts
required at each location. Too many spares, or a large

inventory, could be extremely costly in terms of investment and inventory maintenance. On the other hand, not enough spares could result in a stockout condition which will inturn cause systems to be inoperative, and the defined objectives of the communication network will not be met. This condition may also be quite costly. The goal is to analyze the inventory requirements in terms of a profile similar to the illustration in Figure 4-15, and obtain a balance between the cost of acquiring spares and the cost of maintaining inventory.[12]

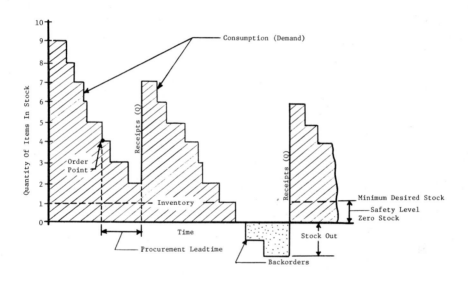

Figure 4-15 Representation of an Inventory Profile

Referring to the figure, the critical factor constitutes consumption or demand, and the probability of having the right type of spare part available when required. Relative to this analysis, demand rates are a function of unit,

---

[12]The "Economic Order Quantity (EOQ)" principle is inferred here. Refer to any text on inventory control; or B. Blanchard, <u>Logistics Engineering And Management</u>, Prentice-Hall, Inc., 1974, Chapter 10.

assembly, module, or part reliability and are based on the
Poisson distribution. Intuitive in the model employed herein
is the expression in Equation (9) which is used in spare
part quantity determination.

$$P = \sum_{n=0}^{n=s} \frac{(R)\left[-K(\ln R)\right]^{n}}{n!} \tag{9}$$

where P = probability of having a spare part of a
            particular type available when required.
       S = the number of spare parts carried in stock.
       R = item reliability (probability of survival),
            or $R = e^{-\lambda\tau}$. In this analysis, reliability
            relates directly to the MTBM factor.
       K = the quantity of a particular part type used
            in the system.

Another consideration is the turnaround time (TAT) and the
transportation time between facilities for repairable items;
i.e., the total time from the point of failure until the
item is repaired and recycled back into the inventory and
ready for use, or the time that it takes to acquire an item
from the source of supply. These time factors are identified
in Figure 4-4, have a significant impact on spare part
requirements, and are considered in the "procurement leadtime"
calculation shown in Figure 4-15.

The process employed for determining the costs associated
with supply support is fairly comprehensive, and all of the
specific detailed steps used in this analysis are not
included here. However, the concepts used are discussed. In
essence, inventory requirements are covered in two categories.
An initial procurement of spare units and assemblies,
basically representing safety stock, is reflected under
initial logistics support cost (i.e., Category C_{PLS}). The
spares required for sustaining support, to include both
repairable and nonrepairable items, are covered in this

category. These items are directly related to consumption
and the quantity of unscheduled maintenance actions identified
in Figure 4-14. The associated costs include both material
costs and the cost of maintaining the inventory. Annual
inventory maintenance is assumed to be 20% of the inventory
value.

   f. Maintenance personnel training cost (C_{OLT}) is covered
in two categories. Initially when the system is first
introducted there is a requirement to train operators and
maintenance technicians. The cost for this initial training
is included in Category C_{PLP}. Subsequently, the cost of
training relates to personnel attrition and the addition of
new operators and/or maintenance technicians. A figure of
$1,300 per year is assumed for formal sustaining training
until that point in time when system phase-out commences.

   g. Test and support equipment cost (C_{OLE}) is presented in
two categories. Category C_{PLT} includes the design and
acquisition of the test and support equipment required for
the intermediate and depot levels of maintenance. This
category includes the sustaining support of these items on
a year-to-year basis; i.e., the unscheduled and scheduled
maintenance actions associated with the test equipment.
Unscheduled maintenance is a function of the use of the test
equipment, which in turn directly relates to the unscheduled
maintenance actions noted in Figure 4-14. In addition, the
reliability and maintainability characteristics of the test
equipment itself will significantly influence the cost of
supporting that test equipment.

   Scheduled maintenance constitutes the periodic 180-day
calibration of certain elements of the test equipment in the
calibration laboratory (refer to Figure 4-4). Calibration is
required to maintain the proper test traceability to primary
and secondary standards.

   The costs associated with test equipment maintenance and
logistics support can be derived through an indepth logistics
support analysis. However, the magnitude of the test
equipment required in this case is relatively small when

compared to other systems. Based on past experience with comparable items, a factor of 5% of the acquisition cost (i.e., \$3,250) is considered to be appropriate for the annual maintenance and logistics cost for the test equipment associated with Alternative "A". A factor of 6.5% (i.e., \$4,225) is assumed for Alternative "B", since the test equipment utilization requirements will be greater.

h. <u>Transportation and handling cost</u> (C_{OLH}) includes the annual costs associated with the movement of materials between the organizational, intermediate, and depot levels of maintenance. This is in addition to the costs of initial distribution and system installation covered in Category C_{ODT}. For the system being analyzed, the movement of materials between the organizational and intermediate levels of maintenance is not considered to be insignificant in terms of relative cost. However, the shipment of materials between the intermediate maintenance facilities and the supplier for depot maintenance is considered to be significant, and can be determined from Equation (10).

$$C_{OLH} = \Big[(\text{cost of transportation}) + (\text{cost of packing}) \Big] \times (\text{quantity of one-way shipments}) \tag{10}$$

where transportation and packing costs are \$30/cwt and \$40/cwt respectively.

The material being moved between the intermediate maintenance facilities and the supplier includes Assembly 5 of Unit C which is supported at the depot level of maintenance (refer to Figure 4-4). The estimated quantity of one-way trips are noted.

	Alternative "A"	Alternative "B"
Year 3	8	10
Year 4	18	22
Years 5-11	30	36
Year 12	10	12
Year 13	4	4

Analysis Results

The problem is to select the best of two alternatives on the basis of total life cycle cost. A comparison of Alternatives "A" and "B" using this criterion is presented in Figure 4-16. Note that the undiscounted costs are listed

Cost Category (Refer to Figures 2-3 and A-1)	Alternative "A" Cost ($)	% of Total	Alternative "B" Cost ($)	% of Total
1. Research & Development Cost (C_R)				
(a) System/Product Management (C_{RM})	247,071	9.8	240,823	9.2
(b) Product Planning (C_{RP})	37,090	1.5	15,960	0.7
(c) Engineering Design (C_{RE})	237,016	9.4	238,119	9.1
(d) Design Data (C_{RD})	48,425	1.9	39,624	1.5
(e) System Test & Evaluation (C_{RT})	67,648	2.7	60,531	2.3
Sub-Total	637,250	25.3	595,057	22.8
2. Production & Construction Cost (C_P)				
(a) System/Product Management (C_{RM})	112,497	4.5	112,497	4.3
(b) Industrial Engineering & Opr. Analysis (C_{PI})	68,200	2.8	66,000	2.5
(c) Manufacturing-Recurring (C_{PMR})	635,100	25.3	657,500	25.2
(d) Manufacturing-Nonrecurring (C_{PMN})	48,900	1.9	55,100	2.1
(e) Quality Control (C_{PQ})	78,502	3.1	72,990	2.8
(f) Initial Logistics Support (C_{PL})				
(1) Supply Support-Initial (C_{PLS})	48,000	1.9	57,020	2.2
(2) Test & Support Equip. (C_{PLT})	70,000	2.8	70,000	2.7
(3) Technical Data (C_{PLD})	5,100	0.2	5,350	0.2
(4) Personnel Training (C_{PLP})	46,400	1.8	46,400	1.8
Sub-Total	1,112,699	44.3	1,142,857	43.8
3. Operation & Support Cost (C_O)				
(a) Operating Personnel (C_{OOP})	24,978	0.9	24,978	0.9
(b) Distribution-Transportation (C_{ODT})	268,000	10.7	268,000	10.4
(c) Unscheduled Maintenance (C_{OLA})	123,130	4.9	151,553	5.8
(d) Maintenance Facilities (C_{OLM})	4,626	0.2	5.705	0.2
(e) Supply Support (C_{OLS})	295,920	11.8	365,040	14.0
(f) Maintenance Personnel Training (C_{OLT})	9,100	0.4	9,100	0.3
(g) Test & Support Equip. (C_{OLE})	32,500	1.3	42,251	1.6
(h) Transportation & Handling (C_{OLH})	5,250	0.2	6.300	0.2
Sub-Total	763,504	30.4	872,927	33.4
GRAND TOTAL	2,513,453	100%	2,610,841	100%

Figure 4-16 Life Cycle Cost Analysis Breakdown

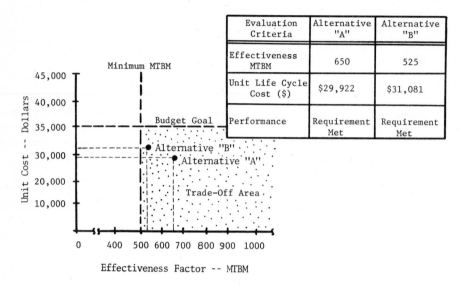

Evaluation Criteria	Alternative "A"	Alternative "B"
Effectiveness MTBM	650	525
Unit Life Cycle Cost ($)	$29,922	$31,081
Performance	Requirement Met	Requirement Met

Effectiveness Factor -- MTBM

Figure 4-17 **Effectiveness Versus Unit Cost**

for those major categories of the cost breakdown structure
that are relevant to this analysis effort. The other
categories of cost that are included in Figure 2-3 and in
Appendix A, and not here, are considered as being not
applicable to this case study.

Referring to the figure, the initial concern is to
determine whether the candidates meet the specified
requirements; i.e., performance; the unit life cycle cost
goal of $35,000; the MTBM of 500 hours; etc. In this
instance, both alternatives meet the requirements and fall
within the trade-off area identified in Figure 4-17.

When evaluating two or more alternatives on a relative
basis, the individual cost projections for each alternative
must be discounted to the present value. The discounted
cost values for Alternatives "A" and "B" are presented in
Figure 4-18, and the cost profiles are illustrated in
Figure 4-19. A 10% discount factor is assumed (refer to the
present value factors in Figure 2-12).

Program Activity	Cost Category Dsgnatn.	1	2	3	4	5	6	7	8	9	10	11	12	13	Total Actual Cost
						Cost By Program Year									
A. Alternative "A"															
1. Research & Development	C_R	162,712	194,357	280,181	—	—									637,250
2. Production/Construction	C_P	—	85,400	307,000	360,270	360,270									1,112,699
3. Operation & Support	C_O	—	—	23,388	56,792	90,954	90,954	90,954	90,954	90,954	90,954	90,954	34,884	11,762	763,504
Total Actual Cost	C	162,712	279,757	610,569	471,062	450,983	90,954	90,954	90,954	90,954	90,954	90,954	34,884	11,762	$2,513,453
Total Discounted Cost	$C_{10\%}$	147,921	231,191	458,720	284,853	280,015	51,344	46,659	42,430	38,574	35,063	31,879	11,114	3,407	$1,663,200
B. Alternative "B"															
1. Research & Development	C_R	166,124	173,317	255,616	—	—									595,057
2. Production/Construction	C_P	—	96,850	305,140	361,510	379,357									1,142,857
3. Operation & Support	C_O	—	—	26,682	64,721	104,037	104,037	104,037	104,037	104,037	104,037	104,037	40,007	13,258	872,927
Total Actual Cost	C	116,124	270,167	587,438	426,231	483,394	104,037	104,037	104,037	104,037	104,037	104,037	40,007	13,258	$2,610,841
Total Discounted Cost	$C_{10\%}$	151,023	223,266	441,342	291,116	300,139	58,729	53,371	48,533	44,122	40,106	36,465	12,746	3,841	$1,704,799

Note: A 10% discount rate is assumed.

Figure 4-18 Cost Allocation by Program Year

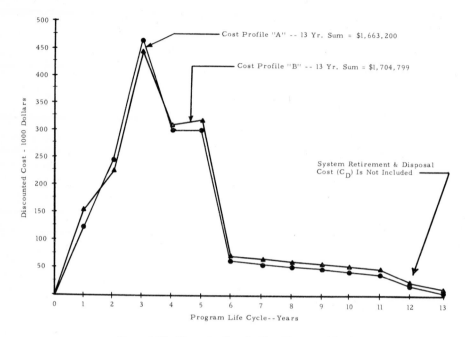

Figure 4-19 Alternative Cost Profiles (Discounted Cost)

   The results of this analysis support <u>Alternative "A"</u> as the
preferred configuration on the basis of life cycle cost.
Note that the research and development (R & D) cost is higher
for Alternative "A"; however, the overall life cycle cost is
lower due to a significantly lower operation and support (O & S)
cost. This would tend to indicate that the equipment design
for reliability, relative to Alternative "A", is somewhat
better. Although this increased reliability results in
higher R & D cost, the anticipated quantity of maintenance
actions is lower resulting in lower O & S costs. The
reliability characteristics in equipment design have a
tremendous effect on life cycle.

   Prior to a final decision on which alternative to select,
the analyst should accomplish a breakeven analysis to
determine the point in time when Alternative "A" becomes
more economical and effective than Alternative "B".

Figure 4-20 indicates that the breakeven point, or the point
in time when Alternative "A" becomes less costly, is
approximately four years and ten months after the program
start. This point is early enough in the life cycle to
support the decision. On the other hand, if this crossover
point were much further out in time, the decision might be
questioned.

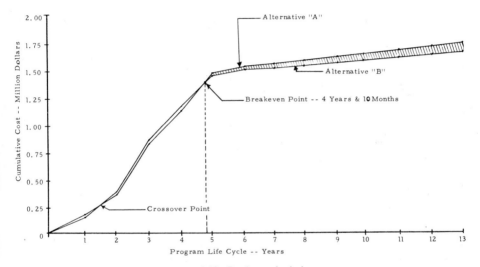

Figure 4-20 Breakeven Analysis

When considering the analysis results in general, it is
noted that the delta cost between the two alternatives is
only $41,599 (refer to Figure 4-18), and that the cost
profiles are relatively close to each other (refer to
Figure 4-20). These factors do not overwhelmingly support a
clear cut decision in favor of Alternative "A" without
introducing some risk. In view of the possible inaccuracies
associated with the input data, the analyst may wish to
perform a sensitivity analysis to determine the effects of
input parameter variations on the life cycle cost analysis
output. The analyst should determine how much variation can
be tolerated before the decision shifts in favor of
Alternative "B".

Referring to Figure 4-16, the analyst should select the
high contributors (those which contribute more than 10% of
the total cost); determine the cause and effect relationships;
and identify the various input data factors that directly
impact cost. In instances where such factors are based on
highly questionable prediction data, the analyst should vary
these factors over a probable range of values and assess the
results. For instance, key input parameters in this analysis
include the system operating time (in hours) and the MTBM
factor. Using the life cycle cost model, the analyst will
apply a multiple factor to the operating time values and the
MTBF, and determine the delta cost associated with each
variation. Trend curves are projected as illustrated in
Figure 4-21.

Through analysis of the information presented, it is quite
evident that a very small variation in operating time
and/or MTBM will cause the decision to shift in favor of
Alternative "B". This provides an indication that there is
a high degree of risk associated with making a wrong decision.
Thus, the analyst should make every effort to reduce this
risk by improving the input data to the greatest extent
possible. Also, where the results are particularly close,
the magnitude of risk associated with the decision must be
determined (refer to Paragraph 3.3).

4.2.2 Case Study Number 2

In defining the detailed maintenance concept and
establishing criteria for equipment design, it is necessary
to determine whether it is economically feasible to repair
certain assemblies or to discard them when failures occur.
If the decision is to accomplish repair, then it is
appropriate to determine the maintenance level at which the
repair should be accomplished; i.e., intermediate maintenance
or supplier/depot maintenance. This case study constitutes
a level of repair analysis based on life cycle cost criterion,

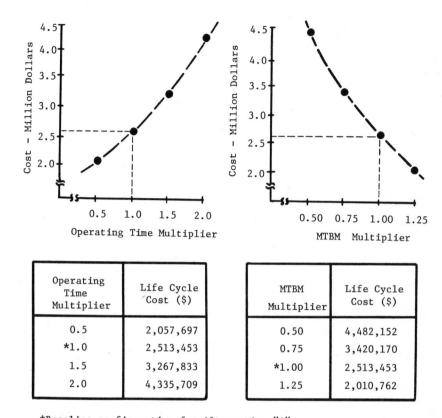

Operating Time Multiplier	Life Cycle Cost ($)
0.5	2,057,697
*1.0	2,513,453
1.5	3,267,833
2.0	4,335,709

MTBM Multiplier	Life Cycle Cost ($)
0.50	4,482,152
0.75	3,420,170
*1.00	2,513,453
1.25	2,010,762

*Baseline configuration for Alternative "A"

Figure 4-21 Sensitivity Analysis

and may be accomplished during preliminary system design.[13]

Definition of the Problem

A computer system will be distributed in quantities of 65 throughout three major geographical areas. The system will

---

[13]It should be noted that some repair level decisions are based on non-economic screening criteria such as safety, technical feasibility, policy, security, contractual provisions, etc. This analysis addresses repair level decisions based on economic criteria.

be utilized to support both scientific and management
functions within various industrial firms and government
agencies. Although the actual system utilization will vary
from one consumer organization to the next, an average
utilization of four hours per day (for a 360-day year) is
assumed.

The computer system is currently in the early development
stage; should be in production in eighteen months; and will
be operational in two years. The full complement of 65
computer systems is expected to be in use in four years, and
will be available through the eighth year of the program
before system phase-out commences. The system life cycle,
for the purposes of the analysis, is 10 years.

Based on early design data, the computer system will be
packaged in five major units with a built-in test capability
that will isolate faults to the unit level. Faulty units
will be removed and replaced at the organizational level
(i.e., consumer's facility), and sent to the intermediate
maintenance shop for repair. Unit repair will be accomplished
through assembly replacement, and assemblies will be either
repaired or discarded. There is a total of 15 assemblies
being considered, and the requirement is to justify the
assembly repair or discard decision on the basis of life
cycle cost criteria. The operational requirements,
maintenance concept, and program plan are illustrated in
Figure 4-22.

Analysis Approach and Results

The stated problem definition primarily pertains to the
analysis of 15 major assemblies of the given computer system
configuration to determine whether the assemblies should be
repaired or discarded when failures occur. In other words,
the various assemblies will be individually evaluated in
terms of: (a) assembly repair at the intermediate level of
maintenance; (b) assembly repair at the supplier or depot
level of maintenance; and (c) disposing of the assembly.

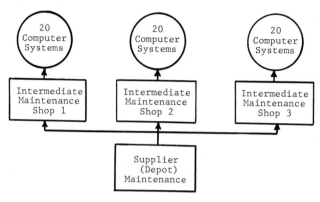

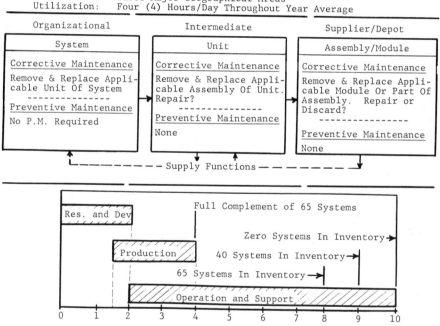

Figure 4-22 Basic System Concepts

Life cycle costs, as applicable to the assembly level, shall
be developed and employed in the alternative selection
process. Total overall computer system costs have been

determined at a higher level, and are not included in this case study.

Given the information in the problem statement, the next step is to develop a cost breakdown structure (CBS) and to establish evaluation criteria. The CBS employed in this analysis is presented in Figures 2-3 and A-1, and the specific cost categories are described in Table A-1 of Appendix A. Not all cost categories in the CBS are applicable in this case; however, the structure is used as a starting point and those categories that are applicable are identified accordingly.

The evaluation criteria include consideration of all costs in each applicable category of the CBS, but the emphasis is on operation and support (O & S) costs as a function of acquisition cost. Thus, the research and development cost and the production cost are presented as one element, while various segments of O & S costs are identified individually. Figure 4-23 presents evaluation criteria, cost data, and a brief description and justification supporting each category. The information shown in the figure covers only one of the 15 assemblies, but is typical for each case.

In determining these costs, the analyst must follow an approach similar to that conveyed in the process illustrated in Figure 3-2 and discussed in Case Study Number 1. That is: operational requirements and a basic maintenance concept must be defined; a program plan must be established; an inventory profile must be identified; a CBS must be established; reliability, maintainability, and logistics support factors must be identified; cost estimating relationships must be developed; and so on.

The next step is to employ the same criteria presented in Figure 4-23 to determine the recommended repair level decision for each of the other 14 assemblies (i.e., Assemblies 2 through 15). Although acquisition costs, reliability and maintainability factors, and certain logistics requirements are different for each assembly, many of the cost estimating relationships are the same. The

Evaluation Criteria	Repair At Intermediate Cost ($)	Repair At Supplier Cost ($)	Discard At Failure Cost ($)	Description and Justification
1. Estimated acquisition costs for Assembly A-1 (to include R & D cost and production cost)	550/Assy. or 35,750	550/Assy. or 35,750	475/Assy. or 30,875	Acquisition cost includes all applicable costs in Categories C_R, C_{PI}, C_{PM}, and C_{PQ} allocated to each Assembly A-1, based on a requirement of 65 systems. Assembly design and production are simplified in the discard area.
2. Unscheduled maintenance cost (C_{OLA})	6,480	8,100	Not Applicable	Based on the 8-year useful system life, 65 systems, a utilization of 4 hours/day, a failure rate (λ) of 0.00045 for Assembly A-1, and a $\overline{M}ct$ of 2 hours, the expected number of maintenance actions is 270. When repair is accomplished, two technicians are required on a full-time basis. The labor rates are $12/hour for intermediate maintenance and $15/hour for supplier maintenance.
3. Supply support - spare assemblies (C_{PLS} and C_{OLS})	3,300	4,950	128,250	For intermediate maintenance 6 spare assemblies are required to compensate for transportation time, the maintenance que, TAT, etc. For supplier/depot maintenance 9 spare assemblies are required. 100% spares are required in the discard case.
4. Supply support - spare modules or parts for assembly repair (C_{PLS} and C_{OLS})	6,750	6,750	Not Applicable	Assume $25 for materials per repair action.
5. Supply support-inventory management (C_{PLS} and C_{OLS})	2,010	2,340	25,650	Assume 20% of the inventory value (spare assemblies, modules, and parts)
6. Test and support equipment (C_{PLT} and C_{OLE})	5,001	1,667	Not Applicable	Special test equipment is required in the repair case. The acquisition and support cost is $25,000 per installation. The allocation for Assembly A-1 per installation is $1,667. No special test equipment is required in the discard case.
7. Transportation and handling (C_{OLH})	Not Applicable	2,975	Not Applicable	Transportation costs at the intermediate level are negligible. For supplier maintenance, assume 340 one-way trips at $175/100 pounds. One assembly weighs 5 pounds.
8. Maintenance training (C_{OLT})	260	90	Not Applicable	Delta training cost to cover maintenance of the assembly is based on the following: Intermediate--26 students, 2 hours each, $200/student week. Supplier--9 students, 2 hours each, $200/student week.
9. Maintenance facilities (C_{OLM})	594	810	Not Applicable	From experience, a cost estimating relationship of $0.55 per direct maintenance manhour is assumed for the intermediate level, and $0.75 is assumed for the supplier level.
10. Technical data (C_{OLD})	1,250	1,250	Not Applicable	Assume 5 pages for diagrams and text covering assembly repair at $250/page.
11. Disposal (C_{DIS})	270	270	2,700	Assume $10/assembly and $1/module or part as the cost of disposal
Total estimated cost	61,665	64,952	187,475	

Figure 4-23 Repair Versus Discard Evaluation (Assembly A-1)

objective is to be <u>consistent</u> in analysis approach and in
the use of input cost factors to the maximum extent possible
and where appropriate. The summary results for all 15
assemblies are presented in Figure 4-24.

Assembly Number	Maintenance Status			Decision
	Repair At Intermediate Cost($)	Repair At Supplier Cost($)	Discard At Failure Cost($)	
A - 1	61,665	64,952	187,475	Repair-Intermediate
A - 2	58,149	51,341	122,611	Repair-Supplier
A - 3	85,115	81,544	73,932	Discard
A - 4	85,778	78,972	65,072	Discard
A - 5	66,679	61,724	95,108	Repair-Supplier
A - 6	65,101	72,988	89,216	Repair-Intermediate
A - 7	72,223	75,591	92,114	Repair-Intermediate
A - 8	89,348	78,204	76,222	Discard
A - 9	78,762	71,444	89,875	Repair-Supplier
A - 10	63,915	67,805	97,212	Repair-Intermediate
A - 11	67,001	66,158	64,229	Discard
A - 12	69,212	71,575	82,109	Repair-Intermediate
A - 13	77,101	65,555	83,219	Repair-Supplier
A - 14	59,299	62,515	62,005	Repair-Intermediate
A - 15	71,919	65,244	63,050	Discard
Policy Cost	1,071,267	1,035,612	1,343,449	Repair-Supplier

Figure 4-24 Summary of Repair Level Costs

The results of the analysis are indicated in Figure 4-24.
Note that the decision for Assembly A-1 favors repair at the
intermediate level; the decision for Assembly A-2 is repair
at the supplier or depot level; the decision for Assembly A-3
is not to accomplish repair at all but to discard the
assembly when a failure occurs; and so on. The figure
reflects recommended policies for each individual assembly.
In addition, the overall policy decision, when addressing
all 15 assemblies as an integral package, favors repair at
the supplier.

Prior to arriving at a final conclusion, the analyst should reevaluate each situation where the decision is close. Referring to Figure 4-23, it is clearly uneconomical to accept the discard decision; however, the two repair alternatives are relatively close. Based on the results of the various individual analyses, the analyst knows that repair level decisions are highly dependent on the unit acquisition cost of each assembly and the total estimated number of replacements over the expected life cycle (i.e., maintenance actions based on assembly reliability. The trends are illustrated in Figure 4-25 where the decision tends to shift from discard to repair at the intermediate level as the unit acquisition cost increases and the number of replacements increases (or the reliability decreases).[14] In instances where the individual analysis result lies close to the crossover lines in the figure, the analyst may wish to review the input data, the assumptions, and accomplish a sensitivity analysis involving the high cost contributors. The purpose is to assess the risk involved and verify the decision. This is the situation for Assembly A-1 where the decision is close relative to repair at the intermediate level versus repair at the supplier's facility (refer to Figure 4-23).

After reviewing the individual analyses of the 15 assemblies to ensure that the best possible decision is reached, the results in Figure 4-24 are updated as required. Assuming that the decisions remain basically as indicated, the analyst may proceed in either of two ways. First, the decisions in Figure 4-24 may be accepted without change, supporting a mixed policy with some assemblies being repaired at each level of maintenance and other assemblies being discarded at failure. With this approach, the analyst should

---

[14]The curves projected in Figure 4-25 are characteristic for this particular life cycle cost analysis and will vary with changes in operational requirements, system utilization, the maintenance concept, production requirements, etc.

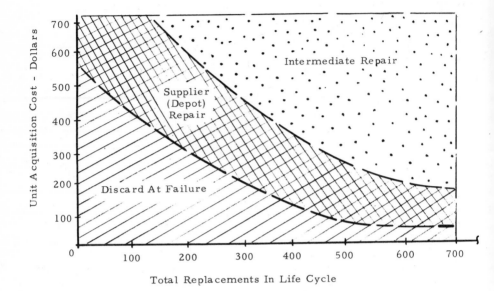

Figure 4-25   Economic Screening Criteria

review the interaction effects that could occur; i.e., the
effects on spares, utilization of test and support equipment,
maintenance personnel utilization, etc. In essence, each
assembly is evaluated individually based on certain
assumptions; the results are reviewed in the context of the
whole; and possible feedback effects are assessed to ensure
that there is no significant impact on the decision.

A second approach is to select the overall "least cost"
policy for all 15 assemblies treated as an entity; i.e.,
assembly repair at the supplier or depot level of maintenance.
In this case, all assemblies are designated as being repaired
at the supplier's facility and each individual analysis
is reviewed in terms of the criteria in Figure 4-23 to
determine the possible interaction effects associated with
the single policy. The result may indicate some changes to
the values in Figure 4-24.

Finally, the output of the repair level analysis must be
reviewed to ensure compatibility with the initially specified

system maintenance concept. The analysis data may either directly support and be an expansion of the maintenance concept, or the maintenance concept will require change as a consequence of the analysis. If the latter occurs, other facets of system design may be significantly impacted. The consequences of such maintenance concept changes must be thoroughly evaluated prior to arriving at a final repair level decision.

4.2.3 Case Study Number 3

This analysis addresses the characteristic problem of selecting an automobile for private use from one of five possible sources. Each of the five automobiles is in the inventory, and the criteria for selection is based on consumer acquisition cost plus operation and support cost.

Definition of the Problem

You as the potential consumer are interested in purchasing a new automobile currently in the inventory. The desired automobile is expected to last for a period of at least five years, and the average usage will be 15,000 miles per year (i.e., 75,000 miles for the defined life cycle). You have narrowed your choice to the five possible candidates listed in Figure 4-26.

ALTERNATIVE	BASIC CHARACTERISTICS	ACQUISITION COST ($)
Automobile A	Large Size, Low Performance, 4-Door, 10 miles/gal.	5,000
Automobile B	Large Size, Medium Performance, 4-Door, 18 miles/gal.	6,000
Automobile C	Medium Size, Medium Performance, 4-Door, 15 miles/gal.	4,200
Automobile D	Small Size, High Performance, 2-Door, 30 miles/gal.	3,600
Automobile E	Medium Size, High Performance, 4-Door, 26 miles/gal.	5,500

Figure 4-26 Alternative Candidates

In evaluating the various candidates, you are interested in acquiring a four-door sedan, but are also willing to consider a small two-door vehicle (i.e., Automobile "D"). The objective is to make a selection based on life cycle cost, where the life cycle cost includes consumer acquisition cost plus the operation and support cost over the five-year period of use.

Analysis Approach

As a start, one should identify the cost breakdown structure or cost categories applicable to the acquisition, operation, and support of an automobile. The significant aspects of cost are noted below.[15]

A. Acquisition Cost

This category constitutes the consumer purchasing price which includes producer R & D cost, production cost, certain initial logistics support costs, product distribution and inventory costs, and the costs associated with the product warranty.

B. Operation Cost

This category includes the cost of the fuel consumed in operating the automobile throughout the life cycle.

C. Support Cost

Support cost is divided between scheduled and unscheduled maintenance. Scheduled maintenance involves the periodic inspections accomplished at 3,000 miles, 6,000 miles, etc., and includes engine oil changes, filter changes, lubrication, and the normal preventive maintenance requirements for a

---

[15]These cost categories, although not specifically identified by the same terms, are included in the CBS in Appendix A.

typical automobile today. Recommended procedures in the
manufacturer's service manual are used as a basis for
determining costs in this area.

Unscheduled maintenance includes visits to the gas station
or garage as a result of suspected problems, repairs due to
failures, new tires, overhauls, and the like. Maintenance
labor cost, the cost of material spares and consumables,
allocated test and support equipment utilization cost,
facilities utilization cost, and related direct and indirect
costs are included.

An analysis of each of the five candidates in terms of
operation and support costs is presented in Figure 4-27.
Operation cost is based on an average utilization rate
throughout the five year life cycle. Support cost relates
to the quantity of scheduled and unscheduled maintenance
actions, and the anticipated logistics support resources

Evaluation Criteria	Automobile	Cost ($) Per Year Of Ownership					Total Cost ($)	Description And Justification
		Year 1	Year 2	Year 3	Year 4	Year 5		
1. Operation--cost of operating the vehicle	A	990	1,035	1,080	1,125	1,245	5,475	Assume an average usage of 15,000 miles per year. Performance characteristics: Car A = 10 mi/gal; Car B = 18 mi/gal; Car C = 15 mi/gal; Car D = 30 mi/gal; Car E = 26 mi/gal. Gas cost is 66¢ in Year 1, 69¢ in Year 2, 72¢ in Year 3, 75¢ in Year 4, and 83¢ in Year 5.
	B	550	575	600	625	691	3,041	
	C	660	690	720	750	830	3,650	
	D	330	345	360	375	415	1,825	
	E	381	398	415	433	479	2,106	
2. Unscheduled maintenance (labor and material)	A	90	240	280	420	500	1,530	Maintenance actions include unscheduled performance checks, repairs, new tires, etc., accomplished at gas station and/or garage.
	B	80	210	290	360	430	1,370	
	C	120	270	320	570	760	2,040	
	D	85	195	200	220	250	950	
	E	100	250	300	400	430	1,480	
3. Scheduled maintenance (labor and material)	A	80	75	75	75	75	380	Maintenance actions include oil changes, filter changes, lubrication, periodic checks, etc., accomplished at gas station and/or garage
	B	70	60	60	60	60	310	
	C	65	50	50	50	50	265	
	D	45	30	30	30	30	165	
	E	50	45	45	45	45	230	

Note: Unscheduled and scheduled maintenance costs include: maintenance personnel labor cost, supply support cost, cost of test and support equipment utilization, cost of facility utilization, and related costs applicable to the consumer.

Figure 4-27 Summary of Operation and Support Cost

required per maintenance action. The concepts discussed in Case Study 1 and 2 are applicable in this instance, although not necessarily to the same level of detail.

Analysis Results

The results of the life cycle cost evaluation indicate that Automobile "D" is clearly favored. Figure 4-28 includes the acquisition plus operation and support cost, and illustrates the consumer life cycle cost profiles for each alternative. Since the various alternatives are compared on an equivalent

Automobile	Acquisition Cost ($)	Consumer Operation And Support Cost ($)					Discounted Total Cost($)
		Year 1	Year 2	Year 3	Year 4	Year 5	
A	5,000	1,074	1,157	1,139	1,191	1,239	10,800
B	6,000	648	724	754	768	804	9,698
C	4,200	782	866	865	1,006	1,115	8,834
D	3,600	426	489	468	453	473	5,909
E	5,500	492	594	603	645	694	8,528

*The assumed discount rate is 8%

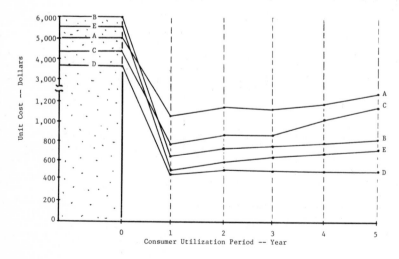

Figure 4-28 Consumer Life Cycle Cost Profile

basis, the costs are discounted to the present value (a discount rate of 8% is assumed). Note that the discounted cost profiles tend to show increasing costs as the various automobiles reach the 45,000 mile point and beyond, which is fairly characteristic of experience with many automobiles to date. If one were to review each alternative individually in terms of inflated budgetary costs, an undiscounted cost profile should be used

If you, the consumer, decide to accept the small high performance 2-door automobile, then the decision is strongly in favor of Automobile "D". However, if your preference is overwhelmingly in favor of a larger 4-door sedan for one reason or another, then Automobile "D" ceases to be a viable alternative, and the other four candidates must be considered. In such a situation, Automobile "E" then assumes the preferable position. Although the acquisition cost is $5,500 (the second highest), the life cycle cost is $8,528 which is the next lowest overall value.

Prior to a final selection of Automobile "E", you may wish to determine the point in time when this automobile assumes the lead position. The breakeven cost projections in Figure 4-29 indicate that Automobile "E" becomes less costly after approximately four years and three months of ownership; i.e., the crossover point between Automobiles "C" and "E". In other words, if you plan to use this automobile for a time period greater than the crossover point, then it is probably worthwhile remaining with "E"; otherwise, your preference may shift to "C".

As a final point, you may wish to address the sensitivities of the input data. For instance, with the present concerns associated with energy and fuels, the cost of fuel over the next five years may increase at a much faster rate than indicated in the quantitative values in Figure 4-27. If this occurs, the breakeven point in Figure 4-29 may shift. Another major input factor that should be evaluated is the frequency of unscheduled maintenance. By varying the quantity of maintenance actions over a realistic range of

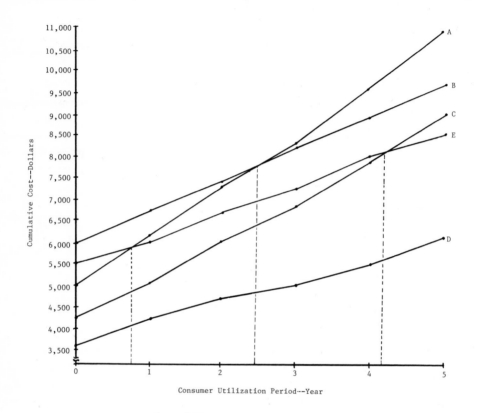

Figure 4-29 Breakeven Cost Analysis

values, you can readily reevaluate your decision in terms of
the projections in Figure 4-29. In any event, you may wish
to test your assumptions through a sensitivity analysis.

4.2.4 Case Study Number 4

This case study addresses the issue of life cycle costing
in connection with the selection and procurement of a capital
equipment item required for the manufacture of a new product.
Both revenues and life cycle costs are used in the evaluation
of two alternative "off-the-shelf" machines.

Definition of the Problem

The ABC Corporation is considering the possibility of introducing Product "X" into the market. A market analysis indicates that the corporation could sell over 500 of these products per year (if available) at a price of $40 each for at least 10 years in the future. The product is not repairable and is discarded at failure.

In order to manufacture the product, the corporation needs to invest in some capital equipment. Based on a survey of potential suppliers, there are two machines available that will fulfill this need. Machine "A" is automatic, will produce up to 340 products per year, and can be purchased at a price of $12,500. Machine "B" is also automatic, will produce 430 products per year, and can be acquired for a price of $15,725. The anticipated machine utilization will be eight hours per day and 270 days per year. Machine output is expected to be one-half during the first year of operation and at full capacity one year after purchase. Machine "A" has an expected reliability MTBF of 275 hours, while Machine "B" has a reliability of 350 hours. Both machines require some preventive maintenance every six months. The salvage value after 10 years of operation is $650 for Machine "A" and $960 for Machine "B".

The problem is to evaluate each of the two machines and to select one of them on the basis of life cycle cost. An 8% discount rate is assumed for evaluation purposes.

Analysis Approach

An initial step is to identify the major categories of revenue and cost that are applicable to the problem at hand. Of primary concern in this instance are the revenues and costs associated with the new product itself and the costs of acquisition, operation, and support of the machine. These factors are discussed further.

A. Product "X" Revenues

It is expected that Machine "A" will manufacture 170
products during Year 1 and 340 products per year thereafter.
Machine "B" will manufacture 215 products during Year 1 and
430 products per year from thereon. All products are sold
during the year of manufacture. From this data, product
revenues are calculated using the $40 selling price as a
basis.

B. Product "X" Manufacturing Cost

Manufacturing costs cover materials and the labor
associated with material procurement, material handling,
product quality control, inspection and test, and packaging.
The effects of learning curves and inflation are considered
and averaged over the life cycle. The estimated average
manufacturing cost is $13 per item, and the cost is
approximately the same for each of the two alternatives
being considered.

C. Product "X" Distribution Cost

This category includes the transportation, warehousing, and
distribution costs associated with the product. The expected
allocated product distribution cost is $3 per item.

D. Machine Operation Cost

The costs included in this category primarily cover the
energy consumption associated with the operation of each
machine. The allocated cost is $1.25 per hour for
Machine "A" and $0.85 per hour for Machine "B".

E. Machine Maintenance Cost

Both scheduled and unscheduled maintenance costs are
included herein. For Machine "A", scheduled (or preventive)

maintenance constitutes two maintenance actions per year at an average cost of $25 per maintenance action. Machine "B" requires three maintenance actions per year at an average cost of $30 per maintenance action.

Unscheduled maintenance cost is based on the estimated quantity of corrective maintenance actions which is a function of the machine reliability. For Machine "A", the average number of maintenance actions per year is 8, and the cost per maintenance action is $150. The average quantity of maintenance actions for Machine "B" is 6, and the cost per maintenance action is $115. The effects of inflation are included in the maintenance cost and averaged over the defined life cycle.

A summary of product manufacturing, distribution, operation, and maintenance costs is presented in Figure 4-30 for each of the two machines being considered. These costs are directly related to the life cycle presented in Figure 4-31 along with

Evaluation Category	Costs Per Program Year – Dollars ($)										Total Undiscounted Cost($)
	1	2	3	4	5	6	7	8	9	10	
A. Machine "A"											
1. Product "X" Manufacturing	2,210	4,420	4,420	4,420	4,420	4,420	4,420	4,420	4,420	4,420	41,990
2. Product "X" Distribution	510	1,020	1,020	1,020	1,020	1,020	1,020	1,020	1,020	1,020	9,690
3. Machine Operation	1,350	2,700	2,700	2,700	2,700	2,700	2,700	2,700	2,700	2,700	25,650
4. Machine Maintenance											
a. Scheduled Maintenance	50	50	50	50	50	50	50	50	50	50	500
b. Unscheduled Maintenance	600	1,200	1,200	1,200	1,200	1,200	1,200	1,200	1,200	1,200	11,400
Total Cost	4,720	9,390	9,390	9,390	9,390	9,390	9,390	9,390	9,390	9,390	89,230
B. Machine "B"											
1. Product "X" Manufacturing	2,795	5,590	5,590	5,590	5,590	5,590	5,590	5,590	5,590	5,590	53,105
2. Product "X" Distribution	645	1,290	1,290	1,290	1,290	1,290	1,290	1,290	1,290	1,290	12,255
3. Machine Operation	918	1,836	1,836	1,836	1,836	1,836	1,836	1,836	1,836	1,836	17,442
4. Machine Maintenance											
a. Scheduled Maintenance	90	90	90	90	90	90	90	90	90	90	900
b. Unscheduled Maintenance	345	690	690	690	690	690	690	690	690	690	6,555
Total Cost	4,793	9,496	9,496	9,496	9,496	9,496	9,496	9,496	9,496	9,496	90,257

Figure 4-30 Summary of Machine Costs

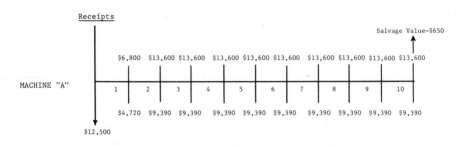

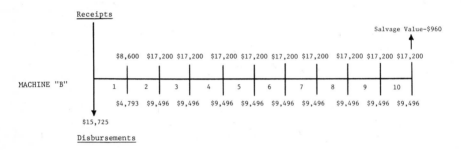

Figure 4-31 Revenue/Cost Projections for Two Alternatives

the initial capital investment, the anticipated revenues from product sales, and the expected salvage value. Figure 4-31 illustrates the cost streams for Machines "A" and "B". It is now necessary to convert these projected revenues and costs to the present value.

Analysis Results

Figure 4-32 shows the present value of the cash flows illustrated in Figure 4-31. Based on the results of this analysis, the selection of Machine "B" is preferred over Machine "A", since the net present value for "B" is $32,803 versus a net present value of only $14,076 for "A".

Program Year	Discount Factor (8%)	Machine "A" Present Value		Machine "B" Present Value	
		Revenues($)	Costs($)	Revenues($)	Costs($)
0	--	--	12,500	--	15,725
1	0.9259	6,295	4,370	7,963	4,438
2	0.8573	11,659	8,050	14,746	8,141
3	0.7938	10,796	7,456	13,653	7,538
4	0.7350	9,996	6,902	12,642	6,980
5	0.6806	9,256	6,391	11,706	6,463
6	0.6302	8,571	5,918	10,839	5,984
7	0.5835	7,936	5,479	10,036	5,541
8	0.5403	7,348	5,073	9,293	5,131
9	0.5002	6,803	4,697	8,603	4,750
10	0.4632	6,601	4,349	8,412	4,399
Total		85,261	71,185	107,893	75,090

Net Present Value Of Machine "A" = $85,261 - $71,185 = $14,076

Net Present Value Of Machine "B" = $107,893 - $75,090 = $32,803

Figure 4-32 Present Value of Cash Flows (Two Machines)

QUESTIONS AND PROBLEMS

1. Select a system or product of your choice; define the system/product life cycle; and describe the possible applications for life cycle cost analyses.

2. Describe in your own words the sequential steps involved in accomplishing a life cycle cost analysis. Identify some of the major input factors.

3. Conduct a literature search and briefly describe the
   items below. Identify each item, its expected content
   relative to applicable data, and its possible use for
   a life cycle cost analysis.
   a. Reliability prediction
   b. Maintainability prediction
   c. Logistics support analysis
   d. Maintenance analysis
   e. Human factors analysis
   f. Functional analysis
   g. Marketing analysis
   h. Feasibility study

4. Refer to Figure 4-2. How would life cycle cost be
   effected if the production schedule is reduced from
   three years to two years (assume that the same quantity
   of items are being produced)?

5. Refer to Figure 4-4. What would be the likely impact
   on life cycle cost if:
   a. The MTBM is decreased?
   b. The $\overline{M}ct$ is increased?
   c. The maintenance manhours per operating hour
      (MMH/OH) figure is increased?
   d. The transportation time between the intermediate
      and supplier levels of maintenance is increased?
   e. The TAT at the intermediate maintenance shop is
      decreased?

6. How does product reliability effect life cycle cost?
   How does maintainability effect life cycle cost?

7. Refer to Figure 4-9. How would modifications during
   the production process effect the learning curves?
   Life cycle cost? Identify all major areas where system
   modifications have an impact.

8. Refer to Figure 4-16. Assume that you have chosen
   Alternative "A" as the preferred approach and wish to
   investigate possible ways in which life cycle cost

could further be reduced. How would you proceed with
your objective? Discuss your approach to the problem
and identify the specific steps that you would follow.

9. Refer to Figure 4-23. If the reliability of Assembly A-1
is five (5) times the value indicated, what would be the
results of the evaluation? What would be the results
if the unit acquisition cost is one-half of the indicated
value and the reliability remained unchanged?

10. Refer to Figure 4-29. Assume that you are interested in
purchasing a 4-door sedan and that you expected to use
the vehicle for the next three years. Which alternative
would you select based on the data provided?

11. Refer to Figure 4-31. At what point in time during the
life cycle does Alternative "B" assume a preferable
position? Draw a breakeven curve.

12. Select one of the following items and perform a life
cycle cost analysis.
   a. A new house
   b. An electric toaster
   c. A washing machine
   d. An airplane or missile
   e. A motorboat
   f. A television set

13. What do you believe is the most important element of
a life cycle cost analysis?

Chapter 5

INTEGRATED MANAGEMENT ASPECTS OF LIFE CYCLE COSTING AND ITS APPLICATIONS

In this era where resources are limited, emphasis must be applied toward increasing productivity. Productivity relates to the effective and efficient utilization of resources. Increased productivity is attained by ensuring that each current and potential program is planned and implemented with the best allocation of resources in mind. The life cycle cost analysis technique is an excellent tool for assessing resource allocation, and for identifying areas where a shift in resources could result in improvement(s).

The life cycle costing technique and its applications are discussed rather thoroughly in the earlier chapters. However, the ultimate benefits of life cycle costing are entirely dependent on management acceptance and the proper use of this technique. One can accomplish the best analysis in the world, but the effort is of little value unless the activity is taken seriously and the results are effectively utilized in the decision-making process. Thus, the successful implementation of life cycle cost analyses is a direct function of management awareness, interest, and emphasis.

This chapter addresses some of the management aspects of life cycle costing as applied to a typical medium-size or

large-scale program. It is recognized that the basic
principles of life cycle costing must also be accepted at the
individual consumer level or by groups of individuals
procuring relatively small products such as an automobile,
an electrical appliance, and so on. However, large projects
such as the acquisition of an airplane, the construction and
operation of a processing plant, the development of a computer
installation, etc., consume enormous quantities of resources
and the potential for savings through the application of life
cycle cost analysis methods is great. Therefore, much of the
discussion is oriented in this direction, although one can
"tailor" the various concepts presented to meet individual
needs. The objective is to briefly discuss the implementation
of the life cycle cost analysis process described earlier.

5.1 PROGRAM PLANNING, IMPLEMENTATION, AND CONTROL

5.1.1 Requirements

The need for life cycle costing has evolved as a result of
the current economic dilemma discussed in Chapter 1. To
attain the total cost visibility desired requires that
emphasis be placed on life cycle cost at program inception.
Thus, market analyses, technical feasibility studies, and
early program planning activities must consider life cycle
cost as a major criterion factor in decision making. This
is particularly essential since decisions early in the life
cycle have the greatest impact on life cycle cost (refer to
Figure 1-7, Chapter 1).

Life cycle cost emphasis can best be applied by initially
setting realistic quantitative cost targets for the system
or product at the start of a program. Such quantitative
factors may be assigned to both material items and program
activities, and should be allocated to the level necessary
to ensure adequate cost monitoring and control. The system/
product cost allocation process is illustrated in Figure 1-9,
Chapter 1. Note that these cost targets include not only

acquisition cost, but life cycle cost. As these cost values
are assigned, they should be included in the appropriate
system/product specifications in the form of required
"design to" criteria; e.g., design to a unit life cycle cost
of $15,000. This is particularly applicable in the
preparation of product specifications for the procurement of
inventoried items from potential suppliers, or in system
specifications covering the development and acquisition of
new systems.

Concurrent with the consideration of life cycle cost as a
system design parameter, early planning data must include a
formal program effort that identifies and provides the
necessary tasks required in establishing the cost targets;
accomplishing life cycle cost analyses on a continuing basis;
generating cost estimating data; measuring and reporting
life cycle cost analysis results; participating in design
reviews and periodic program reviews; initiating the
necessary corrective action when intolerable situations
develop; and so on. In other words, a formal program effort
must be planned and implemented to ensure that the desired
cost targets or goals are met. This activity need not be
extensive, but must be at a level that will provide the
necessary management emphasis to produce a cost-effective
output. The formal life cycle cost task level of effort
should be included in the program plan, and should be
scheduled and organized in a manner similar to any other
program activity. Further, this activity should be
completely integrated into the overall management approach
implemented for the program or project.

5.1.2   Program Planning

Program planning includes: (1) defining the tasks
required to implement life cycle costing activities;
(2) scheduling and organizing these tasks to produce the
desired results in a timely manner; (3) determining the
resources required to accomplish life cycle analyses for a

given program; and (4) establishing the methods by which
task accomplishment can be measured and evaluated.

Figure 1-8 illustrates the application of life cycle
costing throughout the various program phases, and Figure 3-2
shows the process in accomplishing a life cycle cost analysis.
These figures, combined with the case study examples in
Chapter 4, indicate the detailed tasks required in this area.
If one were to group these tasks into functional categories,
the significant functions would likely include the following:

1.   Development of economic factors to include the cost
breakdown structure, cost category descriptions, cost
estimating relationships, and individual cost factors.

2.   Development of system/product operational requirements
and the maintenance concept.

3.   Development of reliability, maintainability, and
logistics support factors.

4.   Development of program planning information to include
the identification of design functions, production functions,
distribution functions, etc.

5.   Development of the analytical methods to facilitate
the life cycle cost analysis process (e.g., models).

Actually, the majority of the functions required for life
cycle costing purposes are inherent in other program
activities. However, the development of the economic factors
and analytical methods required are somewhat unique to the
problem at hand and the analysis activity itself.

As discussed earlier, the life cycle costing effort is a
closely integrated and continuous activity commencing with
the establishment of cost targets and preliminary program
planning data. As the program progresses, the activity serves
not only to assist in system/product design but to assess the
results in terms of the effective and efficient use of
resources. Further, life cycle cost estimates are developed
at designated review points throughout the early phases of
the program and compared against the established targets.
Areas of non-compliance are investigated, and corrective
action is initiated as appropriate.

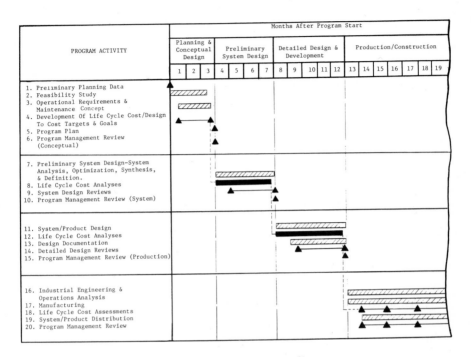

Figure 5-1 Program Milestone Chart

The life cycle costing activity for a medium-sized program requiring system design and development is covered in the milestone chart presented in Figure 5-1.[1] Although analyses are conducted somewhat continuously, composite life cycle cost estimates and special cost reports are required for each program management review. Again, the intent is to compare the up-to-date estimates with the initially specified target values.

---

[1] Figure 5-1 conveys a relatively comprehensive program, and is applicable to medium-size and large-scale systems or products. Obviously, the planning requirements for small products, or those items already developed, are considerably less than that illustrated in the figure. In such instances, the required functions and milestones are tailored accordingly.

As a final point, it should be noted that the major
activity interfaces necessary for life cycle costing are
numerous. Specific elements of data are required in the
areas of reliability, maintainability, logistics support,
production, etc., and the organizational elements responsible
for this data must be integrated into the overall planning
process. Also, the results of the life cycle cost analyses
must be fed back to these sources for decision-making
purposes. These major activity interfaces are illustrated in
Figure 5-2, and the program plan should reflect these
interfaces in the work breakdown structure, schedules (e.g.,
PERT/CPM networks, milestone charts, etc.), supplier
specifications and statements of work, and so on.
Requirements at the top program level must be supported at
each lower level as appropriate.

5.1.3 Organization for Life Cycle Costing

As conveyed earlier, life cycle costing is a technique
primarily employed by managers and engineers for decision-
making purposes. Life cycle cost analyses must be objective,
comprehensive in scope, responsive to specific problem-
oriented needs, and accomplished in a timely manner. The
allotted time for completing a life cycle cost analysis is
often limited to a few days, and response to the "what if"
questions may result in an overnight requirement.

Thus, the organizational component necessary for
accomplishing life cycle costing must be relatively small
and versatile. The individuals within the organization
should be thoroughly familiar with the process discussed in
Chapter 3, the data requirements covered in Chapter 4 and in
Figure 5-2, and the analytical techniques available. It is
recognized that no one individual will possess all of the
skills required. However, a team of specialists with the
proper backgrounds and experience can be assigned to
accomplish the analysis activity itself, with supporting
organizations providing the appropriate data as required.

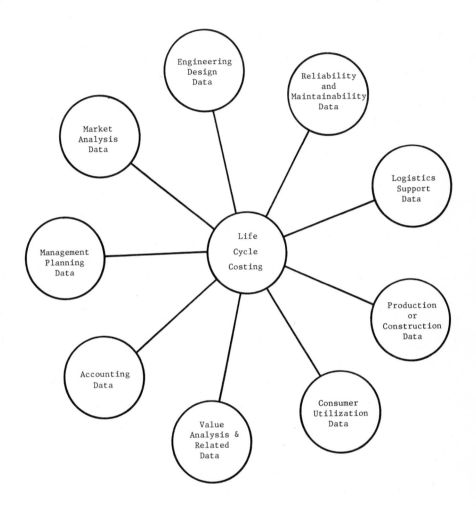

Figure 5-2 Major Activity Interfaces

This team should include some expertise in the area of computer applications and modeling; experience in system/ product operations and logistics support; experience in reliability and maintainability; knowledge of internal producer and supplier activities; and experience in cost estimating and cost analysis.

In some instances, the data requirements for a given

analysis may be rather extensive and the need for detailed
reliability and maintainability predictions, comprehensive
cost estimates, design drawings, etc., is valid. The
participation by supporting organizations is necessary and
should be encouraged as long as the data requirements are
precisely defined, the costs of data preparation are minimal,
and the data are available in a timely manner. It is
relatively easy to misjudge actual needs and ask for too much
data which may turn out to be quite costly and ineffective.

On the other hand, the nature of the problem may allow for
the analysis effort to be accomplished on a relatively
independent basis by the assembled team of specialists. In
such cases, the operational requirements, maintenance concept,
reliability estimates, logistics support factors, cost values,
etc., must be developed by the team, and the team members
should have prior experience in these areas if they are to
produce effective results. Occasionally, additional
expertise may be necessary, and selected personnel are
assigned to the team on a temporary basis in order to
complete the task.

The provisions for accomplishing life cycle cost analyses
will vary, and the organized team must be able to readily
assess the situation. The decision on whether to perform
the analysis independently or with outside assistance is a
function of the nature of the problem, the required analysis
scope and depth, and the time allowed for analysis completion
In any event, the analysis effort must be responsive to
management needs.

As a final point, there are certain organizational
operating conditions that must exist if the life cycle cost
analysis effort is to be successful. These are summarized
below:

1. The analysis activity must be directly accessible to
all levels of program management. A "staff" function is
usually preferred over a "line" function, since the staff
function is not likely to be assigned other concurrent

activities of a possible conflicting nature and is more apt
to be objective in performing the analysis.

2. The analysis activity must not be constrained by any
individual manager or organization in such a way that will
cause incomplete, inaccurate, or untimely reporting.
Changing the data or influencing the results to support a
personal "cause" is self-defeating.

3. The analysis activity must have direct access to all
program cost data and applicable design data, reliability
and maintainability prediction data, production data, and
logistics support data.

4. The analysis effort must be an inherent part of the
program review function. Design decisions should be
supported by life cycle cost data in the formal design
reviews, and life cycle cost projections should be evaluated
as a part of the periodic program management reviews (refer
to Figure 5-1).

5.1.4 Program Review and Control

Once that system design and program requirements have been
established, it is essential that an ongoing review,
evaluation, and control function be initiated. Management
must conduct a periodic assessment to compare current life
cycle cost estimates with the specified requirements.
The selected review points should either be a part of or
tied directly to the normally scheduled program reviews.
Usually, major reviews occur after a significant stage or
level of activity in the program and prior to entering the
next phase. Figure 5-1 identifies the major reviews for one
type of program.

In preparation for each individual program review, a life
cycle cost analysis is accomplished for the system/product
configuration as it exists at that time. The cost breakdown
structure (CBS) in Appendix A may serve as the basis for cost
collection and the latest design data, production data,
reliability and maintainability predictions, logistics

support analyses, etc., are employed to the extent possible in developing the required cost projections. The results may be presented in a manner as shown in Figure 2-8, Chapter 2.

Figure 5-3 identifies the various program review points, and shows a comparison between the target life cycle cost and the estimated value at the third formal review scheduled one year after program start. The projections convey expected cumulative expenditures. Note that the illustration indicates that actual research and development costs did exceed the initial projection (i.e., the costs in the first year); the expected cost at the end of production will exceed the anticipated value; and that the life cycle cost at the end of the 10-year life period will be less than the target due to a reduction in O & S cost.

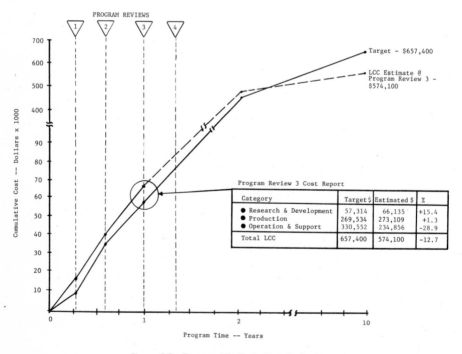

Figure 5-3 Program Life Cycle Cost Projection

If the projected life cycle cost at any given program review exceeds the target value, one should evaluate the different categories of cost in the CBS and identify the high-cost contributors. Also, one should determine the relative relationships of these costs, with each other and with the overall life cycle cost figure, to see if any significant changes have occurred since the previous review; i.e., unusual trends. Areas of concern should be investigated in terms of the possible cause(s) for the high cost, and recommendations for corrective action should be initiated where appropriate. Such recommendations may take the form of design changes, production or process changes, logistics support policy revisions, and/or changes involving the management of resources. Recommendations where significant life cycle cost reduction can be realized should be documented and submitted for management action.

In summary, the program review and control function is an iterative process of life cycle cost assessment. Inherent in this process is not only the accomplishment of life cycle cost analyses, but the feedback and corrective-action that is required when problems occur and requirements are not being met. Management emphasis is necessary in both areas. It is not sufficient to merely review and assess a system/product in terms of life cycle cost unless corrective measures can be taken when required.

5.2 CONSUMER/PRODUCER/SUPPLIER REQUIREMENTS AND INTERFACES

The major interfaces that exist between the producer (i.e., contractor), the supplier of components for the system or product (i.e., subcontractor), and the consumer (i.e., customer) are depicted in Figure 5-4.

Referring to the figure, the initiation of life cycle costing activities commences with the definition of requirements. Consumer requirements are imposed on the producer, and producer requirements are allocated to each

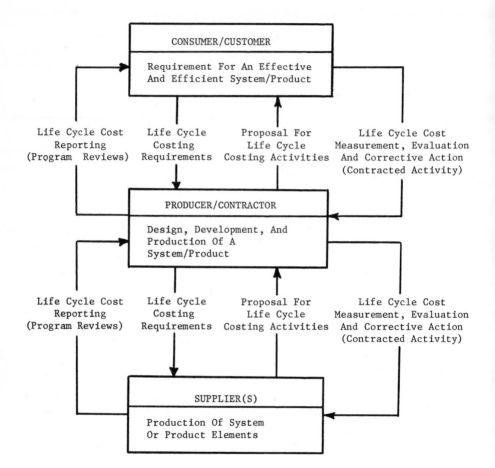

Figure 5-4 Major Consumer/Producer/Supplier Interfaces

supplier as appropriate. Subsequently, there are supplier
proposals, contractual agreements, life cycle cost reporting,
and cost measurement and evaluation activities of one type
or another. These activities create many interfaces between
the consumer, producer, and supplier throughout a program.

Of particular concern when dealing with life cycle costing
are the quantitative cost figures-of-merit that are proposed
and reported overtime. All affected organizations or levels
of activity must be thoroughly familiar with each figure-of-

merit in terms of what is and is not included, how the
figure is derived, and the data base used in deriving the
figure. This is particularly true when various potential
suppliers submit proposals to the producer that include life
cycle costing information. In each instance, the supplier
in all probability has developed a cost structure peculiar
to its own interests and organization, individual cost
estimating relationships, and a cost model. These activities,
which vary from one supplier to the next, result in proposed
life cycle cost figures-of-merit which the producer must
evaluate objectively and in a consistent manner. In other
words, the producer is often faced with the task of
evaluating alternative supplier proposals, including life
cycle cost information, on an equivalent basis. This is
extremely difficult to accomplish (if not impossible) unless
the producer is thoroughly familiar with the factors and
procedures employed by the supplier in developing its life
cycle cost figures.

As an alternative, the producer may develop its own cost
breakdown structure, estimating relationships, cost model,
etc., and employ these tools in evaluating various supplier
proposals. Each supplier, in turn, is requested to provide
specific cost data in a prescribed format, and the producer
uses this information in the evaluation process. The
producer is familiar with the analysis process and the
techniques employed, and the various suppliers may be
evaluated on an equivalent basis. This approach is generally
preferred when there are a number of suppliers being
considered for program support.

Given that contractual agreements exist and there are
program requirements for life cycle cost reporting,
measurement, and evaluation, the problem of proper
communication once again becomes significant. The consumer,
producer, and supplier(s) alike must be thoroughly familiar
with the content and relevance of the information reported
and the techniques used in measurement and evaluation. It
is relatively easy to accept life cycle cost figures at

"face value", but the risks are extremely high unless one
knows and understands the bases for such figures. The
objective, of course, is to minimize this risk through a
better understanding of life cycle cost analysis and its
implications.

5.3 CONTRACTUAL IMPLICATIONS

There are many different applications of contracts used in
the acquisition of systems, products, services, etc.[2] Also,
the type of contract imposed will vary depending on the phase
of system/product development and the anticipated risks in
procurement. For instance, when system/product design is
fairly well established, or in the acquisition of items
already in the inventory, fixed-price contracts are usually
effective. On the other hand, cost-reimbursement type
contracts are relatively flexible and more appropriate for
newly designed items where frequent changes are likely to
occur. In essence, the methods of contracting between the
consumer, producer, and/or supplier are tailored to the
specific program and the related risks.

Associated with each major type of contract is the method
and schedule of payments, incentive and penalty clauses,
warranty and guarantee provisions, and so on. For relatively
large programs, progress payments are often made by the
contractor upon the successful completion and acceptance of
each significant line item specified in the contract. If
incentive contracting is used, an incentive/penalty plan is
often developed and implemented as a supplement to the
schedule for progress payments. Additionally, as a condition

---

[2] Contract types include: firm-fixed-price; fixed-price-
with-escalation; fixed-price-incentive; cost-plus-fixed-
fee; cost-plus-incentive-fee; cost-sharing; time and
material; and letter agreements. For a discussion of
contract types, applications, and negotiations refer to:
B. Blanchard, Engineering Organization And Management,
Prentice-Hall, Inc., 1976, Chapter 15.

in contracting, many systems and products are procured with
the assumption that the contractor will guarantee the item(s)
for a designated period of time after purchase; i.e., the
contractor will accomplish any necessary maintenance and
support at no cost to the consumer.

When addressing life cycle costing in the overall
contractual process, the necessary steps must be taken to
ensure that the life cycle cost activities identified in
in Figure 5-1 receive the proper emphasis, and that the
results of life cycle cost analyses are in some manner tied
directly to the contractual payment structure. The objective
is to convey that life cycle costing is important and should
be taken seriously, and an approach used in attaining this
objective is to positively identify life cycle costing
milestones as part of the contract negotiations between the
consumer, producer, and/or supplier (as applicable). Three
areas of consideration are noted below.

The first area of consideration includes the application
of progress payments directly to the successful completion
of life cycle costing activities, and contingent upon meeting
the anticipated life cycle cost target requirements at that
stage in the program. Referring to Figure 5-1, a progress
payment of sufficient magnitude to be meaningful could be
applied to the System Program Management Review (Task
Number 10) if life cost analyses have been completed, and if
the projected life cycle cost estimate at that stage is less
than the specified target value. On the other hand, if the
life cycle cost estimate does not reflect compliance with
the target value, then the progress payment may be withheld
until such time that the producer (or supplier) implements
corrective action that will cause the necessary reduction in
life cycle cost.

A second consideration relates to incentive contracting
where an incentive/penalty plan is established as a
supplement to the regular contract payment provisions. The
incentive/penalty plan concept is illustrated in Figure 5-5.
Such a plan will specify the application of incentive and

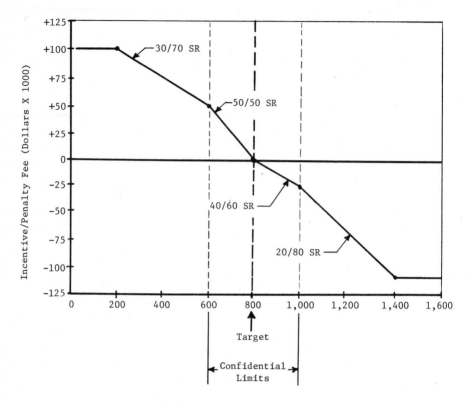

Life Cycle Cost -- Dollars X1000

Figure 5-5   Contractual Incentive/Penalty Plan

penalty payments at a designated point in the program when
there is adequate assurance that the requirements have been
met. For life cycle costing, it is believed that the
application of an incentive/penalty plan would be appropriate
at a point in time after the system or product has acquired
some field experience and realistic life cycle cost
projections can be accomplished using some "real world" data.
Although this specific point in time will vary with the type
of system or product, two to three years of experience seems
appropriate.

Referring to Figure 5-5, the illustrated plan indicates

ordinate values and negotiated sharing ratios (SRs). A
target life cycle cost value of $800,000 is assumed, and
different sharing ratios are developed around this value.
Nearly all incentive plans assume the form of a sharing
arrangement, generally expressed as a percentage ratio. For
instance, the 30/70 SR indicates that if the estimated life
cycle cost is significantly less than the target value
(i.e., $600,000 or less), the value of dollars indicated on
the ordinate would be split, with 30 per cent going to the
customer and 60 per cent being paid to the producer.
Conversely, if the estimated life cycle cost is between
$800,000 and $1,000,000, a penalty payment of 40 per cent of
the indicated ordinate value would be paid by the producer.

The aspect of incentive/penalty plan development and
implementation is a comprehensive subject. There are all
kinds of variations, and the selected approach is highly
dependent on the type of system, the program functions,
development risks, budget limitations, and the formal
negotiated contractual structure.

A third area of consideration involves <u>warranties</u>. For
systems or products where the configuration is relatively
"fixed", it may be appropriate to control O & S costs through
a firm maintenance and support agreement. At this stage,
the producer (or supplier) has established MTBF or MTBM
targets and specific logistics support requirements. As
illustrated in Chapter 4, these factors have a significant
impact on life cycle cost, particularly O & S cost. Thus,
it may be feasible to negotiate a fixed-price contract where
the producer or supplier provides a designated level of
sustaining support for a system/product being utilized by the
consumer. This level of support is based on the frequency
of maintenance (e.g., the reciprocal of the MTBM), and the
logistics support resources required when maintenance actions
occur. If the level of support is higher than anticipated,
then the additional costs are borne by the producer. On the
other hand, if the level is less than predicted, the
producer should realize some savings. In essence, a contract

of this type is basically a warranty established by the producer using reliability, maintainability, and logistics support data to determine the provisions of the warranty.[3]

5.4 SUMMARY

Management considerations pertaining to life cycle costing are numerous and varied. Some of the highlights are noted in this chapter, and many related implications are included in the previous chapters. Life cycle costing constitutes a technique used in the management decision-making process, and must be an integral part of all program activities. As such, it is impossible to cover the entire spectrum of management as it applies to life cycle costing within the confines of this text. However, it is hoped that the points discussed herein will be beneficial in establishing life cycle cost requirements for future programs.

QUESTIONS AND PROBLEMS

1. Identify a system or product of your choice and assume that new design and development is required. Prepare a life cycle cost implementation plan to include activities, schedules, organization, resource needs, and output requirements.

2. Within your own organization, describe in detail how you would fulfill the objectives of life cycle costing.

---

[3] Contractual provisions of a similar nature include Reliability Improvement Warranties (RIWs) which are being applied in many programs today. It is recommended that the reader review the literature covering RIWs.

3. Identify the organizations or groups within your company (or agency) where support is required in the accomplishment of life cycle cost analysis.

4. What individual skills are required to accomplish life cycle cost analyses? Be specific in your discussion.

5. What specific steps would you take to ensure that life cycle costing is being implemented in your program?

Appendix A

COST BREAKDOWN STRUCTURE

When accomplishing a life cycle cost analysis, the analyst must develop a cost breakdown structure illustrating the numerous and varied segments of cost that are combined to provide the <u>total</u> system/product cost. As discussed in Chapter 2, a cost breakdown structure may take various forms depending on the specific need. However, regardless of the format, the analyst must ensure that <u>all</u> life cycle costs are considered, and that the cost breakdown structure reflects the depth required to identify and measure all <u>significant</u> high cost contributors. In other words, the analyst must be able to readily detect and separate those costs which represent high risk areas.

The cost breakdown structure illustrated in Figure A-1 is presented as a typical example of the various elements of cost that when combined, represent total life cycle cost. The categories identified indicate cost collection points which can be summarized upward into broader categories and/or can be collected for different program functions or system elements. The intent is to incorporate a high degree of flexibility in order to provide the necessary visibility for cost allocation, cost measurement, and cost control. This cost breakdown structure can be applied to a variety of programs; however, the depth of coverage may vary from

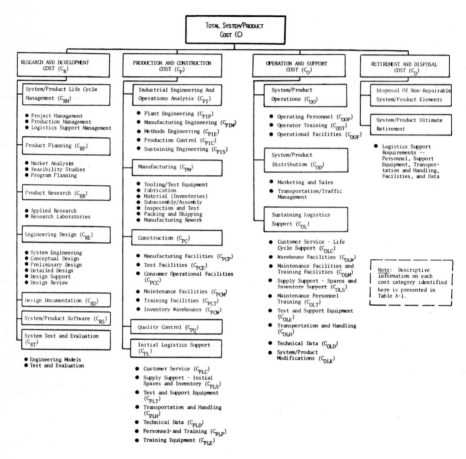

Figure A-1 Cost Breakdown Structure

program to program depending on the emphasis desired.

In viewing cost breakdown structures in general, it is often difficult (if not impossible) to determine the method by which the costs are derived for the various categories. One should not only know what specific cost segments are included, but how each factor is handled and the relationships between the various costs in any given category. Also, it is essential that one completely understand the treatment of not only economic parameters but those non-economic parameters which generate cost.

In an attempt to provide the reader with a better understanding in this area, Table A-1 constitutes a description
of each cost category identified in Figure A-1, along with the
symbology and quantitative relationships used to derive the
overall costs. Referring to Table A-1, the descriptive
information follows the cost breakdown structure on an item-
by-item basis, and the reader by reviewing the entire table
should acquire a good insight as to what the author has
included. In some instances, a more indepth breakdown of
data is necessary for complete cost visibility in certain
areas. However, it is believed that the presentation of
Table A-1 supports the premise that the analyst needs to
develop a comprehensive cost breakdown structure and be
thoroughly familiar with its content.

As a final aid relative to the data presentation in this
appendix, Table A-2 provides a summary of the symbols and
terms utilized throughout Table A-1. These symbols are
listed in alphabetical order for easy reference.

Cost Category (Reference Figure A-1)	Method of Determination (Quantitative Expression)	Cost Category Description and Justification
Total system/product cost (C)	$C = [C_R + C_P + C_O + C_D]$	Includes all future life cycle costs associated with the planning, research, design and development, production and construction, test and evaluation, sustaining operation and logistics support, and retirement of the system or product.
Research and development cost (C_R)	$C_R = [C_{RM} + C_{RP} + C_{RR} + C_{RE} + C_{RD} + C_{RS} + C_{RT}]$	Includes all costs associated with program/project management, product planning, product research, engineering design, design documentation, system/product software, and system test and evaluation. These costs are basically nonrecurring.
System/product life cycle management cost (C_{RM})	$C_{RM} = \sum_{i=1}^{N} C_{RM_i}$ C_{RM_i} = Cost of specific activity "i" N = Number of activities	Costs of all management activities throughout the system/product life cycle applicable to product planning, product research, product design, production/construction, test and evaluation, operation and logistics support, and system/product retirement. This includes project management, engineering management, logistics management, and the like. Management functions relate to C_{RP}, C_{RR}, C_{RE}, C_{RD}, C_{RS}, C_{RT}, C_P, C_O, C_D, and include both producer and consumer activities.
Product planning cost (C_{RP})	$C_{RP} = \sum_{i=1}^{N} C_{RP_i}$ C_{RP_i} = Cost of specific planning activity "i" N = Number of activities	Covers preliminary and detailed market analyses, feasibility studies, development of operational and maintenance concepts, preparation of technical and program proposals, development of program plans and specifications, development of financial plans, etc. This function relates to all planning activity pertaining to C_{RR}, C_{RE}, C_{RD}, C_{RS}, C_{RT}, C_P, C_O, and C_D.

Table A-1 Description of Cost Categories

Cost Category (Reference Figure A-1)	Method of Determination (Quantitative Expression)	Cost Category Description and Justification
Product research cost (C_{RR})	$$C_{RR} = \sum_{i=1}^{N} C_{RR_i}$$ C_{RR_i} = Cost of specific research activity "i" N = Number of activities	Includes all costs associated with applied research, test models, and research laboratory support (i.e., manpower, materials, and facilities).
Engineering design cost (C_{RE})	$$C_{RE} = \sum_{i=1}^{N} C_{RE_i}$$ C_{RE_i} = Cost of specific design activity "i" N = Number of activities	Includes all conceptual design, preliminary design, and detailed design effort associated with the development and/or modification of a system,process, or product. Specific areas include systems engineering; design engineering (electrical, mechanical, structural, chemical, layout and drafting); reliability and maintainability engineering; human factors and safety; functional analysis and allocation; logistics support analysis; components engineering; producibility; and so on. Also, this category covers design support (e.g., computer-aided design capability, procurement activities, etc.) and formal design review functions.
Design documentation cost (C_{RD})	$$C_{RD} = \sum_{i=1}^{N} C_{RD_i}$$ C_{RD_i} = Cost of data item "i" N = Number of data items	This category covers the cost of preparation, printing, publication, distribution, and storage of all data and documentation associated with C_{RR}, C_{RE}, C_{RD}, and C_{RT}. Specific elements include R and D reports; design data (drawings, parts lists, specifications, layouts); analyses; test plans, test procedures, and reports; preliminary operational, installation, and maintenance procedures; and design-related supporting documentation. Program proposals and plans are included in C_{RP}.

TABLE A-1. Description of Cost Categories (Continued)

Cost Category (Reference Figure A-1)	Method of Determination (Quantitative Expression)	Cost Category Description and Justification
System/product software cost (C_{RS})	$C_{RS} = [C_{RSD} + C_{RSM} + C_{RSP}]$ C_{RSD} = Software development C_{RSM} = Software modification C_{RSP} = Software production	All initial development (requirements, procedures, layout, logic flows, etc.), modification, and production of software is included in this category. This covers both recurring and nonrecurring costs.
System test and evaluation cost (C_{RT})	$C_{RT} = [C_{RTA} \cdot N_{RT} + C_{RTB} \cdot N_{RT}$ $+ \sum_{i=1}^{N} C_{RTT_i}]$ C_{RTA} = Cost of engineering model fabrication and assembly labor C_{RTB} = Cost of engineering model material C_{RTT_i} = Cost of test operations and support associated with specific test "i" N_{RT} = Number of engineering models N = Number of identifiable tests	The fabrication, assembly, test and evaluation of engineering breadboards, engineering models, and pre-production prototype models (in support of system/product design--C_{RE}) is included herein. Specifically, this constitutes fabrication and assembly of hardware and software; material procurement and handling; instrumentation; quality control and inspection; logistics support (personnel, training, supply support, test and support equipment, facilities, etc.); data collection and analysis; and the evaluation of engineering models. Test and evaluation plans, procedures, and reports are included in C_{RD}. Recurring production tests are included in C_P.
Production and construction cost (C_P)	$C_P = [C_{PI} + C_{PM} + C_{PC} + C_{PQ}$ $+ C_{PL}]$	This category includes all recurring and nonrecurring costs associated with industrial engineering and operations analysis, product manufacturing, construction of new facilities, and initial logistics support.

TABLE A-1. Description of Cost Categories (Continued)

Cost Category (Reference Figure A-1)	Method of Determination (Quantitative Expression)	Cost Category Description and Justification
Industrial engineering and operations analysis cost (C_{PI})	$C_{PI} = [C_{PIP} + C_{PIM} + C_{PIE} + C_{PIC} + C_{PIS}]$ C_{PIP} = Cost of plant engineering C_{PIM} = Cost of manufacturing engineering C_{PIE} = Cost of methods engineering C_{PIC} = Cost of production control C_{PIS} = Cost of sustaining engineering	Includes all recurring and nonrecurring costs associated with the initial engineering and sustaining engineering functions of manufacturing and construction. Specifically, this constitutes: (1) plant engineering (e.g., design of production and storage facilities, utility requirements, capital equipment needs, material handling provisions, etc.); (2) manufacturing engineering (e.g., make or buy decisions, process design, design of special tools/fixtures/test equipment, process design, design of special tools/fixtures/test equipment, man-machine functions, etc.); (3) methods engineering (e.g., work methods, job skill requirements, standards, design of subassembly and assembly operations, etc.); (4) production control operations (e.g., production lot quantities and batch sizes, economic order quantities and inventory levels, work-order processing and assignment); and (5) sustaining engineering support throughout the production/construction phase.
Manufacturing cost (C_{PM})	$C_{PM} = [C_{PMR} + C_{PMN}]$ C_{PMR} = Recurring manufacturing C_{PMN} = Nonrecurring manufacturing cost	This covers all recurring and nonrecurring costs associated with the production, test, and initial distribution of the prime product. Costs associated with manufacturing facilities are covered in C_{PC}. The cost of spare parts, test and support equipment (used for life cycle system/product support), and training equipment are included in C_{PL}. (1) Recurring manufacturing cost -- fabrication and assembly labor cost, material and inventory cost, inspection and test cost, product rework cost (as required), packing and initial transportation cost, and direct engineering support cost.

TABLE A-1. Description of Cost Categories (Continued)

Cost Category (Reference Figure A-1)	Method of Determination (Quantitative Expression)	Cost Category Description and Justification
		(2) Nonrecurring manufacturing cost -- labor and material costs associated with the installation and support of factory tools, fixtures, and test equipment. Design costs are included in C_{PIM}.
Construction cost (C_{PC})	$C_{PC} = [C_{PCP} + C_{PCE} + C_{PCC} + C_{PCM}$ $+ C_{PCT} + C_{PCW}]$ C_{PCP} = Cost of manufacturing facilities C_{PCE} = Cost of special test facilities C_{PCC} = Acquisition cost of consumer facilities (system operations) C_{PCM} = Acquisition cost of maintenance facilities C_{PCT} = Acquisition cost of training facilities C_{PCW} = Acquisition cost of inventory warehouses	Includes all initial acquisition costs and certain support costs associated with manufacturing facilities, special test facilities, consumer/user operational facilities, maintenance repair and product rework facilities, special training facilities, and product warehouses. Facilities constitute real property, plant, capital equipment, and utilities (gas, electric power, water, telephone, heat, air conditioning, etc.). Facility costs cover the design and development of new buildings, the modification of existing facilities, and/or the occupancy of existing facilities without modification. Work areas and family housing are considered as appropriate. Category costs include preliminary surveys and environmental impact studies, real estate, building construction, roads and pavement, railroad sidings, helicopter pads, etc. Specifically, this category covers: (1) Manufacturing facilities which support the functions described in C_{PI} and C_{PM}. Initial acquisition and sustaining maintenance costs are included herein. (2) Special test facilities necessary to cover unique and peculiar test and evaluation requirements (above and beyond available facilities for engineering and manufacturing test as covered in C_{RT} and C_{PM}). Initial acquisition and sustaining maintenance costs are included herein.

TABLE A-1. Description of Cost Categories (Continued)

Cost Category (Reference Figure A-1)	Method of Determination (Quantitative Expression)	Cost Category Description and Justification
		(3) Special facilities required for the day-to-day operation of large systems/products by the consumer or user. Acquisition costs are included herein and sustaining costs are covered in C_{OOF}.
		(4) Special facilities required for the sustaining support of maintenance needs of the system throughout its programmed life cycle (e.g., repair, rework, periodic calibration, overhaul, modification, etc.). Recurring sustaining costs are covered in C_{OLM}.
		(5) Special facilities required for training consumer or user personnel in the operation and maintenance of the system/product (e.g., large simulator). Sustaining costs are covered in C_{OOT} and C_{OLT}.
		(6) Special warehousing required for system/product storage and distribution. Sustaining costs are covered in C_{OLW}.
Quality control cost (C_{PQ})	$$C_{PQ} = [C_{PQA} + \sum_{i=1}^{N} C_{PQC} + \sum_{i=1}^{N} C_{PQS}]$$ C_{PQA} = Quality assurance cost C_{PQC} = Cost of qualification test "i" C_{PQS} = Cost of production sampling test "i"	This category covers the recurring cost of maintaining an on-going quality assurance or quality control capability throughout production and construction, and directly supports activities in C_{RT}, C_{PI}, C_{PM}, C_{PC}, and C_{PL}. In addition, the specific nonrecurring costs associated with initial system/product qualification testing and the periodic sampling tests accomplished throughout production are included. The inspection and acceptance testing for individual items in production is covered in C_{PM}.

TABLE A-1. Description of Cost Categories (Continued)

Cost Category (Reference Figure A-1)	Method of Determination (Quantitative Expression)	Cost Category Description and Justification
Initial logistics support cost (C_{PL})	N = Number of individual tests $C_{PL} = [C_{PLC} + C_{PLS} + C_{PLT} + C_{PLH}$ $+ C_{PLD} + C_{PLP} + C_{PLE}]$ C_{PLC} = Initial customer service cost C_{PLS} = Initial supply support cost C_{PLT} = Initial test and support equipment cost C_{PLH} = Initial transportation and handling cost C_{PLD} = Initial technical data cost C_{PLP} = Initial training cost C_{PLE} = Initial training equipment cost	This overall category covers: the acquisition of major elements of logistics which are necessary to support the system/product throughout its programmed life cycle; and the interim support capability often required as the system/product evolves from production to ultimate operational use by the consumer. This transition may constitute a short-term interim support period of a few months or a longer period of a few years. (1) Initial customer service (C_{PLC}) -- as the system or product is initially deployed for consumer use often there are installation requirements, servicing requirements, etc., where engineering support is necessary. This category covers the cost of such services for a designated period of time. Sustaining customer service is included in O_{LC}. (2) Initial supply support cost (C_{PLS}) -- this includes: (a) Initial inventory management costs -- preparation of documentation required for the procurement and acquisition of spare/repair parts for all elements of the system or product at each level of maintenance. Provisioning, cataloging, listing, coding, etc., of spares entering the inventory are covered.

TABLE A-1. Description of Cost Categories (Continued)

Cost Category (Reference Figure A-1)	Method of Determination (Quantitative Expression)	Cost Category Description and Justification
		(b) Initial spare/repair part <u>material</u> costs — material spares and repair parts stocked in warehouses or at various inventory points to support maintenance needs of the prime product, test and support equipment, transportation and handling equipment, training equipment, and facilities at all levels of maintenance. These spares/repair parts are usually based on predicted demand data for the designated period of interim support. Sustaining supply support cost is covered in C_{OLS}. Inventory cost associated with production/construction operations is included in C_{PM} and C_{PC}.
		(3) Initial test and support equipment cost (C_{PLT}) — the design, development, and acquisition of test equipment needed to accomplish maintenance of the system/product in the field. The sustaining maintenance of test and support equipment throughout the life cycle is covered in C_{OLE}.
		(4) Initial transportation and handling cost (C_{PLH}) — the design, development, and acquisition of special transportation and handling equipment needed to support operations and maintenance of the system/ product in the field (e.g., stands, dollies, containers, etc.). The sustaining maintenance of these items throughout the life cycle is covered in C_{OLH}.

TABLE A-1. Description of Cost Categories (Continued)

Cost Category (Reference Figure A-1)	Method of Determination (Quantitative Expression)	Cost Category Description and Justification
System/product operations cost (C_{OO})		(5) Initial technical data cost (C_{PLD}) -- preparation of operating and maintenance instructions, installation and test procedures, overhaul and calibration procedures, maintenance cards, etc., is included. Data revisions are included in C_{OLD}. (6) Initial personnel training cost (C_{PLP}) -- the training of producer and/or consumer personnel who are initially assigned to the system/product in the field. Training costs include instructor time, supervision, student salary and allowances, student transportation and per diem, class material and data, etc. Training accomplished on a sustaining basis throughout the system/product life cycle (due to personnel attrition) is covered in C_{OOT} and C_{OLT}. (7) Initial training equipment cost (C_{PLE}) -- the design development, acquisition, and support of training equipment required for personnel training in C_{PLP}.
Operation and support cost (C_O)	$C_O = [C_{OO} + C_{OD} + C_{OL}]$	This category includes all costs associated with system/product distribution, system/product operational use (by the consumer), and the sustaining life cycle logistics support of the system/product in the field.
System/product operations cost (C_{OO})	$C_{OO} = [C_{OOP} + C_{OOT} + C_{OOF}]$ C_{OOP} = Operating or user personnel cost C_{OOT} = Cost of operation training C_{OOF} = Cost of operational facilities	Includes all costs associated with the actual operation (not maintenance) of the system or product throughout its programmed life cycle. Specific areas are the costs of system/product operational personnel (system operator); the formal training of operators; and operational facilities. Both producer and consumer (or user) costs should be addressed.

TABLE A-1. Description of Cost Categories (Continued)

Cost Category (Reference Figure A-1)	Method of Determination (Quantitative Expression)	Cost Category Description and Justification
Operating personnel cost (C_{OOP})	$C_{OOP} = [(C_{OPP})(Q_{OP})(T_O)(N_{OP}) \times$ (% Allocation)] C_{OPP} = Cost of operator labor Q_{OP} = Quantity of operators per system N_{OP} = Number of operating systems T_O = Hours of system operation	This category covers the costs of operating personnel as allocated to the system or product. In some instances costs may be assumed by the producer; in other cases the costs are borne by the consumer; or there may be a combination of both. A system may require more than one operator, a single operator full time, or a single operator on a part-time basis. In any event, costs should be allocated to an individual system or product, and should include base salary, overhead (i.e., fringe benefits, insurance, medical, retirement), travel, etc. Both direct and indirect costs are included.
Operator training cost (C_{OOT})	$C_{OOT} = [(C_{OTT})(Q_{OT})(T_T) +$ (C_{OTS}) (% Allocation)] C_{OTT} = Cost of operator training ($/student-week) C_{OTS} = Cost of training equipment and facility support Q_{OT} = Quantity of student operators T_T = Duration of training (weeks)	Initial operator training is included in C_{PLP} and C_{PLE}. This category covers the formal training (not on-the-job training) of personnel assigned to operate the system, and who either require periodic upgrading or are new replacements due to attrition. Total costs include instructor time; supervision; student salary and allowances while in school; student transportation and per diem; class material and data; training equipment support; and training facilities support (allocation of that portion of equipment and facilities required specifically for formal training).
Operational facilities cost (C_{OOF})	$C_{OOF} = [(C_{OFS} + C_{OFU})(N_{OF}) \times$ (% Allocation)]	Initial operator facility cost is included in C_{PCC}. This category covers the annual recurring costs associated with the occupancy and maintenance (utilities, taxes, facility repair, etc.) of operational facilities throughout the system programmed life cycle. Facility

TABLE A-1. Description of Cost Categories (Continued)

Cost Category (Reference Figure A-1)	Method of Determination (Quantitative Expression)	Cost Category Description and Justification
	C_{OFS} = Cost of operational facility support ($/site) C_{OFU} = Cost of utilities ($/site) N_{OF} = Number of operational sites <u>Alternate approach</u> – it may be more feasible to relate facility cost in terms of: ($/square meter of space/site) X (number of operational sites); or on the basis of volume requirements ($/cubic meter)	and utility costs are proportionately allocated to each system.
System/product distribution cost (C_{OD})	$C_{OD} = [C_{ODM} + C_{ODT} + C_{ODI}]$ C_{ODM} = Cost of marketing and sales C_{ODT} = Cost of transportation and traffic management C_{ODI} = Cost of inventory in warehouses	This category includes: (1) The cost of product marketing and sales — advertising, exhibits, personnel costs associated with marketing and distribution, etc. (2) The cost of transportation and traffic management — initial or first destination transportation from the producer's factory to the various warehouses, and the subsequent transportation from warehouses to the point(s) of distribution to the consumer. In addition, traffic management and control functions are included herein. (3) The cost of inventory in warehouses — that inventory in various distribution warehouses which is not included in C_{PM}, C_{PLS}, and/or C_{OLS}.

TABLE A-1. Description of Cost Categories (Continued)

Cost Category (Reference Figure A-1)	Method of Determination (Quantitative Expression)	Cost Category Description and Justification
Sustaining logistics support cost (C_{OL})	$C_{OL} = [C_{OLC} + C_{OLW} + C_{OLM} + C_{OLS} + C_{OLT} + C_{OLE} + C_{OLH} + C_{OLD} + C_{OLK}]$	This category includes all costs associated with the maintenance and support of the system/product throughout its life cycle after delivery of the system to the consumer (or user). These costs are above and beyond the initial logistics support costs in C_{PL}.
Customer service cost (C_{OLC})	$C_{OLC} = [C_{OLA} + C_{OLB}]$ C_{OLA} = Cost of unscheduled or corrective maintenance C_{OLB} = Cost of scheduled or preventive maintenance Total cost (C_{OLC}) is the summation of C_{OLA} and C_{OLB} for all levels of maintenance support.	Includes all day-to-day labor costs associated with the accomplishment of scheduled (preventive) and unscheduled (corrective) maintenance on the system or product. When a system/product malfunctions or when a scheduled maintenance action is performed, personnel manhours are expended, the handling of spare parts and related material takes place, and maintenance action reports are completed. This category includes all direct and indirect related costs. Initial customer service cost for the designated early system/product transition period is included in C_{PLC}.
Unscheduled/corrective maintenance cost (C_{OLA})	$C_{OLA} = [(C_{OUL})(M_{MHU})(Q_{MAU}) + (Q_{MAU})(C_{OUM}) + (Q_{MAU}) \cdot (C_{OUD})](N_{MS})$ C_{OUL} = Unscheduled maintenance labor cost ($/M_{MHU}$) M_{MHU} = Unscheduled maintenance manhours per maintenance action Q_{MAU} = Quantity of unscheduled maintenance actions $Q_{MAU} = (T_O)(\lambda)$	This category covers the personnel activity costs associated with the accomplishment of unscheduled or corrective maintenance on the system/product. Related spares, test and support equipment, transportation, training, and facilities are covered in C_{OLS}, C_{OLE}, C_{OLH}, C_{OLT}, and C_{OLM}. Total cost (C_{OLA}) includes the sum of the individual costs for each maintenance action multiplied by the number of maintenance action anticipated over the entire system/product life cycle. A maintenance action constitutes any requirement for unscheduled maintenance resulting from catastrophic failures, dependent failures, operator/maintenance induced failures, latent manufacturing or construction

TABLE A-1. Description of Cost Categories (Continued)

Cost Category (Reference Figure A-1)	Method of Determination (Quantitative Expression)	Cost Category Description and Justification
	C_{OUM} = Cost of material handling per unscheduled maintenance action C_{OUD} = Cost of documentation per unscheduled maintenance action N_{MS} = Number of maintenance sites T_O = Hours of system operation λ = System/product failure rate in failures/hour Determine unscheduled maintenance cost for each appropriate level of maintenance.	defects, etc. The cost per maintenance action includes the personnel labor expended for accomplishment of all direct tasks (fault localization and isolation, remove and replace, repair, verification and checkout), associated administrative/logistics support actions, and maintenance documentation (failure reports, supply issue reports, and so on). The unscheduled maintenance labor cost, C_{OUL}, will of course vary with the skill levels and classification of the personnel required for task performance. Both direct labor and overhead costs are included.
Scheduled/preventive maintenance cost (C_{OLB})	$C_{OLB} = [(C_{OSL})(M_{MIS})(Q_{MAS}) + (Q_{MAS}) \cdot$ $(C_{OSM}) + (Q_{MAS})(C_{OSD})](N_{MS})$ C_{OSL} = Scheduled maintenance labor cost ($/M_{MSH}$) M_{MHS} = Scheduled maintenance man-hours per maintenance action Q_{MAS} = Quantity of scheduled maintenance actions. Q_{MAS} relates to fpt. C_{OSM} = Cost of material handling per scheduled maintenance action C_{OSD} = Cost of documentation per scheduled maintenance action N_{MS} = Number of maintenance sites	This category covers the personnel activity costs associated with the accomplishment of scheduled or preventive maintenance on the system/product. Related spares and consumables, test and support equipment, transportation, training, and facilities are covered in C_{OLS}, C_{OLE}, C_{OLH}, C_{OLT}, and C_{OLM}. Total cost (C_{OLB}) includes the sum of the individual costs for each maintenance action multiplied by the number of maintenance actions anticipated over the system/product life cycle. A scheduled or preventive maintenance action includes servicing, lubrication, inspection, critical item replacements, periodic system checkouts, overhaul, calibration, and the like. The cost per maintenance action includes the personnel labor expended for accomplishment of all direct tasks, associated administrative/logistics support actions, and maintenance documentation. The scheduled maintenance labor cost, C_{OSL}, will of

TABLE A-1. Description of Cost Categories (Continued)

Cost Category (Reference Figure A-1)	Method of Determination (Quantitative Expression)	Cost Category Description and Justification
	fpt = Frequency of scheduled maintenance Determine scheduled maintenance cost for each appropriate level of maintenance.	course vary with the skill levels and classification of the personnel required for task performance. Both direct labor and overhead costs are included.
Warehouse facilities cost (C_{OLW})	$C_{OLW} = [(C_{OWS} + C_{OWU})(N_{OW})] \times$ (% Allocation) C_{OWS} = Cost of warehouse facility support ($/warehouse) C_{OWU} = Cost of utilities ($/warehouse) N_{OW} = Number of warehouses	Initial warehouse acquisition costs are included in C_{PCW}. This category covers the annual recurring costs associated with the occupancy and maintenance (utilities, taxes, facility repair, etc.) of warehouses throughout the programmed life cycle. Warehouse facility and utility costs are proportionately allocated to each system.
Maintenance facilities and training facilities cost (C_{OLM})	$C_{OLM} = [(C_{OMM})(N_{OM}) + (C_{OMT})(N_{OR})] \times$ (% Allocation) C_{OMM} = Cost of maintenance facility support N_{OM} = Number of maintenance facilities C_{OMT} = Cost of training facility support N_{OT} = Number of maintenance training facilities	The initial acquisition costs of maintenance facilities and training facilities are covered in C_{PCM} and C_{PCT} respectively. This category includes: (1) The annual recurring costs associated with the up-keep of maintenance facilities at each level of maintenance. These facilities are used to support unscheduled and scheduled maintenance actions identified in C_{OLA} and C_{OLB}. (2) The annual recurring costs associated with the upkeep of facilities primarily utilized for maintenance training purposes. The cost of occupancy, facility repair, taxes, utilities, etc., are included in each category. Maintenance-facility and training facility costs are proportionately allocated to each system as appropriate.

TABLE A-1. Description of Cost Categories (Continued)

Cost Category (Reference Figure A-1)	Method of Determination (Quantitative Expression)	Cost Category Description and Justification
Supply support cost (C_{OLS})	$C_{OLS} = [C_{OSO} + C_{OSI} + C_{OSD} + C_{OSS} + C_{OSC}]$ C_{OSO} = Cost of spare/repair parts at organizational level C_{OSI} = Cost of spare/repair parts at intermediate level C_{OSD} = Cost of spare/repair parts at depot level C_{OSS} = Cost of spare/repair parts at supplier C_{OSC} = Cost of consumables $$C_{OSO} = \sum_{N_{MS}} [(C_A)(Q_A) + \sum (C_{M_i})(Q_{M_i})] + \sum_{i=1} (C_{H_i})(Q_{H_i})]$$ C_A = Average cost of material purchase order ($/order) Q_A = Quantity of purchase orders C_{M_i} = Cost of spare part "i" Q_{M_i} = Quantity of "i" items demanded	Initial supply support costs are covered in C_{PLS}. This category includes all replenishment spare/repair parts and consumable materials (e.g., oil, gas, lubricants, fuel, etc.) that are required to support scheduled and unscheduled maintenance activities associated with prime equipment, transportation and handling equipment (C_{OLH}) test and support equipment (C_{OLE}), at training equipment at each level of maintenance. Traditional levels of maintenance include organizational (on-site), intermediate depot, and/or supplier. Supply support cost covers the cost of purchasing items; the actual cost of the material itself; and the cost of holding or maintaining items in inventory. For multiple quantities of like items, the Economic Order Quantity (EOQ) principle is used. Otherwise, procurements may be based on calendar date, levels of inventory, and/or on a one-for-one replacement concept. Supply support costs are assigned to the applicable level of maintenance.

TABLE A-1. Description of Cost Categories (Continued)

Cost Category (Reference Figure A-1)	Method of Determination (Quantitative Expression)	Cost Category Description and Justification
	C_{H_i} = Cost of maintaining spare item "i" in the inventory ($/$ value of the inventory) Q_{H_i} = Quantity of "i" items in the inventory N_{MS} = Number of maintenance sites C_{OSI}, C_{OSD}, and C_{OSS} are determined in a similar manner.	
Maintenance personnel training cost (C_{OLT})	$C_{OLT} = [(C_{OTM})(Q_{OM})(T_T) + (C_{OLL})$ (% Allocation)] C_{OTM} = Cost of maintenance training ($/student week) Q_{OM} = Quantity of maintenance students C_{OLL} = Cost of training equipment support T_T = Direction of training (weeks)	Initial maintenance personnel training cost is included in C_{PLP} and C_{PLE}. This category covers the formal training (not on-the-job training) of personnel assigned to maintain the system, and who either require periodic upgrading or are new replacements due to attrition. Total costs include instructor time; supervision; student salary and allowances while in school; student transportation and per diem; class material and data; and training equipment support. Facility support for maintenance training is covered in C_{OLM}.
Test and support equipment cost (C_{OLE})	$C_{OLE} = [C_{OEO} + C_{OEI} + C_{OED}]$ C_{OEO} = Cost of maintenance of the test and support equipment at organizational level	The initial acquisition cost for the test and support equipment intended for the life cycle maintenance support of the system/product is covered in C_{PLT}. This category includes the annual recurring life-cycle maintenance cost for the test and support equipment itself at each level of maintenance. Support equipment operation costs are actually covered by the tasks performed in C_{OLC}. Maintenance constitutes both unscheduled

TABLE A-1. Description of Cost Categories (Continued)

Cost Category (Reference Figure A-1)	Method of Determination (Quantitative Expression)	Cost Category Description and Justification
	C_{OEI} = Cost of maintenance of the test and support equipment at intermediate level C_{OED} = Cost of maintenance of the test and support equipment at depot and supplier level $C_{OEO} = [C_{OEU} + C_{OES}]$ C_{OEU} = Cost of equipment unscheduled maintenance C_{OES} = Cost of equipment scheduled maintenance C_{OEI} and C_{OED} are derived in a similar manner.	(corrective) and scheduled (preventive) maintenance, and the costs are derived on a similar basis with the prime system/product (C_{OLA} and C_{OLB}). That is: the overall cost is a function of labor cost ($/maintenance manhour); manhours per maintenance action; quantity of maintenance actions; material handling per maintenance action; documentation per maintenance action; tools and test equipment for maintenance of the support equipment for each maintenance action; and the number of maintenance sites where the test and support equipment is located. In some situations, specific items of test and support equipment are utilized for more than a single system and in such cases, the associated costs are allocated proportionately to each system as appropriate.
Transportation and handling cost (C_{OLH})	$C_{OLH} = [(C_T)(Q_T) + (C_S)(Q_T) + C_X]$ C_T = Cost of transportation C_S = Cost of packing Q_T = Quantity of one-way shipments C_X = Cost of transportation and handling equipment maintenance	Initial transportation and handling equipment acquisition costs are covered in C_{OLH}, and first destination transportation costs from the producer to the consumer are included in C_{ODT}. This category includes: (1) All transportation and handling (or shipping) between organizational, intermediate, depot, and supplier facilities in support of maintenance operations. This covers the return of faulty material items to a higher level of maintenance for repair and overhaul, and the transportation of items to a higher level for preventive maintenance.

TABLE A-1. Description of Cost Categories (Continued)

Cost Category (Reference Figure A-1)	Method of Determination (Quantitative Expression)	Cost Category Description and Justification
	$C_T = [(W)(C_{TC})]$ W = Weight of item (kilogram) C_{TC} = Shipping cost (\$/kilogram) $C_S = [(W)(C_{SC})]$ C_{SC} = Packing cost (\$/kilogram) Shipping cost will vary with the distance (in kilometers) of the one-way shipment. Packing cost and weight will vary depending on whether reusable containers are employed.	(2) The transportation and handling (or shipping) of spare/repair parts, personnel, data, test and support equipment, etc., from the supplier to the organizational, intermediate, and depot levels of maintenance; to the consumer operation sites; and/or to inventory warehouses. (3) The sustaining maintenance costs associated with transportation and handling equipment
Technical data cost (C_{OLD})	$C_{OLD} = \sum_{i=1}^{N} C_{OLD_i}$ C_{OLD_i} = Cost of specific data item i N = Number of data items	The initial preparation of technical documentation and data (e.g., operating and maintenance instructions, test procedures, etc.) is covered in C_{PLD}. Individual data reports associated with scheduled and unscheduled maintenance actions are covered in C_{OLA} and C_{OLB}. This category includes any additional data developed throughout the life cycle to support system operation and maintenance functions. This may include special notices of caution, helpful suggestions on system operation, revision of instructions and procedures, and so on.
System/product modifications (C_{OLK})	$C_{OLK} = \sum_{i=1}^{N} C_{OLK_i}$ C_{OLK_i} = Cost of specific modifications i	Throughout the system/product life cycle (after the system is delivered to the consumer), modifications are often proposed and initiated to improve system performance, effectiveness, safety, correct deficiencies, or a combination thereof. This category covers design costs associated with the modification (R and D); the production

TABLE A-1. Description of Cost Categories (Continued)

Cost Category (Reference Figure A-1)	Method of Determination (Quantitative Expression)	Cost Category Description and Justification
	N = Number of system/product modifications	of modification kits; preparation of modification kit installation instructions; formal training (as required) to cover the new or revised configuration; personnel to install the modification and verify system operation; spare/repair parts for the new system elements; test and support equipment changes for compatibility with the modified system/product; and facility changes as appropriate. The objective is to record all costs associated with any given modification.
Retirement and disposal cost (C_D)	$C_D = [(F_C)(Q_{MAU})(C_{DIS} - C_{REC})]$ $+ C_{DR}$ F_C = Condemnation factor Q_{MAU} = Quantity of unscheduled maintenance actions C_{DIS} = Cost of item disposal C_{REC} = Reclamation value C_{DR} = Cost of system/product ultimate retirement	As the system/product evolves through its programmed life cycle, there are non-repairable items which fail and must be discarded. In addition, there are items which are normally repairable but that are damaged beyond economic repair and consequently, are also discarded. These condemned items are usually tied to the unscheduled maintenance actions in C_{OLA}. A second major consideration occurs when the system (or product) as an entity is retired from the inventory due to obsolescence, wearout, or for some reason of an environmental nature. The system/product must then be phased-out and the impact of phase-out should not be detrimental to the environment. The process of phase-out and disposal may involve disassembly, decomposition, reforming, reprocessing, and so on. This in turn may require extensive logistics support and can be quite costly.

TABLE A-1. Description of Cost Categories (Continued)

C	Total system/product life cycle cost
C_A	Average cost of material purchase order (\$/order)
C_D	Total system/product retirement and disposal cost
C_{DIS}	Cost of item disposal
C_{DR}	Cost of system/product ultimate retirement
C_H	Cost of maintaining a spare item in inventory
C_M	Cost of spare part (material)
C_O	Total operation and support cost
C_{OD}	System/product distribution cost
C_{ODI}	Cost of inventory in warehouses
C_{ODM}	Cost of marketing and sales
C_{ODT}	Cost of transportation and traffic management
C_{OED}	Cost of maintenance of the test and support equipment at the depot and supplier level
C_{OEI}	Cost of maintenance of the test and support equipment at the intermediate level
C_{OEO}	Cost of maintenance of the test and support equipment at the organizational level
C_{OES}	Cost of test and support equipment scheduled maintenance
C_{OEU}	Cost of test and support equipment unscheduled maintenance
C_{OFS}	Cost of operational facility support (\$/site)
C_{OFU}	Cost of utilities (\$/site)
C_{OL}	Sustaining logistics support
C_{OLA}	Cost of unscheduled or corrective maintenance
C_{OLB}	Cost of scheduled or preventive maintenance
C_{OLC}	Customer service (life cycle support) cost
C_{OLD}	Technical data cost
C_{OLE}	Test and support equipment
C_{OLH}	Transportation and handling cost
C_{OLK}	Cost of special modification kits
C_{OLL}	Cost of training equipment support
C_{OLM}	Maintenance facilities and training facilities cost
C_{OLS}	Supply support (spares and inventory support) cost
C_{OLT}	Maintenance personnel training cost
C_{OLW}	Warehouse facilities cost
C_{OMM}	Cost of maintenance facility support
C_{OMT}	Cost of training facility support
C_{OO}	System/product operations cost
C_{OOF}	Cost of operational facilities
C_{OOP}	Operating or user personnel cost
C_{OOT}	Cost of operator training
C_{OPP}	Cost of operator labor (\$/hour)
C_{OSC}	Cost of consumables
C_{OSD}	Cost of spare/repair parts at the depot level
C_{OSI}	Cost of spare/repair parts at the intermediate level

Table A-2 Summary of Terms (Reference Figure A-1)

C_{OSL}	Scheduled or preventive maintenance labor cost ($\$/M_{MHS}$)
C_{OSO}	Cost of spare/repair parts at the organizational level
C_{OSS}	Cost of spare/repair parts at the supplier level
C_{OTM}	Cost of maintenance training ($\$$/student week)
C_{OTS}	Cost of training equipment and facility support
C_{OTT}	Cost of operator training ($\$$/student-week)
C_{OUD}	Cost of documentation per unscheduled maintenance action
C_{OUL}	Unscheduled or corrective maintenance labor cost ($\$/M_{MHU}$)
C_{OUM}	Cost of material handling per unscheduled maintenance action
C_{OWS}	Cost of warehouse facility support ($\$$/warehouse)
C_{OWU}	Cost of utilities ($\$$/warehouse)
C_P	Total production and construction cost
C_{PC}	Construction cost
C_{PCC}	Acquisition cost of consumer facilities (system operations)
C_{PCE}	Cost of special test facilities
C_{PCM}	Acquisition cost of maintenance facilities
C_{PCP}	Cost of manufacturing facilities
C_{PCT}	Acquisition cost of training facilities
C_{PCW}	Acquisition cost of inventory warehouses
C_{PI}	Industrial engineering and operations analysis cost
C_{PIC}	Cost of production control
C_{PIE}	Cost of methods engineering
C_{PIM}	Cost of manufacturing engineering
C_{PIP}	Cost of plant engineering
C_{PIS}	Cost of sustaining engineering
C_{PL}	Initial logistics support cost
C_{PLC}	Initial customer service cost
C_{PLD}	Initial technical data cost
C_{PLE}	Initial training equipment cost
C_{PLH}	Initial transportation and handling cost
C_{PLP}	Initial training cost
C_{PLS}	Initial supply support cost
C_{PLT}	Initial test and support equipment cost
C_{PM}	Manufacturing cost
C_{PMN}	Nonrecurring manufacturing cost
C_{PMR}	Recurring manufacturing cost
C_{PQ}	Quality control/quality assurance cost
C_{PQA}	Quality assurance cost
C_{PQC}	Cost of qualification test
C_{PQS}	Cost of production sampling test
C_R	Total research and development cost
C_{RD}	Design documentation cost
C_{RE}	Engineering design cost
C_{REC}	Reclamation value

TABLE A-2. Summary Of Terms (Continued)

C_{RM}	System/product life cycle management cost
C_{RP}	Product planning cost
C_{RR}	Product research cost
C_{RS}	System/product software cost
C_{RSD}	Software development cost
C_{RSM}	Software modification cost
C_{RSP}	Software production cost
C_{RT}	System test and evaluation cost
C_{RTA}	Cost of engineering model fabrication and assembly labor
C_{RTB}	Cost of engineering model material
C_{RTT}	Cost of test operations and support (engineering model)
C_S	Cost of packing
C_{SC}	Packing cost ($/kilogram)
C_T	Cost of transportation
C_{TC}	Shipping cost ($/kilogram)
C_X	Cost of transportation and handling equipment maintenance
F_C	Condemnation factor
f_{pt}	Frequency of scheduled or preventive maintenance
M_{MHS}	Scheduled maintenance manhours per maintenance action
M_{MHU}	Unscheduled maintenance manhours per maintenance action
N_{MS}	Number of maintenance sites
N_{OF}	Number of operational sites
N_{OM}	Number of maintenance facilities
N_{OP}	Number of operating systems
N_{OT}	Number of maintenance training facilities
N_{OW}	Number of warehouses
N_{RT}	Number of engineering models
Q_A	Quantity of purchase orders
Q_H	Quantity of items in the inventory
Q_M	Quantity of spare items demanded or required
Q_{MAS}	Quantity of scheduled maintenance actions
Q_{MAU}	Quantity of unscheduled maintenance actions
Q_{OM}	Quantity of maintenance students
Q_{OP}	Quantity of operators per system
Q_{OT}	Quantity of student operators
Q_T	Quantity of one-way shipments
T_O	Hours of system operation
T_T	Duration of training (weeks)
W	Weight of item (kilogram)
λ	System/product failure rate (failures/hour)

TABLE A-2. Summary of Terms (Continued)

Appendix B

INTEREST TABLES PRESENT VALUE/FUTURE VALUE FACTORS

Table B-1 includes present value and future value factors for different interest rates. The application of these factors is discussed in Chapter 2, Paragraph 2.4. These factors usually are included in most engineering economy textbooks. (Refer to Appendix E.)

	1% Interest Factors		2% Interest Factors		3% Interest Factors		4% Interest Factors		5% Interest Factors	
	Single Payment		Single Payment		Single Payment		Single Payment		Single Payment	
	Compound amount factor	Present worth factor	Compound amount factor	Present worth factor	Compound amount factor	Present worth factor	Compound amount factor	Present worth factor	Compound amount factor	Present worth factor
n	To find F Given P F/P i,n	To find P Given F P/F i,n	To find F Given P F/P i,n	To find P Given F P/F i,n	To find F Given P F/P i,n	To find P Given F P/F i,n	To find F Given P F/P i,n	To find P Given F P/F i,n	To find F Given P F/P i,n	To find P Given F P/F i,n
1	1.010	0.9901	1.020	0.9804	1.030	0.9709	1.040	0.9615	1.050	0.9524
2	1.020	0.9803	1.040	0.9612	1.061	0.9426	1.082	0.9246	1.103	0.9070
3	1.030	0.9706	1.061	0.9423	1.093	0.9152	1.125	0.8890	1.158	0.8638
4	1.041	0.9610	1.082	0.9239	1.126	0.8885	1.170	0.8548	1.216	0.8227
5	1.051	0.9515	1.104	0.9057	1.159	0.8626	1.217	0.8219	1.276	0.7835
6	1.062	0.9421	1.126	0.8880	1.194	0.8375	1.265	0.7903	1.340	0.7462
7	1.072	0.9327	1.149	0.8706	1.230	0.8131	1.316	0.7599	1.407	0.7107
8	1.083	0.9235	1.172	0.8535	1.267	0.7894	1.369	0.7307	1.477	0.6768
9	1.094	0.9143	1.195	0.8368	1.305	0.7664	1.423	0.7026	1.551	0.6446
10	1.105	0.9053	1.219	0.8204	1.344	0.7441	1.480	0.6756	1.629	0.6139
11	1.116	0.8963	1.243	0.8043	1.384	0.7224	1.539	0.6496	1.710	0.5847
12	1.127	0.8875	1.268	0.7885	1.426	0.7014	1.601	0.6246	1.796	0.5568
13	1.138	0.8787	1.294	0.7730	1.469	0.6810	1.665	0.6006	1.886	0.5303
14	1.149	0.8700	1.319	0.7579	1.513	0.6611	1.732	0.5775	1.980	0.5051
15	1.161	0.8614	1.346	0.7430	1.558	0.6419	1.801	0.5553	2.079	0.4810
16	1.173	0.8528	1.373	0.7285	1.605	0.6232	1.873	0.5339	2.183	0.4581
17	1.184	0.8444	1.400	0.7142	1.653	0.6050	1.948	0.5134	2.292	0.4363
18	1.196	0.8360	1.428	0.7002	1.702	0.5874	2.026	0.4936	2.407	0.4155
19	1.208	0.8277	1.457	0.6864	1.754	0.5703	2.107	0.4747	2.527	0.3957
20	1.220	0.8196	1.486	0.6730	1.806	0.5537	2.191	0.4564	2.653	0.3769
21	1.232	0.8114	1.516	0.6598	1.860	0.5376	2.279	0.4388	2.786	0.3590
22	1.245	0.8034	1.546	0.6468	1.916	0.5219	2.370	0.4220	2.925	0.3419
23	1.257	0.7955	1.577	0.6342	1.974	0.5067	2.465	0.4057	3.072	0.3256
24	1.270	0.7876	1.608	0.6217	2.033	0.4919	2.563	0.3901	3.225	0.3101
25	1.282	0.7798	1.641	0.6095	2.094	0.4776	2.666	0.3751	3.386	0.2953
26	1.295	0.7721	1.673	0.5976	2.157	0.4637	2.772	0.3607	3.556	0.2813
27	1.308	0.7644	1.707	0.5859	2.221	0.4502	2.883	0.3468	3.733	0.2679
28	1.321	0.7568	1.741	0.5744	2.288	0.4371	2.999	0.3335	3.920	0.2551
29	1.335	0.7494	1.776	0.5631	2.357	0.4244	3.119	0.3207	4.116	0.2430
30	1.348	0.7419	1.811	0.5521	2.427	0.4120	3.243	0.3083	4.322	0.2314
31	1.361	0.7346	1.848	0.5413	2.500	0.4000	3.373	0.2965	4.538	0.2204
32	1.375	0.7273	1.885	0.5306	2.575	0.3883	3.508	0.2851	4.765	0.2099
33	1.389	0.7201	1.922	0.5202	2.652	0.3770	3.648	0.2741	5.003	0.1999
34	1.403	0.7130	1.961	0.5100	2.732	0.3661	3.794	0.2636	5.253	0.1904
35	1.417	0.7059	2.000	0.5000	2.814	0.3554	3.946	0.2534	5.516	0.1813
40	1.489	0.6717	2.208	0.4529	3.262	0.3066	4.801	0.2083	7.040	0.1421
45	1.565	0.6391	2.438	0.4102	3.782	0.2644	5.841	0.1712	8.985	0.1113
50	1.645	0.6080	2.692	0.3715	4.384	0.2281	7.107	0.1407	11.467	0.0872
55	1.729	0.5785	2.972	0.3365	5.082	0.1968	8.646	0.1157	14.636	0.0683
60	1.817	0.5505	3.281	0.3048	5.892	0.1697	10.520	0.0951	18.679	0.0535
65	1.909	0.5237	3.623	0.2761	6.830	0.1464	12.799	0.0781	23.840	0.0420
70	2.007	0.4983	4.000	0.2500	7.918	0.1263	15.572	0.0642	30.426	0.0329
75	2.109	0.4741	4.416	0.2265	9.179	0.1090	18.945	0.0528	38.833	0.0258
80	2.217	0.4511	4.875	0.2051	10.641	0.0940	23.050	0.0434	49.561	0.0202
85	2.330	0.4292	5.383	0.1858	12.336	0.0811	28.044	0.0357	63.254	0.0158
90	2.449	0.4084	5.943	0.1683	14.300	0.0699	34.119	0.0293	80.730	0.0124
95	2.574	0.3886	6.562	0.1524	16.578	0.0603	41.511	0.0241	103.035	0.0097
100	2.705	0.3697	7.245	0.1380	19.219	0.0520	50.505	0.0198	131.501	0.0076

Table B-1   Present Value/Future Value Interest Factors

n	6% Interest Factors Single Payment		7% Interest Factors Single Payment		8% Interest Factors Single Payment		9% Interest Factors Single Payment		10% Interest Factors Single Payment	
	Compound amount factor	Present worth factor	Compound amount factor	Present worth factor	Compound amount factor	Present worth factor	Compound amount factor	Present worth factor	Compound amount factor	Present worth factor
	To find F Given P F/P i,n	To find P Given F P/F i,n	To find F Given P F/P i,n	To find P Given F P/F i,n	To find F Given P F/P i,n	To find P Given F P/F i,n	To find F Given P F/P i,n	To find P Given F P/F i,n	To find F Given P F/P i,n	To find P Given F P/F i,n
1	1.060	0.9434	1.070	0.9346	1.080	0.9259	1.090	0.9174	1.100	0.9091
2	1.124	0.8900	1.145	0.8734	1.166	0.8573	1.188	0.8417	1.210	0.8265
3	1.191	0.8396	1.225	0.8163	1.260	0.7938	1.295	0.7722	1.331	0.7513
4	1.262	0.7921	1.311	0.7629	1.360	0.7350	1.412	0.7084	1.464	0.6830
5	1.338	0.7473	1.403	0.7130	1.469	0.6806	1.539	0.6499	1.611	0.6209
6	1.419	0.7050	1.501	0.6664	1.587	0.6302	1.677	0.5963	1.772	0.5645
7	1.504	0.6651	1.606	0.6228	1.714	0.5835	1.828	0.5470	1.949	0.5132
8	1.594	0.6274	1.718	0.5820	1.851	0.5403	1.993	0.5019	2.144	0.4665
9	1.689	0.5919	1.838	0.5439	1.999	0.5003	2.172	0.4604	2.358	0.4241
10	1.791	0.5584	1.967	0.5084	2.159	0.4632	2.367	0.4224	2.594	0.3856
11	1.898	0.5268	2.105	0.4751	2.332	0.4289	2.580	0.3875	2.853	0.3505
12	2.012	0.4970	2.252	0.4440	2.518	0.3971	2.813	0.3555	3.138	0.3186
13	2.133	0.4688	2.410	0.4150	2.720	0.3677	3.066	0.3262	3.452	0.2897
14	2.261	0.4423	2.579	0.3878	2.937	0.3405	3.342	0.2993	3.798	0.2633
15	2.397	0.4173	2.759	0.3625	3.172	0.3153	3.642	0.2745	4.177	0.2394
16	2.540	0.3937	2.952	0.3387	3.426	0.2919	3.970	0.2519	4.595	0.2176
17	2.693	0.3714	3.159	0.3166	3.700	0.2703	4.328	0.2311	5.054	0.1979
18	2.854	0.3504	3.380	0.2959	3.996	0.2503	4.717	0.2120	5.560	0.1799
19	3.026	0.3305	3.617	0.2765	4.316	0.2317	5.142	0.1945	6.116	0.1635
20	3.207	0.3118	3.870	0.2584	4.661	0.2146	5.604	0.1784	6.728	0.1487
21	3.400	0.2942	4.141	0.2415	5.034	0.1987	6.109	0.1637	7.400	0.1351
22	3.604	0.2775	4.430	0.2257	5.437	0.1840	6.659	0.1502	8.140	0.1229
23	3.820	0.2618	4.741	0.2110	5.871	0.1703	7.258	0.1378	8.954	0.1117
24	4.049	0.2470	5.072	0.1972	6.341	0.1577	7.911	0.1264	9.850	0.1015
25	4.292	0.2330	5.427	0.1843	6.848	0.1460	8.623	0.1160	10.835	0.0923
26	4.549	0.2198	5.807	0.1722	7.396	0.1352	9.399	0.1064	11.918	0.0839
27	4.822	0.2074	6.214	0.1609	7.988	0.1252	10.245	0.0976	13.110	0.0763
28	5.112	0.1956	6.649	0.1504	8.627	0.1159	11.167	0.0896	14.421	0.0694
29	5.418	0.1846	7.114	0.1406	9.317	0.1073	12.172	0.0822	15.863	0.0630
30	5.744	0.1741	7.612	0.1314	10.063	0.0994	13.268	0.0754	17.449	0.0573
31	6.088	0.1643	8.145	0.1228	10.868	0.0920	14.462	0.0692	19.194	0.0521
32	6.453	0.1550	8.715	0.1148	11.737	0.0852	15.763	0.0634	21.114	0.0474
33	6.841	0.1462	9.325	0.1072	12.676	0.0789	17.182	0.0582	23.225	0.0431
34	7.251	0.1379	9.978	0.1002	13.690	0.0731	18.728	0.0534	25.548	0.0392
35	7.686	0.1301	10.677	0.0937	14.785	0.0676	20.414	0.0490	28.102	0.0356
40	10.286	0.0972	14.974	0.0668	21.725	0.0460	31.409	0.0318	45.259	0.0221
45	13.765	0.0727	21.002	0.0476	31.920	0.0313	48.327	0.0207	72.890	0.0137
50	18.420	0.0543	29.457	0.0340	46.902	0.0213	74.358	0.0135	117.391	0.0085
55	24.650	0.0406	41.315	0.0242	68.914	0.0145	114.408	0.0088	189.059	0.0053
60	32.988	0.0303	57.946	0.0173	101.257	0.0099	176.031	0.0057	304.482	0.0033
65	44.145	0.0227	81.273	0.0123	148.780	0.0067	270.846	0.0037	490.371	0.0020
70	59.076	0.0169	113.989	0.0088	218.606	0.0046	416.730	0.0024	789.747	0.0013
75	79.057	0.0127	159.876	0.0063	321.205	0.0031	641.191	0.0016	1271.895	0.0008
80	105.796	0.0095	224.234	0.0045	471.955	0.0021	986.552	0.0010	2048.400	0.0005
85	141.579	0.0071	314.500	0.0032	693.456	0.0015	1517.932	0.0007	3298.969	0.0003
90	189.465	0.0053	441.103	0.0023	1018.915	0.0010	2335.527	0.0004	5313.023	0.0002
95	253.546	0.0040	618.670	0.0016	1497.121	0.0007	3593.497	0.0003	8556.676	0.0001
100	339.302	0.0030	867.716	0.0012	2199.761	0.0005	5529.041	0.0002	13780.612	0.0001

n	12% Interest Factors Single Payment		15% Interest Factors Single Payment		20% Interest Factors Single Payment		25% Interest Factors Single Payment		30% Interest Factors Single Payment	
	Compound amount factor	Present worth factor	Compound amount factor	Present worth factor	Compound amount factor	Present worth factor	Compound amount factor	Present worth factor	Compound amount factor	Present worth factor
	To find F Given P $F/P\ i,n$	To find P Given F $P/F\ i,n$	To find F Given P $F/P\ i,n$	To find P Given F $P/F\ i,n$	To find F Given P $F/P\ i,n$	To find P Given F $P/F\ i,n$	To find F Given P $F/P\ i,n$	To find P Given F $P/F\ i,n$	To find F Given P $F/P\ i,n$	To find P Given F $P/F\ i,n$
1	1.120	0.8929	1.150	0.8696	1.200	0.8333	1.250	0.8000	1.300	0.7692
2	1.254	0.7972	1.323	0.7562	1.440	0.6945	1.563	0.6400	1.690	0.5917
3	1.405	0.7118	1.521	0.6575	1.728	0.5787	1.953	0.5120	2.197	0.4552
4	1.574	0.6355	1.749	0.5718	2.074	0.4823	2.441	0.4096	2.856	0.3501
5	1.762	0.5674	2.011	0.4972	2.488	0.4019	3.052	0.3277	3.713	0.2693
6	1.974	0.5066	2.313	0.4323	2.986	0.3349	3.815	0.2622	4.827	0.2072
7	2.211	0.4524	2.660	0.3759	3.583	0.2791	4.768	0.2097	6.275	0.1594
8	2.476	0.4039	3.059	0.3269	4.300	0.2326	5.960	0.1678	8.157	0.1226
9	2.773	0.3606	3.518	0.2843	5.160	0.1938	7.451	0.1342	10.605	0.0943
10	3.106	0.3220	4.046	0.2472	6.192	0.1615	9.313	0.1074	13.786	0.0725
11	3.479	0.2875	4.652	0.2150	7.430	0.1346	11.642	0.0859	17.922	0.0558
12	3.896	0.2567	5.350	0.1869	8.916	0.1122	14.552	0.0687	23.298	0.0429
13	4.364	0.2292	6.153	0.1625	10.699	0.0935	18.190	0.0550	30.288	0.0330
14	4.887	0.2046	7.076	0.1413	12.839	0.0779	22.737	0.0440	39.374	0.0254
15	5.474	0.1827	8.137	0.1229	15.407	0.0649	28.422	0.0352	51.186	0.0195
16	6.130	0.1631	9.358	0.1069	18.488	0.0541	35.527	0.0282	66.542	0.0150
17	6.866	0.1457	10.761	0.0929	22.186	0.0451	44.409	0.0225	86.504	0.0116
18	7.690	0.1300	12.375	0.0808	26.623	0.0376	55.511	0.0180	112.455	0.0089
19	8.613	0.1161	14.232	0.0703	31.948	0.0313	69.389	0.0144	146.192	0.0069
20	9.646	0.1037	16.367	0.0611	38.338	0.0261	86.736	0.0115	190.050	0.0053
21	10.804	0.0926	18.822	0.0531	46.005	0.0217	108.420	0.0092	247.065	0.0041
22	12.100	0.0827	21.645	0.0462	55.206	0.0181	135.525	0.0074	321.184	0.0031
23	13.552	0.0738	24.891	0.0402	66.247	0.0151	169.407	0.0059	417.539	0.0024
24	15.179	0.0659	28.625	0.0349	79.497	0.0126	211.758	0.0047	542.801	0.0019
25	17.000	0.0588	32.919	0.0304	95.396	0.0105	264.698	0.0038	705.641	0.0014
26	19.040	0.0525	37.857	0.0264	114.475	0.0087	330.872	0.0030	917.333	0.0011
27	21.325	0.0469	43.535	0.0230	137.371	0.0073	413.590	0.0024	1192.533	0.0008
28	23.884	0.0419	50.066	0.0200	164.845	0.0061	516.988	0.0019	1550.293	0.0007
29	26.750	0.0374	57.575	0.0174	197.814	0.0051	646.235	0.0016	2015.381	0.0005
30	29.960	0.0334	66.212	0.0151	237.376	0.0042	807.794	0.0012	2619.996	0.0004
31	33.555	0.0298	76.144	0.0131	284.852	0.0035	1009.742	0.0010	3405.994	0.0003
32	37.582	0.0266	87.565	0.0114	341.822	0.0029	1262.177	0.0008	4427.793	0.0002
33	42.092	0.0238	100.700	0.0099	410.186	0.0024	1577.722	0.0006	5756.130	0.0002
34	47.143	0.0212	115.805	0.0086	492.224	0.0020	1972.152	0.0005	7482.970	0.0001
35	52.800	0.0189	133.176	0.0075	590.668	0.0017	2465.190	0.0004	9727.860	0.0001

Table B-1 Present Value/Future Value Interest Factors (Continued)

Appendix C

SAMPLE COST MODELS

Chapter 3 (Paragraph 3.2) introduces the subject of models and typical model applications. A model constitutes a simplified representation of a real world situation, and is employed to assist the decision maker in addressing and analyzing certain problems.

Models can vary from a simple mathematical expression to a complex computer program. The specific type of model required depends on the nature of the problem at hand and is a function of the number of alternatives, quantity and characteristics of the variables, and the complexity of operation. Further, since each problem application is somewhat different, models are likely to vary from one situation to the next. The decision maker must define the problem at hand, choose the techniques appropriate for problem resolution, and select or develop a model that properly employs these techniques.

As stated in Chapter 3, life cycle cost analyses are accomplished in all phases of the system/product life cycle to varying degrees, and models of different levels of complexity are employed to assist in fulfilling the analysis objectives. The case studies presented in Chapter 4 constitute simplified examples of model variations. Ten sample cost models briefly described below are additional

examples of actual models in use today. This listing is not
intended to be all inclusive by any means since there are
many cost models in existence; however, the models included
herein are considered typical with broad application in mind.

1. Acquisition Based On Consideration Of Logistics Effects
    (ABLE) Model. This model computes life cycle cost by
    item by cost type (stockage, repair, training, technical
    data, etc.), and sums the costs for all items in the
    system. The model can be used in detailed design, but
    is intended primarily for developing and specifying
    contract incentives regarding logistics. Refer to:
    Operations Analysis Office, Air Force Logistics Command,
    Wright-Patterson AFB, Ohio 45433.

2. Cost Optimization And Analysis Of Maintenance Policies
    (COAMP). The prime application of this model is to
    determine life cycle costs and operational availability
    for any type of system or product by analyzing its
    logistics support configuration. The objective is to
    identify the most cost-effective solution. Refer to:
    Maintenance Director, U.S. Army Armament Command, Rock
    Island, Illinois 61201.

3. Level Of Repair Analytical Techniques For Naval Air
    Systems Command Avionics Equipment (LOR MOD III),
    MIL-STD-1390A. The general purpose of the level of
    repair model is to determine, for each replaceable
    item in a system, actions that are to be taken when the
    item fails in order to minimize the life cycle costs
    associated with these actions. The action decisions
    include: (a) whether the item should be discarded or
    repaired upon failure; and (b) if repaired, at what
    level should the item be repaired; i.e., organizational,
    intermediate, depot, or supplier level of maintenance.
    Refer to: Naval Air Systems Command, AIR-4115,
    Washington, D. C. 20360.

4. <u>Logistics Support Cost (LSC) Model</u>. This model is used
    to estimate the support costs that may be incurred by
    adopting a specific system/product design configuration.
    The model is intended for application in two areas:
    (a) to estimate the differential logistics support
    costs between the proposed design configuration of two
    or more potential suppliers during source selection; and
    (b) to serve as a decision aid when discriminating among
    design alternatives during the advanced development and
    detailed design phases of a program. Refer to:
    "Logistics Support Cost (LSC) Model User's Handbook",
    AFLC/AQMLA, Wright-Patterson AFB, Ohio 45433, January
    1976.

5. <u>Navy Life Cycle Cost (NLCC) Model</u>. The NLCC model is a
    computerized mathematical tool which addresses life
    cycle costs utilizing four major cost categories:
    (a) acquisition costs; (b) development costs:
    (c) initial logistics set up costs; and (d) recurring
    operations and support costs. Cost categories may be
    further sub-divided into the following elements: prime
    contractor, other contractor, testing, prime system,
    training, supply support, technical data, support
    equipment, operations, and maintenance. Total life
    cycle cost is the sum of all cost elements for all cost
    categories. Refer to: Naval Weapons Engineering
    Support Activity (ESA 84), Washington Navy Yard,
    Washington, D.C. 20390.

6. <u>Optimum Repair Level Analysis (ORLA)</u>, AFLCM/AFSCM 800-4.
    This model is the baseline programming application for
    repair versus discard decisions. The model computes
    the logistics resource costs associated with the
    following maintenance options: (a) discard-at-failure;
    (b) intermediate level repair; and (c) depot level
    repair. The model considers program parameters and
    item characteristics to determine logistics support

costs for each alternative. The model has been tailored
for numerous applications. Refer to: Air Force
Logistics Command, AFALD/XRS, Wright-Patterson AFB,
Ohio 45433. Documenting is also available through the
Defense Logistics Studies Information Exchange,
DLSIE 31330MA, Fort Lee, Virginia 23801.

7. Systems Analysis Repair Cost (SARC). This model permits
   manipulation of various cost and related repair factors
   to determine how these factors affect life cycle costs.
   It aids in economic decisions regarding discard-at-
   failure and level of repair. Refer to: U.S. Army
   Missile Command, AMSM1-SA, Redstone Arsenal, Alabama
   35809.

8. System Cost And Operational Resource Evaluation (SCORE)
   Model. This model estimates life cycle costs (RDT & E,
   Investment, Operations) for up to 15 years for various
   system component elements, and aggregates these into
   a total cost estimate for a system. Cost estimates are
   based on historical accounting records and on cost
   estimating relationships. Costs are arranged in a two-
   dimensional matrix (program element and time). Refer to:
   Systems Analysis and Engineering Department, Naval Air
   Development Center, Johnsville, Warminster, Pennsylvania
   18974.

9. System Support Cost Analysis Model (SCAM). This model
   computes the 10-year discounted life cycle cost by item
   for a system. It also computes optimal stock levels and
   aids in determining optimal maintenance posture and
   support equipment requirements. Refer to: Office of the
   Assistant Chief of Staff, Studies and Analysis,
   Headquarters USAF, Washington, D.C. 20330.

10. Weapon System Life Cycle Cost Model (WSCOM). This model
    provides the life cycle costs of a system by work

breakdown structure, and in total for the specified
life cycle. The model is applicable to any development
program in which costs must be monitored and
recalculated for frequent changes in cost related
parameters. Refer to: Naval Air Systems Command,
720 Jefferson Plaza 2, Washington, D. C. 20360.

The cost models described herein are frequently supported
through the use of other models required for data generation
purposes. Compiling costs in an additive manner is basically
an accounting function; however, the data required to
determine system/product operational requirements, production
requirements, inventory and quality control levels, product
distribution and transportation policies, logistics support
policies, etc., are often generated from models of a
different nature. Accomplishing life cycle cost analyses
not only requires the use of accounting techniques, but one
must be knowledgeable of other techniques and models and
their applications; e.g., models employed in production
operations, inventory models, distribution models, quality
control models, queueing models, and logistics models.
Since it is impossible to cover the numerous classes of
models within the confines of this text, a few references
are included to encourage further study in this area.

1. Fabrycky, W.J., P.M. Ghare, and P.E. Torgersen,
   Industrial Operations Research, Prentice-Hall, Inc.,
   Englewood Cliffs, New Jersey, 1972.

2. Collins, D.E., "Analysis of Available Life Cycle Cost
   Models And Their Application", Joint AFSC/AFLC
   Commanders' Working Group On Life Cycle Cost, Wright-
   Patterson AFB, Ohio 45433, June 1976.

3. "Department Of Defense Catalog Of Logistics Models",
   Defense Logistics Information Exchange, U.S. Army
   Logistics Management Center, Fort Lee, Virginia 23801,
   January 1976.

4. NAVFAC P-443, "Catalog Of Navy Systems Commands Systems
    Analysis/Operations Research Models", 2nd Edition,
    Department of the Navy, Naval Facilities Engineering
    Command, Washington, D.C. 20390, March 1972.

5. R-550-PR, "Using Logistics Models In Systems Design And
    Early Support Planning", The RAND Corporation, 1700
    Main Street, Santa Monica, California 90406, 1971. This
    document is available through Defense Logistics Studies
    Information Exchange, DLSIE LD No. 26432MA, Fort Lee,
    Virginia 23801.

Appendix D

SELECTED TERMS AND DEFINITIONS

The majority of terms and definitions considered necessary
for an understanding of the principles and concepts of life
cycle costing are included throughout the five chapters in
this text. However, there are a few definitions that need
some expansion, particularly in view of their relevance to
life cycle costing. The purpose here is to briefly expand
in the areas of cost effectiveness, logistics,
maintainability, maintenance, reliability, system
effectiveness, etc. It is hoped that a review of this
material will facilitate an understanding of some of the key
assumptions upon which life cycle cost estimates are based.
This listing is certainly not intended to be all-inclusive.

A. Benefit-cost ratio. A popular method in determining
    the best among various alternative projects is to
    compute the benefit-cost ratio, a function of equivalent
    benefits and equivalent costs. In life cycle management,
    equivalent benefits are often presented in terms of
    revenues over the entire economic life cycle, and are
    then compared to life cycle costs accumulated throughout
    the same period of time. A benefit-cost ratio in this
    context is presented in Equation (D-1).

$$\text{B.C.} = \frac{\text{Equivalent Life Cycle Benefits}}{\text{Equivalent Life Cycle Costs}} \qquad \text{(D-1)}$$

B. Cost effectiveness. Cost effectiveness relates to a
measure of a system/product in terms of need or mission
fulfillment (system effectiveness) and total life cycle
cost. Mission fulfillment may be expressed differently
(one or more figures-of-merit), depending on the type of
system/product and its objective. Some commonly employed
cost effectiveness figures-of-merit (FOMs) are noted in
Equations (D-2) through (D-5).

$$\text{C.E. FOM} = \frac{\text{System Effectiveness}}{\text{Life Cycle Cost}} \qquad \text{(D-2)}$$

$$\text{C.E. FOM} = \frac{\text{Product Availability}}{\text{Life Cycle Cost}} \qquad \text{(D-3)}$$

$$\text{C.E. FOM} = \frac{\text{System Capacity}}{\text{Life Cycle Cost}} \qquad \text{(D-4)}$$

$$\text{C.E. FOM} = \frac{\text{Supply Support Effectiveness}}{\text{Life Cycle Cost}} \qquad \text{(D-5)}$$

And Others

C. Logistics. Logistics is the art and science of
management, engineering, and technical activities
concerned with requirements, design, and supplying and
maintaining resources to support objectives, plans and
operations. (This definition was established by the
Society of Logistics Engineers, 1974.) The elements of
logistics support include personnel and training, test
and support equipment, supply support (provisioning,
spare/repair parts, distribution, warehousing,

inventories, etc.), transportation and handling, facilities, and technical data.

Logistics is also a term often employed in manufacturing and commerce to describe the broad range of activities concerned with the efficient movement of finished products from the end of the production line to the consumer, and in some cases includes the movement of raw materials from the source of supply to the beginning of the production line. (Refer to Davis, G.M., and S.W. Brown, Logistics Management, Lexington Books, D. C. Heath and Company, 1974.) The elements of logistics in this context include material acquisition or procurement, inventory requirements, warehousing, packing and containerization, physical distribution, transportation and traffic management, customer service, etc.

In essence, logistics involves a broad range of activities throughout program planning, design, test and evaluation, production or construction, and sustaining system/product support. The impact of logistics on life cycle cost is significant, particularly relevant to production/construction costs and operation and support (O & S) costs.

D. Logistics support analysis (LSA). The LSA is an iterative analytical process that is employed throughout the system life cycle to: (a) aid in the initial determination and establishment of logistics support criteria which influence or impact on the system/product design; (b) aid in the evaluation of various configurations in terms of the inherent supportability characteristics already incorporated in the system/ product design; (c) aid in the identification and provisioning of the various logistics support elements required for system/product sustaining life cycle

support; and (d) to aid in the final analysis of the
system/product design to assess its total logistics
support effectiveness. An output of the LSA is the
identification and documentation of maintenance
frequencies (i.e., scheduled and unscheduled maintenance
actions), and the logistics support resource requirements
when maintenance actions occur. Resource requirements
include test and support equipment, supply support
(spares and repair parts, inventory control and
maintenance, etc.), maintenance personnel and training,
transportation and handling, maintenance facilities and
warehouses, and technical data. The LSA often includes
maintenance analyses and the evaluation of various
alternative support policies, and the results of this
effort constitute a significant input into life cycle
cost analyses in all program phases and at varying
levels of detail. The LSA is covered in: B. Blanchard,
Logistics Engineering Management, Prentice-Hall, Inc.,
Englewood Cliffs, New Jersey, 1974, Chapter 6 and
Appendix B; and MIL-STD-1388, "Logistics Support
Analysis", U.S. Navy, Tabor Avenue, Philadelphia,
Pennsylvania. (Refer to Appendix E for references.)

E. Maintainability. Maintainability is an inherent
    characteristic of equipment design and installation
    which is concerned with the ease, economy, safety and
    accuracy in the performance of maintenance actions
    (i.e., scheduled and unscheduled maintenance). It is
    concerned with maintenance times, supportability
    characteristics in system/product design, and
    maintenance costs. Maintainability is the ability of a
    piece of equipment to be maintained, versus maintenance
    which constitutes a series of actions to be taken to
    restore or retain an item in a satisfactory operational
    state. Maintainability is a design parameter and
    maintenance is a result of design. Thus, maintainability
    has a significant impact on life cycle cost, particularly

operation and support (O & S) cost. If the system/ product design is not maintainable, the logistics support resources required in the accomplishment of maintenance actions are extensive which, in turn, is costly. On the other hand, a prime objective in the design for maintainability is to minimize logistics support resource requirements in the event that maintenance actions are required.

Maintainability can also be defined in a more limited sense as "a characteristic of design and installation which is expressed as the probability that an item will be retained in or restored to a specified condition within a given period of time when maintenance is performed in accordance with prescribed procedures and resources". (Refer to MIL-STD-721, "Definition Of Effectiveness Terms For Reliability, Maintainability, Human Factors, And Safety".)

Maintainability can be specified, predicted, and measured. The primary measures of maintainability are in terms of a combination of maintenance times, supportability factors, and projected maintenance cost. Those measures most commonly applicable in life cycle cost analyses are described below:

1. Mean Time Between Maintenance (MTBM) is a function of both scheduled and unscheduled maintenance, and represents the average time between all maintenance actions for a specified period or for the life cycle. MTBM includes consideration of reliability MTBF and MTBR, and is determined from Equation (D-6).

$$MTBM = \frac{1}{1/MTBM_u + 1/MTBM_s} \qquad (D-6)$$

where $MTBM_u$ is the mean interval of unscheduled
(corrective) maintenance, and $MTBM_s$ is the mean
interval of scheduled (preventive) maintenance.
$MTBM_u$ must consider: (a) inherent reliability
characteristics; (b) manufacturing or process
defects; (c) wear-out characteristics; (d) dependent
or secondary failures resulting from a chain
reaction; (e) operator-induced failures;
(f) maintenance induced failures; and (g) equipment
damage due to handling.   Idealistically, $MTBM_u$
should generally be equivalent to the reliability
MTBF factor.   The reciprocal of MTBM is the
frequency of maintenance which is a significant
factor in deriving O & S costs.   (Refer to:
B. Blanchard, Logistics Engineering And
Management, Prentice-Hall, Inc., 1974, Chapter 2
and Appendix B).

2. Mean Time Between Replacement (MTBR) is the mean
    interval of time between item replacements due to
    either scheduled or unscheduled maintenance actions,
    and usually generates spare/repair part requirements.
    MTBR is not necessarily synonymous with $MTBM_u$ or
    MTBF.

3. Mean Corrective Maintenance Time ($\overline{Mct}$) is the mean
    elapsed time to complete the corrective maintenance
    cycle for all unscheduled maintenance actions.   The
    corrective maintenance cycle is illustrated in
    Figure D-1. $\overline{Mct}$ is expressed in Equation (D-7).

$$\overline{Mct} = \frac{\sum (\lambda_i)(Mct_i)}{\sum \lambda_i} \qquad (D-7)$$

where "λ_i" is the failure rate of the individual
(ith) element of the item being measured,
generally expressed in failures per item operating

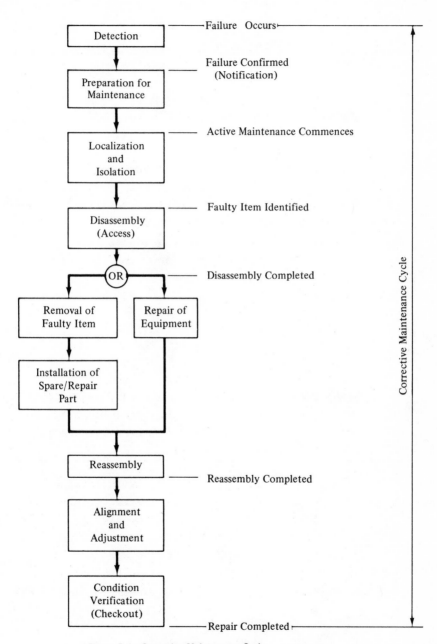

Figure D-1 Corrective Maintenance Cycle
(Source: B. S. Blanchard, *Engineering Organization and Management,* Prentice-Hall, Inc. 1976. By Permission.)

hour; and "Mct_i" is the elapsed time to complete
the maintenance cycle for each individual (ith)
maintenance action. $\overline{Mct}$ considers only active
maintenance time, or that time which is spent
working directly on the system or product, and is
the weighted average of the individual Mct_i values.

4. Mean Preventive Maintenance Time ($\overline{Mpt}$) is the mean
   (or average) elapsed time required to perform
   preventive or scheduled maintenance on an item. This
   may include servicing, inspection, calibration, and
   overhaul; and can be accomplished when the system/
   product is in full operation, or could result in
   downtime. $\overline{Mpt}$, resulting in downtime, can be
   determined from Equation (D-8).

$$\overline{Mpt} = \frac{\sum (fpt_i)(Mpt_i)}{\sum fpt_i} \qquad (D\text{-}8)$$

   where "fpt_i" is the frequency of the individual
   (ith) preventive maintenance action, generally
   expressed in actions per item operating hour; and
   "Mpt_i" is the elapsed time required for the ith
   preventive maintenance action.

5. Mean Active Maintenance Time ($\overline{M}$) is the mean or
   average elapsed time required to perform scheduled
   (preventive) and unscheduled (corrective)
   maintenance. It excludes logistics supply and
   administrative delay time, and is expressed in
   Equation (D-9).

$$\overline{M} = \frac{(\lambda)(\overline{Mct}) + (fpt)(\overline{Mpt})}{\lambda + fpt} \qquad (D\text{-}9)$$

   where "λ" is the corrective maintenance rate and
   "fpt" is the preventive maintenance rate.

6. <u>Maintenance Downtime (MDT)</u> is the total elapsed time
   that a system/product is not operationally
   available or in use due to scheduled or unscheduled
   maintenance. MDT includes active maintenance time
   ($\overline{M}$), downtime due to logistics support delays, and
   downtime due to administration delays of one form
   or another. Logistic delay time is that portion of
   nonactive maintenance time during which maintenance
   is delayed solely because of not having a spare part
   available, the unavailability of test and support
   equipment, the unavailability of facilities, etc.
   Administrative delay time (or waiting time) is that
   portion of nonactive maintenance time during which
   maintenance is delayed for reasons of an
   administrative nature; i.e., personnel assignment
   priority, inadequate manning, organization constraint,
   etc.

7. <u>Maintenance Manhours Per System Operating Hour</u>
   <u>(MMH/OH)</u> is the ratio of the total manhours
   expended in maintenance to the hours of system/
   product operation or use.

Additional coverage of maintainability is found in:
B. Blanchard and E. Lowery, <u>Maintainability Principles</u>
<u>And Practices</u>, McGraw-Hill Book Company, N.Y., 1969;
(b) A. Goldman and T. Slattery, <u>Maintainability - A</u>
<u>Major Element Of System Effectiveness</u>, John Wiley &
Sons, Inc., N.Y., 1967; and (c) C. Cunningham and
W. Cox, <u>Applied Maintainability</u>, John Wiley & Sons, Inc.,
N.Y., 1972.

F. <u>Maintenance</u>. Maintenance includes all scheduled and
   unscheduled actions necessary for retaining an item in,
   or restoring it to, an operational condition.
   Maintenance includes repair, remove and replace, testing,
   modification, inspection, servicing, calibration,

overhaul, condition verification, and so on. Maintenance
may or may not result in system/product downtime
(depending on the situation), but is usually a major
contributor to life cycle cost.

G. Maintenance Concept. The maintenance concept constitutes
    a series of statements and/or illustrations that define
    criteria covering maintenance strategy, maintenance
    levels, support policies, major support functions at
    each maintenance level, effectiveness factors
    (e.g., maintenance time constraints, supply effectiveness,
    pipeline and turnaround times, etc.), and basic logistics
    support requirements. The maintenance concept is a
    prerequisite to system/product design and development,
    and forms the basis for determining O & S costs in life
    cycle cost analyses.

H. Maintenance Level. Maintenance levels may be classified
    as divisions of maintenance responsibility, functions,
    or tasks; e.g., organization level maintenance,
    intermediate level maintenance, depot level maintenance,
    supplier maintenance, etc. Refer to: B. Blanchard,
    Logistics Engineering Management, Prentice-Hall, Inc.,
    Englewood Cliffs, N.J., 1974, Chapter 4.

I. Reliability. Reliability is the probability that a
    system or product will operate in a satisfactory manner
    for a specified period of time when used under stated
    conditions. When related to the fulfillment of a given
    need, reliability may be defined as the probability of
    successfully meeting that need under specified use
    conditions. Reliability, sometimes equated to the
    probability of survival, may be determined from
    Equation (D-10).

$$R = e^{-\lambda t} \qquad\qquad (D\text{-}10)$$

where "e" is the Napierian or natural logarithm base (2.7183); "λ" is the failure rate in failures per hour (λ = 1/MTBF); and "t" is the total operating time in hours.

Reliability is usually related to the exponential function as illustrated in Figure D-2. Assuming that an item has a constant failure rate (λ), the reliability can be determined from the exponential distribution curve. Test and field data covering a variety of items have indicated that if the design of a system/product is mature, the failure rate (λ) is relatively constant throughout a defined period of the system's operational life. In addition, when an item is first produced and introduced into the field, there are usually more failures during a "debugging" period. Likewise, when an item reaches a certain age, there is a "wearout" period when failures tend to increase. A typical failure-rate curve is depicted in Figure D-3.

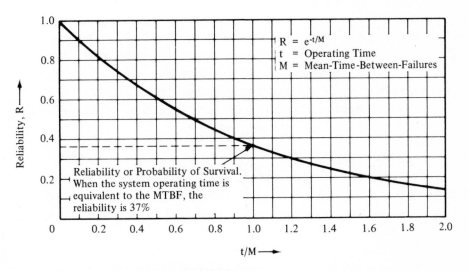

Figure D-2   Basic Reliability Curve
(Source: B. S. Blanchard, *Engineering Organization and Management*, Prentice-Hall, Inc. 1976. By Permission.)

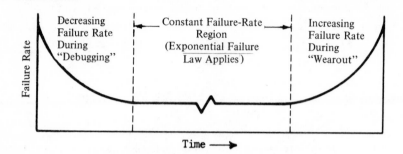

Figure D-3   Typical Failure Rate Curve
(Source: B. S. Blanchard, *Engineering Organization*
***and Management*, Prentice-Hall, Inc., 1976.**
By Permission.)

However, it should be noted that this curve may vary
considerably depending on the type of system, the
operating conditions of the system, whether system
modifications are introduced, and so on. The curve in
Figure D-3 represents a relative set of conditions.

Reliability, which is often expressed in terms of MTBF,
basically reflects the frequency of unscheduled
maintenance (i.e., $MTBM_u$). As such, this factor is a
major parameter in determining O & S costs in life
cycle cost analyses. The analyst must acquire a basic
knowledge of reliability if he (or she) is to effectively
accomplish life cycle costing objectives. Additional
sources covering reliability are indicated in the
selected bibliography, Appendix E.

J.   System Effectiveness. System effectiveness may be
     defined as the probability that a system or product can
     successfully meet an overall operational demand within
     a given time when operated under specified conditions,
     or the capability of a system to do the job for which it
     was intended. System effectiveness relates to the
     ability of a system to fulfill a defined need and is a
     function of performance, capacity, availability,
     readiness, reliability, maintainability, supportability,

dependability, and so on. System effectiveness, or some element there of, is often related with life cycle cost in the evaluation of systems or products.

K. System Engineering. System engineering involves the application of scientific and engineering efforts to:

(1) transform an operational need into a description of system/product performance parameters and a preferred system configuration through the use of an iterative process of functional analysis, allocation, synthesis, optimization, definition, design, test, and evaluation; (2) integrate related technical parameters to assure compatibility of all physical, functional, and program interfaces in a manner which optimizes the total system definition and design; and (3) integrate reliability maintainability, human factors, logistics support, safety, producibility, cost, and other related specialities into the total engineering effort.

The system engineering process, in its evolving of functional detail and design requirements, has as its goal the achievement of the proper balance between operational, performance, logistics support, and economic factors. The process employs a sequential and iterative approach in arriving at cost-effective solutions. Life cycle costing is an integral part of this process. Refer to: (1) MIL-STD-499A, "Engineering Management", U.S. Air Force, AFSC/SDDE, Andrews AFB, Maryland 20331; and (2) B. Blanchard, Logistics Engineering And Management, Prentice-Hall, Inc., Englewood Cliffs, N.J., 1974, Chapter 1.

L. Terotechnology. Terotechnology is defined as "a combination of management, financial, engineering, and other practices applied to physical assets in pursuit of economic life cycle costs". Terotechnology is a multi-disciplinary approach to ensure optimum life cycle costs

in the development and use of equipment and facilities.
It includes the design of various assets with the
objective of attaining the proper balance of
performance, reliability, maintainability, supportability,
quality, and related features. Terotechnology
constitutes the "cradle-to-grave" management of
resources in an efficient and effective manner, and
includes functions in all phases of the life cycle;
i.e., feasibility studies, research and development,
design, production, operation, maintenance and
logistics support, replacement and disposal.

Terotechnology is a relatively new term developed by
the British in the early 1970s in response to the
increasing problems of waste and the high costs of
doing business. A Committee for Terotechnology was
formed in the United Kingdom in April 1970 to establish
terotechnology in British industry and commercial life.
The objective is to "bring together" existing
capabilities and methods in a way which can be used to
improve the management of physical assets. As a result
of this effort, the British have established a
National Terotechnology Centre for the promotion of
these concepts and objectives. Refer to The National
Terotechnology Centre, Cleeve Road, Leatherhead,
Surrey KT227SA, United Kingdom.

Appendix E

SELECTED BIBLIOGRAPHY

When addressing the various aspects of life cycle costing, design to cost, cost estimating, cost effectiveness, cost analysis, etc., there are many documents that one may review for guidance in accomplishing life cycle costing functions. The majority of references on life cycle costing cover a specific application or case study, while there are a few references that are considered appropriate in acquiring the fundamental knowledge necessary to understand and successfully complete life cycle cost analyses in general.

The author has attempted to select a few references with the intent of facilitating an understanding of life cycle cost/design to cost objectives. In addition, the references covering accounting, finance, engineering economy, reliability, logistics, etc., are considered appropriate when considering the "tools" necessary in completing a life cycle cost analysis effort. The list presented below is by no means all inclusive.

1. Accounting - managerial and cost accounting.

    a. Gordon, M.J., and G. Shillinglaw, Accounting - A Managerial Approach, 3rd Edition, Richard D. Irwin, Inc., Homewood, Illinois, 1964.

b.   Horngren, C.T., <u>Cost Accounting - A Managerial</u>
     <u>Emphasis</u>, 3rd Edition, Prentice-Hall, Inc.,
     Englewood Cliffs, N.J., 1972.

2. Cost estimating and cost factors.

a.   Gillespie, C., <u>Standard And Direct Costing</u>,
     Prentice-Hall, Inc., Englewood Cliffs, N.J., 1962.
b.   Jelen, F.C. (Ed.), <u>Cost And Optimization Engineering</u>,
     McGraw-Hill Book Company, N.Y., 1970.
c.   Ostwald, P.F., <u>Cost Estimating For Engineering And</u>
     <u>Management</u>, Prentice-Hall, Inc., Englewood Cliffs,
     N.J., 1974.
d.   Popper, <u>Modern Cost Engineering Techniques</u>,
     McGraw-Hill Book Company, N.Y., 1970.

3. Department of Defense, Army, Navy, Air Force, and
    related documentation.

a.   AD 702-424, "An Introduction To Equipment Cost
     Estimating", RAND Corporation, Defense Documentation
     Center, December 1969.
b.   AFLCM/AFSCM 800-4, "Optimum Repair-Level Analysis
     (ORLA)", Department of the Air Force, June 1971.
c.   AFR 173-10, "Cost Analysis - USAF Cost And
     Planning Factors", Department of the Air Force,
     February 6, 1975.
d.   AFR 800-11, "Life Cycle Costing", Department of the
     Air Force, Headquarters USAF, Washington, D. C.
     20330, August 1973.
e.   AMCP 700-6 (Army), NAVMAT P5242 (Navy), AFLCP/AFSCP
     800-19 (Air Force), "Joint Design-To-Cost Guide, A
     Conceptual Approach For Major Weapon System
     Acquisition", Department of Army/Navy/Air Force,
     October 1973.
f.   "Bibliography On Design To Cost, Life Cycle Cost,
     and Cost Models", Defense Logistics Studies
     Information Exchange (DLSIE), U.S. Army Logistics

Management Center, Ft. Lee, Virginia 23801

g. Department of Defense Directive 5000.28, "Design to Cost", Department of Defense, May 1975.

h. Department of Defense Guide LCC-1, "Life Cycle Costing Procurement Guide", U.S. Government Printing Office, Washington, D.C. 20402, July 1970.

i. Department of Defense Guide LCC-2, "Casebook - Life Cycle Costing In Equipment Procurement", U.S. Government Printing Office, Washington, D.C. 20402, July 1970.

j. Department of Defense Guide LCC-3, "Life Cycle Costing Guide For System Acquisition", U.S. Government Printing Office Washington, D.C. 20402, January 1973.

k. Department of Defense Instruction 7041.3, "Economic Analysis and Program Evaluation for Resource Management", U.S. Government Printing Office, Washington, D.C. 20402, October 18, 1972.

l. "Life Cycle Cost", Defense Management Journal, Volume 12, Number 1, U.S. Government Printing Office, Washington, D.C. 20402, January 1976.

m. McClure, L., "Life Cycle Costing - A Selected Bibliography", RB 330-1, Martin Marietta Aerospace Corp., Orlando, Florida 32805, October 1976.

n. MIL-STD-1390A (Navy), "Level Of Repair", Naval Publications and Form Center, 5801 Tabor Avenue, Philadelphia, Pennsylvania 19120, April 1974.

o. NADC-73240-50, "NADC Life Cycle Costing Methodology And Applications", Naval Air Development Center, Warminster, Pennsylvania 18974, November 1973.

p. NAVFAC P-443, <u>Catalog Of Navy Systems Commands Systems Analysis/Operations Research Models</u>, 2nd Edition, Department Of The Navy, Naval Facilities Engineering Command, Washington, D.C. 20390. This document includes a description of some cost estimating models.

q. NSIA AD HOC Committee Report, "Life Cycle Cost, Findings And Recommendations", Prepared for Assistant Secretary of Defense (I&L), April 1976.

r. Paulson, R.M., R.B. Waina, and L.H. Zacks, Using Logistics Models In System Design And Early Support Planning, R-550-PR, A Report Prepared for U.S. Air Force, RAND Corporation, 1700 Main Street, Santa Monica, California 90406, February 1971. This document includes a description of some cost models.

s. TTO-ORT-032-76B-V3, "Cost Effectiveness Program Plan for Joint Tactical Communications, Volume III, Life Cycle Costing", Joint Tactical Communications Office, Ft. Monmouth, New Jersey, June 1976.

t. Betaque, N.E., and M.R. Fiorello, Aircraft System Operating And Support Costs: Guidelines For Analysis, Logistics Management Institute, 4701 Sangamore Road, Washington, D. C. 20016, March 1977.

u. Menker, L.J., Life Cycle Cost Analysis Guide, Joint AFSC/AFLC Commander's Working Group On Life Cycle Cost, ASD/ACL, Wright-Patterson AFB, Ohio 45433, November 1975.

v. Collins, D.E., Analysis Of Available Life Cycle Cost Models Add Their Applications, Joint AFSC/AFLC Commander's Working Group On Life Cycle Cost, ASD/ACL, Wright Patterson AFB, Ohio 45433, June 1976.

w. Kernan, J.E., and L.J. Menker, Life Cycle Cost Procurement Guide, Joint AFSC/AFLC Commander's Working Group On Life Cycle Cost, ASD/ACL, Wright-Patterson AFB, Ohio 45433, July 1976.

x. "Life Cycle Cost Reference Library Bibliography", Compiled by A. Srofe, Joint AFSC/AFLC Commanders' Working Group On Life Cycle Cost, Wright-Patterson AFB, Ohio 45433, March 1976.

4. Engineering economy, economic analysis, and cost analysis.

a. Barish, N.N., <u>Economic Analysis For Engineering And Managerial Decision Making</u>, McGraw-Hill Book Company, N.Y., 1962.

b. Canada, J.R., <u>Intermediate Economic Analysis For Management And Engineering</u>, Prentice-Hall, Inc., Englewood Cliffs, N.J., 1971.

c. English, J.M. (Ed), <u>Cost-Effectiveness - The Economic Evaluation Of Engineering Systems</u>, John Wiley & Sons, Inc., N.Y., 1968.

d. Fabrycky, W.J., and G.J. Thuesen, <u>Economic Decision Analysis</u>, Prentice-Hall, Inc., Englewood Cliffs, N.Y., 1974.

e. Fisher, G.H., <u>Cost Considerations In Systems Analysis</u>, American Elsevier Publishing Company, Inc., N.Y., 1971.

f. Grant, E.L., W.G. Ireson, and R.S. Leavenworth, <u>Principles Of Engineering Economy</u>, 6th Edition, The Ronald Press Company, N.Y., 1976.

g. Kendall, M.G. (Ed), <u>Cost-Benefit Analyses</u>, American Elsevier Publishing Company, Inc., N.Y., 1971

h. Park, W.R., <u>Cost Engineering Analysis</u>, John Wiley & Sons, N.Y., 1973.

i. Riggs, J.L., <u>Economic Decision Models For Engineers And Managers</u>, McGraw-Hill Book Company, N.Y., 1968.

j. Seiler, C., <u>Introduction To Systems Cost Effectiveness</u>, John Wiley & Sons, Inc., N.Y., 1969.

k. Thuesen, H.G., W.J. Fabrycky, and G.J. Thuesen, <u>Engineering Economy</u>, 5th Edition, Prentice-Hall, Inc., Englewood Cliffs, N.J., 1977.

5. Finance and financial management.

a. Van Horne, J.C., <u>Financial Management And Policy</u>, 3rd Edition, Prentice Hall, Inc., Englewood Cliffs, N.J., 1974.

6. Reliability, maintainability, and logistics support.

    a. Blanchard, B.S., <u>Logistics Engineering And
        Management</u>, Prentice-Hall, Inc., Englewood Cliffs,
        N.J., 1974. This document includes life cycle cost
        data and covers cost analysis applications.
    b. Blanchard, B.S., and E.E. Lowery, <u>Maintainability
        Principles And Practices</u>, McGraw-Hill Book Company,
        N.Y., 1969.
    c. Cunningham, C., and W. Cox, <u>Applied Maintainability</u>,
        John Wiley & Sons, Inc., N.Y., 1972.
    d. Davis, G., and S. Brown, <u>Logistics Management</u>,
        Lexington Books, D. C. Heath & Company, Lexington,
        Mass., 1974.
    e. Goldman, A., and T. Slattery, <u>Maintainability - A
        Major Element Of System Effectiveness</u>, John Wiley
        & Sons, Inc., N.Y., 1967.
    f. Heskett, J.L., R. Ivie, N. Glaskowsky, <u>Business
        Logistics</u>, <u>Management Of Physical Supply And
        Distribution</u>, 2nd Edition, The Ronald Press Co.,
        N.Y., 1973.
    g. Kapur, K.C., and L.R. Lamberson, <u>Reliability In
        Engineering Design</u>, John Wiley & Sons, Inc., N.Y.,
        1977.
    h. Jardine, A.K.S., <u>Maintenance, Replacement, and
        Reliability</u>, Halsted Press, Division of John Wiley
        & Sons, Inc., N.Y., 1973.
    i. Von Alven, W. (Ed.), <u>Reliability Engineering</u>,
        Prentice-Hall, Inc., Englewood Cliffs, N.J., 1964.

7. Additional references.

    a. "Engineering And Process Economics -- An International
        Journal For Industry", Published Quarterly,
        Elsevier Scientific Publishing Company, P.O. Box 211,
        Amsterdam, The Netherlands.
    b. Haworth, D.P., "The Principles Of Life Cycle
        Costing", Industrialization Forum, Volume 6,

Number 3-4, Department Of Architecture, Graduate
School of Design, Harvard University, Cambridge,
Massachusetts 02138, 1975.

c. "Spectrum", Published Quarterly, The Society Of
Logistics Engineers, 3322 South Memorial Parkway,
Suite 2, Huntsville, Alabama 35801.

d. MIL-STD-499A (USAF), "Engineering Management",
Headquarters, Air Force Systems Command, Attention
SDDE, Andrews AFB, Maryland 20331. This document
covers life cycle costing as an integral part of the
systems engineering process.

e. "Terotechnology - An Introduction To The Management
Of Physical Resources", The National Terotechnology
Centre, Cleeve Road, Leatherhead, Surrey KT227SA,
United Kingdom, 1976. Terotechnology includes the
concept of life cycle costing.

INDEX

System:
  definition of, 1
  effectiveness, 11, 79, 238
  engineering, 239
  life cycle process, 16
  operational requirements, 73, 111, 151
  maintenance concept, 73, 118, 151, 236

        T

Terotechnology, 239
Turnaround time, 118

        U

Uncertainty, 99

        W

Warranty, 187